HARLEM IS A COLONY

Fighting to liberate itself and to find its place in the black revolution . . .

John Henrik Clarke

Harlem is also a wealthy source of literary creation. In this collection, critic and author John Henrik Clarke has gathered twenty tales by black writers who evoke the many moods of their beloved Harlem. The stories are united by the many threads of love, optimism, despair and understanding of the ghetto which is, and always has been, the soul of Black America.

Here is Harlem as it was and is today—from the period when, as Langston Hughes wryly noted, "the Negro was in vogue" to today's black literary renaissance. Here, too, the gentle dignity of Paule Marshall and Maya Angelou, the superb craftsmanship of Ann Petry, the evocative reality of Claude McKay and Louise Meriwether, the passion and anger of James Baldwin, LeRoi Jones, and John O. Killens, and the poignant humor of Langston Hughes and Ray Meaddough—all are represented in this definitive anthology which spans three generations and recreates what it meant and what it means to be black and coming of age in Harlem.

Harlem

Edited with a new Introduction by

John Henrik Clarke

First published in 1970 by
Signet
Republished 1993

A&B BOOKS PUBLISHERS
149 Lawrence Street
Brooklyn, New York
11201

ACKNOWLEDGMENTS

"All Day Long" by Maya Angelou. Used by permission of the author.

"Roy's Wound" by James Baldwin. Originally published in *New World Writings No. 2*, New American Library, 1952. Reprinted by permission of the Robert Lantz-Candida Donadio Literary Agency.

"Revolt of the Angels" by John Henrik Clarke. Originally published in *Freedomways* Magazine, Summer, 1963. Reprinted by permission of the author.

"One Way to Heaven" by Countee Cullen. Chapter 6 of *One Way to Heaven* by Countee Cullen. Copyright, 1932, by Countee Cullen; renewed 1960 by Ida M. Cullen. Reprinted by permission of Harper & Row, Publishers.

"Verisimilitude" by John P. Davis. Originally published in *Ebony and Topez,* 1927. Reprinted by permission of the author.

"Miss Cynthie" by Rudolph Fisher. Originally published in *Story* Magazine, 1933. Reprinted by permission of Jane Ryder Fisher.

"The Harlem Teacher" by Lorraine Freeman. Copyright © 1970 by Lorraine Freeman. Used by permission of the author.

"Harlem on the Rocks" by Loyle Hairston. Originally published in *Freedomways* Magazine, Spring, 1969. Reprinted by permission of the author.

"So Softly Smiling" by Chester Himes. Originally published in *The Crisis,* October 1943. Reprinted by permission of the author and his agents, Franz J. Horch Associates, Inc.

"Who's Passing For Who?" by Langston Hughes. Reprinted by permission of Harold Ober Associates Incorporated. Copyright 1952 by Langston Hughes.

"Unfinished" by LeRoi Jones. Copyright © 1967 by LeRoi Jones. Reprinted by permission of The Sterling Lord Agency.

"A Good Long Sidewalk" by William Melvin Kelley. Copyright © 1964 by William Melvin Kelley, from *Dancers on the Shore*. Reprinted by permission of Doubleday & Company, Inc. and Hutchinson Publishing Group Ltd., London, England.

"Rough Diamond" by John Oliver Killens. Copyright © 1970 by John Oliver Killens. Used by permission of the author.

"Some Get Wasted" by Paule Marshall. Originally published in *Harlem U.S.A.,* 1964. Reprinted by permission of the author.

"Home to Harlem" by Claude McKay. Chapter II and III of *Home to Harlem* by Claude McKay. Copyright 1928 by Harper & Brothers; renewed 1956 by Hope McKay Virtue. Reprinted by permission of Harper & Row, Publishers.

"The Other Side of Christmas" by R. J. Meaddough. Originally published in *Freedomways* Magazine, Fall, 1967. Reprinted by permission of the author.

"Daddy Was a Numbers Runner" by Louise Meriwether. From *The Antioch Review* (XXVII), Fall, 1967. Reprinted by permission of the Ad Schulberg Agency.

"In Darkness and Confusion" by Ann Petry. Originally published in *Crosscurrents,* 1947. Reprinted by permission of Russell & Volkening, Inc.

"Now That Henry Is Gone" by Clayton Riley. Originally published in *Liberator Magazine,* July 1965. Reprinted by permission of the author.

"Jack in the Pot" by Dorothy West. Published by the *New York Daily News,* 1940. Reprinted by permission of the author.

A&B BOOKS PUBLISHERS
149 Lawrence Street
Brooklyn, New York
(718) 596-3389

PRINTED IN THE UNITED STATES OF AMERICA

Dedication

To Mrs. Dorothy R. Homer, former Head Librarian, Countee Cullen Branch, New York Public Library

and

Mrs. Jean Blackwell Hutson, Curator, Schomburg Collection, New York Public Library

A small token of appreciation for your friendship and encouragement during my early years in Harlem.

Contents

INTRODUCTION

Since this book was first published in 1970, there have been changes, challenges and conflicts in the Harlem community that might call for the need of a new appraisal of this community beyond fiction and fact. Some of the best recent writings on the community have been in the field of factual reporting. The best novel on the Harlem community in recent years is Grace Yearwood's book, *In the Shadow of the Peacock*. Ann Petry, who wrote the novel, *The Street*, has written very little about Harlem since then, except the story included here: "In Darkness and Confusion." John Killen's book, *Cotillion*, was about social climbing in the Harlem across the river, Bedford-Stuyvesant, Brooklyn.

Harlem continues to be the world's most famous ethnic community. It is a community in transition searching for itself. Harlem was once the culture capital of the African world, the meeting place and the proving ground for organizations, messiahs, and just plain money-changers. With the encroachment of something called gentrification, Black Americans who live in Harlem and who love that community are in danger of losing it to real-estate speculators and urban developers. A political fight with many undercurrents has been in motion for a number of years by Blacks who want to save Harlem and preserve its special uniqueness.

A number of writers in this volume were beginning their careers at the time of this publication. Maya Angelou is now noted as a poet, lecturer, biographer and performer. John Killens and Ray Meaddough have passed during the interim.

LeRoi Jones has been known for a number of years as Amiri Baraka. Paule Marshall, soon after her last novel, *The Daughters*, won the MacArthur fellowship. I have always considered her to be one of the most talented of living Black women writers. Louise Meriwether now functions both as a writer and as a teacher of writing. James Baldwin passed in 1990, ending a brilliant career that lasted for more than a generation.

Langston Hughes and Chester Himes, now deceased, are still with us in the many books they wrote and published in their lifetime. Langston Hughes' urban folk hero, Jesse B. Semple, has outlived its creator.

The stories in this volume are, indeed, the voices from the soul of Black America. In the re-publication of this book, I thought and hoped that another generation of readers would want to hear those voices again.

JOHN HENRIK CLARKE
Professor Emeritus
African World History
Department of African and PuertoRican Studies
Hunter College
New York City
July, 1993

Verisimilitude

by John P. Davis

I am a rather young man, with no especial knack for writing, who has a story to tell. I want to tell it as I feel it —without restraint—but I can't do that. Critics are already waxing sarcastic about this way of doing things. They think it is too emotional, too melodramatic. I am going to attempt to tell the story I have in me without any fuss or sensation. To achieve "grandeur of generality," to attain the "universal" rather than the "specific"—these are the things I am trying to do. I want you to say when you have finished reading: "That reminds me of . . . ," or "There are thousands like that character; I may never have known one, but there are thousands, thousands. There must be."

Now you can help me, if you will forget everything else in the world except this story. Whether it actually happened or not is of little consequence. The important thing is that it might have happened, that, in mathematical or scientific terms, given such causes working on such characters, the results about which I am going to tell you would have happened. If at any time you feel that there is something in the story that couldn't happen on your own main street, then stop reading. I don't want to create monsters, but real, living characters.

Now this is the story of a man. A man is the hero of most stories. Man is the hero of life. This man was a Negro.

15

Negroes are common enough. There are fifteen million, more or less, in the United States alone. This Negro man was in love. Love is the theme of ninety percent of all fiction. I doubt that it is the theme of ninety percent of life. But no matter, it is common enough in these days.

The next fact in the plot may seem to point the way to something grotesque, something that veers away off from the center of normal human existence like a comet. The Negro man loved a white woman. Are you disappointed already? Well, I am sorry. But I was a census-taker in Virginia. And you would be surprised at the number of cases of intermarriage I found. That is why they passed an anti-intermarriage law there. There are such laws in nearly all southern states. There must be a reason back of these statutes. Legislatures don't pass laws for nothing. So it wouldn't be strange if I wrote a story about a Negro man who loved a white woman and married her. But I have no intention of marrying my characters. In fact my plot exists because they did not marry. I say only that he loved her. Whether she loved him, I leave you to judge when you have read the story.

This Negro man was tall, young, and brown. There is nothing to quarrel with here. I haven't said he was handsome. Surely, young, tall, brown Negro bundle-wrappers in downtown New York department stores are common enough not to shock you out of belief. And just as ordinary and matter-of-fact are slim, little, rather nice-looking white salesgirls.

You see these two characters now, don't you? You see them working side by side ten hours a day. One is selling yard after yard of vari-colored cambric to fat housewives who are harder to please than you would expect Mrs. J. Pierpont Morgan to be. You see these termagants snarl at the shopgirl and then go to buy cambric at a cheaper price in one of the cut-rate stores. Of course, it is the most natural thing in the world that the shopgirl should get angry and stick her tongue out at them when they have turned their backs.

Take a look at the other character. He is at the end of the counter wrapping up package after package which the girl hands him. He hears the housewives' quarrelsome babble. He sees the girl make faces at them. He sympathizes and smiles at her as if to say: "I understand how it is with you." The girl has caught the smile and thrown it back. She wants to talk about that last old biddy who put on the airs of her mistress. And she doesn't see why she shouldn't talk to this bundle-wrapper. He smiled; he would understand. She goes over while there is a lull in the sale of cambric and chats with him about "that old fool who expected to get something for nothing and blamed me because Gimbels charged a cent less per yard for cambric than we did. Why the heck didn't she go there in the first place?" He laughs at the way she got back at the woman. She laughs. The tension is broken. They understand. Isn't all this about as natural and plausible as may be? Put yourself in place of either of the characters. Would you have acted differently?

Common suffering leads to mutual interest. That's why men forced to fight against tyranny form friendships for one another. It is just as plausible, then, that this girl and this man, united by laughter, should form a combine against stupid customers. Talk with a man and you find out that he isn't so different after all. "You can't know a man and hate him," said Woodrow Wilson. The girl, Mame (we might as well call her that as anything else), probably never heard that statement, but she was human nature just the same. She talked with this bundle-wrapper. Let's call him "Paul." Mame found that Paul went to movies, read the *Daily Graphic,* and was on the whole a normal human being. She forgot to notice any difference in him. And in the little respites from selling cambric she liked to talk to him about this, that, or the other thing. What they actually said doesn't matter. This will serve as a specimen of what they might have said.

Mame: "I'll sure be glad when six o'clock comes."

Paul: "So will I."

Now right here I had better tell you that I am not trying to reproduce Paul's southern accent or Mame's American cockney dialect. How they said things doesn't matter. It is sufficient to give you the impression of what they thought. Your imagination will have to do the rest.

Paul: "Have you heard anything about the new rule for closing on Saturdays beginning in June?"

Mame: "I haven't heard anything definite, but I certainly hope they do."

But enough of this. The things they talked about, then, were just everyday matters-of-fact about work, life, and movies. Paul never tried to go any farther. Mame never said more than: "See you tomorrow," when she pulled the

black cloth over the cambric counter and arranged her
cloche hat on her sleek round head.

In real life things don't continue as they began ever.
You come to know a person as an acquaintance. Then you
are thrown into more intimate contact with him. After
that it isn't long before you like him better or like him
less. That was the case with Abelard and Heloise. It was
true of Paul and Mame.

It won't take much imagination to suppose that Mame
lived on 119th Street and Paul on 131st. White people live
on 119th; black people inhabit 131st. It shouldn't strain
your fancy either to imagine that they both usually rode
home from work on top of a Seventh Avenue bus. Suppose that coming out from work one evening, some two or
three months after their first laugh together, Mame should
be waiting for a bus at the same time and the same corner
as Paul. This might not have happened. Paul might have
lived in Brooklyn and Mame have been accustomed to
going home on the subway. But it isn't being sensational to
throw characters together to aid the action of the plot. So
they did meet each other one night about a quarter after
six o'clock waiting for a bus. Paul tipped his hat; Mame
smiled. Bus Number Two came along crowded. They went
up to the top. There was one seat vacant. They sat down
together. They talked of everything you think they would
talk about. There were no distractions to interrupt their
conversation. They talked as they passed throngs of tired
everyday toilers pouring out of stores and warehouses at
42nd Street. They talked as they passed alongside Central
Park. They talked as the bus trundled into upper Seventh
Avenue. Mame got off at 119th Street. She smiled and
said good-bye. There are flaws in this little episode, I
admit. A little too much coincidence. A bit too little moti-
vation. But if you are not too fastidious a reader, I think
you will let it pass. For at least it is within the realms of
plausibility.

Let us say that Paul and Mame did not meet again for a
week, two weeks, a month. But don't let us say they never
met again. They did. Perhaps Paul covertly planned it.
Perhaps Mame did. That doesn't matter. They met. That
is sufficient. And they met several times. In fact, it became
a habit for them to ride up on the bus together. Am I losing reality? I think not. You see, after all, the thing I am
suggesting is a mere mechanical detail. Although I handle
it clumsily, the intrinsic design of the life I am trying to
depict cannot be destroyed.

"So far so good," you say, "but whither go we?" or, if
you incline to slang, "What has their riding home from
work together got to do with the wholesale price of on-
ions?" The answer is simple. It was on such occasions that
Mame found in Paul something she liked. What was the
"something," you ask? Say Mame discovered that Paul was
going to night school in preparation for a clerical examination for a position in the municipal department of New
York. Not much to admire from your point of view. But
suppose all Mame's life had been one of crowded tene-
ments. Say she lived with a cross old aunt, wanted an escape, wanted to get away from humdrum life, to be something better, to marry a decent man—(God knows every
woman wants that). Every woman admires a man who is
doing things. And Paul from Mame's point of view was
doing things. She said to herself: "This colored fellow is
different from anybody else I've ever known. He is a man.
I like him. I wish Albert (let Albert be what we Americans would call Mame's "steady feller") I wish Albert
would go to night school."

And Paul probably thought: "This white girl is a lot less
stuck-up than some colored girls I know. She's darn decent to talk with me like this. I wonder if she would go to
the movies some night with me."

Here we are hundreds of sentences and thousands of
words from the beginning and never a sign of complications. Well, they will be with us in a moment. First I must
get Paul and Mame in love. I could spare myself a great
deal of tedious detail by just saying they came to love one
another. But you would not believe me. All readers come
from Missouri. Anyway, I am going to compromise with
principle and say that Paul came to love Mame first because of novelty and then because he was forced to admire a woman who broke convention to love him. And
Mame fell in love with Paul because to her he represented
a somewhat better man than any other she had ever
known. The process of falling in love is an evasive thing at
best. You somehow know you are in love, but when and
how and, above all, why defy analysis. It is an elusive
something. Say, then, that these two characters fell in love.
If you want a dash of sentiment say they saw dawn in each
other's eyes. There are lovers that do. If you are practical
say Mame saw possibilities of a three room apartment and
no more drudgery. Repeat for emphasis: they fell in love.
What about Albert. Well, let Albert be a wastrel, a drunk-

ard, a loafer. You will find a great many like him. Doubt-
less, you know a few.

I promised you complications. Life demands them as
well as you. Complications? Here they are. Paul takes
Mame to see Lya de Putti in *Variety* at the Rialto. A colored fellow whom he knows sees them. Next morning all
Harlem is gossiping about Paul who has turned "pink-
chaser"—(apologies to Mr. Carl Van Vechten).
When Harlem talks about you it means that you feel curious eyes staring at you. The spirit of scandal stalks your
path. People you know avert their eyes as you pass. Stand
on the street corner and you stand alone. That is the effect
of the colored Mrs. Grundy on a man. The white Mrs.
Grundy may look different, but "the lady and Judy
O'Grady are sisters under the skins." On 119th Street
houses have just as many eyes as on 131st. So when Mame
let Paul take her home once or twice, people talked. Albert heard about it and "raised Hell." The aunt heard
about it and threatened to kick Mame out if she didn't
stop "going around with a nigger." Mame looked guilty.

Does this suit you? You have the sunshine and now you
see the clouds. Are you worried? You should be. I am not
one to lead you up to tragedy and then turn aside to talk
about flowers. Well, you know and I know that life
wouldn't let this end happily. There has got to be death,
there has got to be sorrow. And since it must be, let it
come soon.

But I am not quite ready for the showdown. Like a
woman who powders her nose before every great moment
of her life, I must hesitate, demur—in a word—build up
suspense. We need emotional intensification here. For that
purpose let Paul be happy enough with Mame to forget
the snubs of his own people. Let Mame pacify her aunt
temporarily by threatening to leave and thus deplete the
family revenue eleven dollars a week. The eleven dollars rep-
resents Mame's contribution for room and board. Leave
a cancerous wound in the souls of both characters, if you
must; but let them live yet awhile. For, like Alamanzor,
they have "not leisure yet to die."

Don't be provoked with me. Don't accuse me of "playing in wench-like words with something serious." Peace!
brother. Peace! sister. All will be clear in only a little
while. Soon you will know. Soon you will sit back in your
chair and see Mame and Paul as duly garnished sacrifices.

And whether you like them or not, you will know them as they are.

Paul and Mame were happy. They went to Staten Island on picnics. They went to movies. Paul gave Mame candy. Mame gave Paul a tie for his birthday. And love—the ideal of humanity—lived in their hearts. Or if this is too poetic, just say they enjoyed being with one another. I have not explained their love fully enough, maybe—but can you explain it better? If you can, please fill in the facts for yourself.

When two persons become intimate with one another they lose their sense of proportion. They respect neither time, custom, nor place. This fact got Paul and Mame into trouble. They didn't know when it was time to stop talking and pay attention to their work. You see, it was one thing to exchange a few commonplaces while at work; but it was quite another to delay customers or to smile at each other while the world was waiting for a yard of cambric. Businessmen know such delays irritate their customers. That is why they hire floor-managers to snoop on their salesgirls. You see what I am driving at, don't you? I am getting Paul and Mame into more trouble. Soon I'll have them discharged. But not before I give a sidelight on the episode.

Shopgirls have had love affairs before. They have kept customers waiting before; and have got away with it under the very eyes of floor-managers. It isn't enough, therefore, for me to offer this as the only excuse for getting Mame and Paul discharged. But I can suggest others. A young Negro man talking to a young white woman for more than five minutes is always subject to suspicion. And when this is repeated again and again, scandal gets busy. You know this as well as I do. There is still another reason. Perhaps you remember Albert. I shouldn't have had any justification for naming him if I did not intend to weave him into the plot. It would have been faulty technique. So Albert comes in here. He enters through the department store door and makes his way to the cambric counter. Now he is on the scene. He is half-drunk and a little loud. It is ten-thirty in the morning and Albert has come to tell Paul that he had better "damn sight" leave his woman alone—all white women, in fact. That's just what Albert did. He "bawled Paul out" right before a crowd of people. And Mame couldn't keep her temper. She turned red in the face. She dug her nails in her hands and wanted

to fly at Albert. Paul held her back. He put his arm
around her. The crowd grew larger. A policeman took Albert away. That. is all there is for Albert to do in this
story. The floor-manager whispered something to Paul and
about two hours later both Paul and Mame had their sala-
ries in little manila envelopes. You can't blame the floor-
manager very much. It was for the good of the business.
Anyway, as he told Paul, he had noticed for some time
that they were not paying attention to business. He didn't
get angry. He was simply hard, cold, and matter-of-fact.
That was all.

Here we are facing the climax of this personally conducted tour of a short story. Mame and Paul are out of a
job. They have to live. Mame is crying. Life seems unfair,
bitter, unkind. Don't weep because Mame did. Stand on
the sidelines and see the show. What are Hecuba's tears to
you, or Mame's? I only record that she wept because,
under the circumstances, I think she would have done so.
Paul gritted his teeth. They would get a job soon, he told
her. And it wouldn't be long before he would be able to
take the clerical examination. Then they could get married
and go to Atlantic City for a honeymoon. All that is
needed here is a little time and a little sanity. But life
would cease to be a tragedy, if time would wait for us.
The harsh reality, the bitterness of life comes because everything in the world is run by clocks and whistles. Time
to get up. Time to retire. Time to live. And time to die.
To use a slang expression—Mame and Paul "didn't get the
break."

If you have ever hunted for a job in New York, you
know what it is like to do so. Your feet hurt after the first
two or three days. You get tired of being told that there
are no vacancies. Sometimes you go back to the same
place on five or six occasions before you can find the employment manager in his office, and then he only shakes
his head. Sometimes you think you've got a job; then you
are asked where you worked last, how long, why you quit,
if you have any references. Your heart sinks and you go
out of the door of the inner office, through the outer office, down the elevator and out into the street. And all the
time you are saying to yourself: "Oh God, dear God, am I
your creature?" A man can stand a great deal more of this
sort of thing than a woman. Mame gave up; Paul lasted.
There were other reasons for Mame's surrender but this
had its share in the result.

Mame, I have said, contributed eleven dollars a week to her aunt. A week or so after she was fired her contributions ceased. Mame hadn't saved up much. Soon that was gone. You understand how that might happen, I know. Money doesn't come from the skies. And the girl's name was Mame and not Cinderella. Mame's aunt was angry with Mame in the first place for "taking up with a nigger." She was angrier when Mame lost her job. "I-told-you-so's" dinned in Mame's ears and buzzed in her head. It was too much for the aunt to stand when Mame couldn't pay her the eleven dollars. Mame had to do one thing or the other: "either get out or give up that nigger." Those were the aunt's own words. Do you think that the aunt is too hard a character? Read any metropolitan daily. The world is getting hard and cold. All the world wants is money. Money was all Mame's aunt wanted. So she turned Mame out. But she wasn't altogether cold. She didn't really mean to turn her out. She wanted only to teach Mame a lesson. After all, blood is thicker than water. She didn't believe Mame would really go. She wanted her to stop being a fool and come down to earth. There were plenty of decent young white men she could marry. It was infatuation or something that got Mame this way. If she had her way, she'd either put Mame in the insane asylum or that "nigger" in jail. Whoever heard of such "carryings-on!" She was tired of having people talk about her. She wasn't going to be related to a "nigger" even by marriage.

Don't blame Mame's aunt any more than you did the floor-manager or Albert. All—all of them are just cogs in the wheels of the world. If you must fume and fret, say simply that all the world's a pasture and each one in the world, a jackass.

This is what human beings such as Mame's aunt and Albert and the floor-manager might have done to such a girl as Mame. What would Mame have done? Probably, gone to Paul. She did. But he could not take care of her. He had no money. He was being threatened himself with being put out of his rooming house because he didn't pay his rent. It was a poor time to try to bring a young, unmarried white woman into a respectable Harlem rooming house. Go . . . go where? Somewhere, you say? But where? There are streets. But streets in New York are either covered with soft, cold snow, or melted by the rays of a hot blazing sun. Try living in New York without money. Try living anywhere without money. Friends, you suggest?

I wish I could. But where are friends when your aunt turns you out of doors and you have done what Mame had done? Then, who with pride would go a-begging? Only one thing remains: it whispers in your ear every time there seems no way out—suicide.

Suicide isn't normal. Only abnormal people think of it. Joy may drop from you like a dead bird from a leafless tree, but, somehow, life is still sweet. But too much defeat, too much bitterness make people abnormal. Consider a woman who has drudged all her life; put her in Mame's place. You will find that she is like the string on a violin: draw her too tightly and she snaps. Something snapped in Mame. She kissed Paul goodnight in the park, spent her last dollar and a half to get a room in a settlement house —and turned on the gas. Don't blame Paul. He didn't know she was going to commit suicide. He thought he would see her the next day. Don't say Mame isn't true to life. If you believe she is not, live her life over. Spend two months looking for a job; wandering willy-nilly. Then put her back into the picture as a human being. I think you will succeed.

What about Paul. There isn't much to tell. He stood it. He stood Mame's death. But how he stood it I leave you to imagine. You will agree that he grew bitter. You will not agree that he would commit suicide. That is the sort of melodramatic thing I want to avoid. I am sorry Mame had to commit suicide. But I don't see how she could help it. Do you?

Suppose that after Mame's death Paul got a job as a longshoreman on the New York docks. Not as clerk in the municipal department, mind you. He had given up night school when he lost his job. Then Mame had died and he hadn't gone back. He was bitter, he grew cynical. . . . No money, no job, Mame, were the causes. He might have got over it some time, but that time didn't come. Is this anti-climactic? Not quite. Remember Paul is really the chief character.

When you have gone through what Paul went through, you won't be happy and optimistic. You are apt to look on the world and people in it as just so much damned rot. You are apt to walk around with a chip on your shoulder. And a chip on your shoulder doesn't help you any if you are a longshoreman. They are hard-working, hard-swearing, sweating Negroes, Irish and whatnots—these longshore gangs. And the dock is no place for Hamlet. Even

Falstaff would have a hard time getting along. You've got to laugh loudly, work hard, and mix with the gang. Paul did none of these things. He felt just a little above them. He was always moody, introspective, hard to get along with. Even Negroes despised him. You can imagine the opinion that the Irish held.

Under the circumstances can't you imagine Paul becoming a flaming pillar of rage when an Irish longshore boss yelled at him: "Hey, nigger, stop dreaming and go to work. Yes I mean you, you son of a——." But the Irish fellow didn't finish his oath. Paul hit him over the head with a chisel. Chisels are common on the docks. They are used to open boxes. Paul opened the fellow's head with one. He didn't kill him. The Irish foreman lived to testify against Paul. He was quite well when the District Attorney painted a gaudy word-picture of how Paul lost his last job. He saw twelve ordinary men, readers of the *Daily Graphic,* cigar salesmen, shopkeepers, butchers, insurance agents—all, somehow, a little influenced by the way Paul glared at people in the courtroom and by the District Attorney's subtle suggestion that Paul had been the cause of a white woman's suicide. Of course, they thought more about the affair than actually happened. Can't you see that District Attorney? He's running on the state ticket next year. He's got to make a record. Some cases he can't prosecute to win. Politics won't let him. Here is one in which he can have a free hand. Here he can make a name for himself. Look at the jury. They don't know much about sociology, but they know where to get the best beer in New York City. Look at the judge. He's a scholarly man, but he's sick of the crime wave. Something's got to be done. And Paul to him is obviously a criminal. Look at the young man who calls himself a lawyer. He is defending Paul and he means well. But his best is not good enough. Maybe next year or year after he'll be a good lawyer. Paul won't smile, he won't plead. He is obstinate. I think you will find little fault with the verdict. Guilty. The law is the law. He was lucky to get only seven years.

I have outlined this story and set it in New York. If you like you may write it to please your taste and set it any place under the sun. The results would not vary a great deal. If you must have a happy ending, pardon Paul, or, bring him back from prison and regenerate him. But I doubt if you will succeed. It is hard to get a pardon. It is harder to reform a man who looks on life pessimistically for seven years. At least grant that what I have outlined is true or might be true. As someone has writen (a Jewish poet, I think):

> The sum and substance of the tale is this
> The rest is but the mise en scène
> And if I have painted it amiss
> I am a prattler and a charlatan.

Oh yes, you will want a moral. I had forgot. Take it from Shakespeare:

> Golden lads and girls all must
> Like chimney sweepers come to dust.

Home To Harlem

by Claude McKay

Jake was paid off. He changed a pound note he had brought with him. He had fifty-nine dollars. From South Ferry he took an express subway train for Harlem.

Jake drank three Martini cocktails with cherries in them. The price, he noticed, had gone up from ten to twenty-five cents. He went to Bank's and had a Maryland fried-chicken feed—a big one with candied sweet potatoes.

He left his suitcase behind the counter of a saloon on Lenox Avenue. He went for a promenade on Seventh Avenue between One Hundred and Thirty-fifth and One Hundred and Fortieth Streets. He thrilled to Harlem. His blood was hot. His eyes were alert as he sniffed the street like a hound. Seventh Avenue was nice, a little too nice that night.

Jake turned off on Lenox Avenue. He stopped before an ice-cream parlor to admire girls sipping ice-cream soda through straws. He went into a cabaret. . . .

A little brown girl aimed the arrow of her eye at him as he entered. Jake was wearing a steel-gray English suit. It fitted him loosely and well, perfectly suited his presence. She knew at once that Jake must have just landed. She rested her chin on the back of her hands and smiled at him. She was brown, but she had tinted her leaf-like face to a ravishing chestnut. She had on an orange scarf over a green frock, which was way above her knees, giving an

27

adequate view of legs lovely in fine champagne-colored stockings. . . .

Her shaft hit home. . . . Jake crossed over to her table. He ordered Scotch and soda.

"Scotch is better with soda or even water," he said. "English folks don't take whisky straight, as we do."

But she preferred ginger-ale in place of soda. The cabaret singer, seeing that they were making up to each other, came expressly over to their table and sang. Jake gave the singer fifty cents. . . .

Her left hand was on the table. Jake covered it with his right.

"Is it clear sailing between us, sweetie?" he asked.

"Sure thing. You just landed from over there?"

"Just today."

"But there wasn't no boat in with soldiers today, daddy."

"I made it in a special one."

"Why, you lucky baby. . . . I'd like to go to another place, though. What about you?"

"Anything you say, I'm game," responded Jake.

They walked along Lenox Avenue. He held her arm. His flesh tingled. He felt as if his whole body was a flaming wave. She was intoxicated, blinded under the overwhelming force.

But nevertheless she did not forget her business.

"How much is it going to be, daddy?" she demanded.

"How much? How much? Five?"

"Aw no, daddy . . ."

"Ten?"

She shook her head.

"Twenty, sweetie," he said gallantly.

"Daddy," she answered, "I wants fifty."

"Good," he agreed. He was satisfied. She was responsive. She was beautiful. He loved the curious color on her cheek.

They went to a buffet flat on One Hundred and Thirty-seventh Street. The proprietress opened the door without removing the chain and peeked out. She was a matronly mulatto woman. She recognized the girl, who had put herself in front of Jake, and she slid back the chain and said, "Come right in."

The windows were heavily and carefully shaded. There was beer and wine, and there was plenty of hard liquor. Black and brown men sat at two tables in one room, playing poker. In the other room a phonograph was grinding

out a "blues," and some couples were dancing, thick as
maggots in a vat of sweet liquor, and as wriggling.

Jake danced with the girl. They shuffled warmly, glo-
riously about the room. He encircled her waist with both
hands, and she put both of hers to his shoulders and laid
her head against his breast. And they shuffled around.

"Harlem! Harlem!" thought Jake. "Where else could I
have all this life but Harlem? Good old Harlem! Harlem,
I've got you' number down. Lenox Avenue, you're a bear,
I know it. And, baby honey, sure enough you'se a pippin
for your pappy. Oh, boy! . . ."

After Jake had paid for his drinks, that fifty-dollar note
was all he had left in the world. He gave it to the
girl. . . .

"Is we going now, honey?" he asked her.

"Sure, daddy. Let's beat it."

Oh, to be in Harlem again after two years away. The
deep-dyed color, the thickness, the closeness of it. The
noises of Harlem. The sugared laughter. The honey-talk
on its streets. And all night long ragtime "blues" playing
somewhere . . . singing somewhere, dancing somewhere!
oh, the contagious fever of Harlem. Burning everywhere
in dark-eyed Harlem. . . . Burning now in Jake's sweet
blood. . . .

He woke up in the morning in a state of perfect peace.
She brought him hot coffee and cream and doughnuts. He
yawned. He sighed. He was satisfied. He breakfasted. He
washed. He dressed. The sun was shining. He sniffed the
fine dry air. Happy, familiar Harlem.

"I ain't got a cent to my name," mused Jake, "but ahm
as happy as a prince, all the same. Yes, I is."

He loitered down Lenox Avenue. He shoved his hand in
his pocket and pulled out the fifty-dollar note. A piece of
paper was pinned to it on which was scrawled in pencil:

"Just a little gift from a baby girl to a honey boy!"

"Great balls of fire. Looka here! See mah luck." Jake
stopped in his tracks . . . went on . . . stopped again . . .
retraced his steps . . . checked himself. "Guess I won't go
back right now. Never let a woman think you're too crazy
about her. But she's a particularly sweet piece of business. Me and her again tonight. . . . Handful o' luck shot
straight outa heaven. Oh, boy, Harlem is mine."

Jake went rolling along Fifth Avenue. He crossed over
to Lenox Avenue and went into Uncle Doc's saloon,

where he had left his bag. Called for a glass of Scotch.
"Gimme the siphon, Doc. I'm off the straight stuff."

"Iszh you? Counta what?"

"Hits the belly better this way. I l'arned it over the
other side."

A slap on the shoulder brought him sharply round.
"Zeddy Plummer! What grave is you risen from?" he
cried.

"Buddy, you looks so good to me, I could kish you,"
Zeddy said.

"Where?"

"Everywhere . . . French style."

"One on one cheek and one on the other."

"Savee-vous?"

"Parlee-vous?"

Uncle Doc set another glass on the counter and poured
out pure bourbon. Zeddy reached a little above Jake's
shoulders. He was stocky, thick-shouldered, flat-footed,
and walked like a bear. Some more customers came in and
the buddies eased round to the short side of the bar.

"What part of the earth done belch you out?" demanded Zeddy. "Nevah heard no God's tidings a-you
sence we missed you from Brest."

"And how about you?" Jake countered. "Didn't them
Germans git you scrambling over the top?"

"Nevah see'd them, buddy. None a-them showed the
goose-step around Brest. Have a shot on me. . . . Well,
dawg bite me, but—say, Jake, we've got some more stuff to
booze over."

Zeddy slapped Jake on his breast and looked him over
again. "Tha's some stuff you're strutting in, boh. 'Taint
'Merican and it ain't French."

"English." Jake showed his clean, white teeth.

"Mah granny an' me! You been in that theah white
folks' country, too?"

"And don't I look as if I's been? Where else could a fellow git such good and cheap man clothes to cover his
skin?"

"Buddy, I know it's the truth. What you doing today?"

"No, when you make me think ov it, particular thing.
And you?"

"I'm alongshore, but I ain't gwine to work this day."

"I guess I've got to be heaving along right back to it,
too, in pretty short time. I got to get me a room but—"

Uncle Doc reminded Jake that his suitcase was there.

"I ain't nevah fohgitting all mah worldly goods," responded Jake.

Zeddy took Jake to a poolroom where they played.
Jake was the better man. From the poolroom they went to
Aunt Hattie's chitterling joint in One Hundred and
Thirty-second Street, where they fed. Fricassee chicken
and rice. Green peas. Stewed corn.

Aunt Hattie's was renowned among the lowly of Harlem's black belt. It was a little basement joint, smoke-col-
ored. And Aunt Hattie was weather-beaten, dark-brown,
cherry-faced, with two rusty-red front teeth sticking together conspicuously out of her twisted, spread-away
mouth. She cooked delicious food—home-cooked food
they called it. None of the boys loafing round that section
of Fifth Avenue would dream of going to any other place
for their "poke chops."

Aunt Hattie admired her new customer from the
kitchen door and he quite filled her sight. And when she
went with the dish rag to wipe the oilcloth before setting
down the cocoanut pie, she rubbed her breast against
Jake's shoulder and a sensual light gleamed in her aged
smoke-red eyes.

The buddies talked about the days of Brest. Zeddy recalled the everlasting unloading and unloading of ships
and the toting of lumber. The house of the Young Men's
Christian Association, overlooking the harbor, where colored soldiers were not wanted. . . . The central Rue de
Siam and the point near the Prefecture of Marine, from
which you could look on the red lights of the Quartier Reserve. The fatal fights between black men and white in the
Maisons closes. The encounters between apaches and
white Americans. The French sailors that couldn't get the
Yankee idea of amour and men. And the cemetery, just
beyond the old medieval gate of the town, where he left
his second-best buddy.

"Poor boh. Was always bellyaching for a chance over
the top. Nevah got it nor nothing. Not even a baid in the
hospital. Strong like a bull, yet just knocked off in the
dark through raw cracker cussedness. Some life it was,
buddy, in them days. We was always on the defensive as if
the boches, as the froggies called them, was right down on
us."

"Yet you stuck t'rough it, toting lumber. Got back to
Harlem all right, though."

"You bet I did, boh. You kain trust Zeddy Plummer to
look out for his own black hide. . . . But you, buddy.

How come you just vanished that way like a spook? How did you take your tail out ov it?"

Jake told Zeddy how he walked out of it straight to the station in Brest. Le Havre, London. The West India docks. And back home to Harlem.

"But you must keep it dark, buddy," Zeddy cautioned. "Don't go shooting off your mouth too free. Gov'mant still smoking out deserters and draft dodgers."

"I ain't told no niggers but you, boh. Nor ofay, neither. Ahm in your confidence, chappie."

"That's all right, buddy." Zeddy put his hand on Jake's knee. "It's better to keep your business close all the time. But I'll tell you this for your perticular information. Niggers am awful close-mouthed in some things. There is fellows here in Harlem that just telled the draft to mount upstairs. Police and soldiers were hunting ev'where foh them. And they was right here in Harlem. Fifty dollars foh them. All their friends knowed it and not a one gived them in. I tell you, niggers am amazing sometimes. Yet other times, without any natural reason, they will just go vomiting out their guts to the ofays about one another."

"God; but it's good to get back home again! . . ." said Jake.

"I should think you was hungry foh a li'l brown honey. I tell you trute, buddy. I made mine ovah there, spittin ov ev'thing. I l'arned her a little z'inglese and she l'arned me beaucoup plus the French stuff. The real stuff, buddy. But I was tearing mad and glad to get back all the same. Take it from me, buddy, there ain't no honey lak to that theah comes out of our own belonging-to-us honeycomb."

"Man, what you telling me?" cried Jake. "Don't I know it? What else you think made me leave over the other side? And dog mah doggone ef I didn't find it just as I landed."

"K-hhhhh! Khhhhh!" Zeddy laughed. "Dog mah cats! You done tasted the real life a'ready?"

"Last night was the end of the world, buddy, and to-night ahm going back there," chanted Jake as he rose and began kicking up his heels round the joint.

Zeddy also got up and put on his gray cap. They went back to the poolroom. Jake met two more fellows that he knew and got into a ring of Zeddy's pals. . . . Most of them were longshoremen. There was plenty of work, Jake learned. Before he left the poolroom he and Zeddy agreed to meet the next evening at Uncle Doc's.

"Got to work tomorrow, boh," Zeddy informed Jake.

"Good old New York! The same old wench of a city. Elevated racketing over you' head. Subway bellowing under you' feet. Me foh wrastling round them piers again. Scratching down to the bottom of them ships and scrambling out. All alongshore for me now. No more fooling with the sea. Same old New York. Everybody dashing round like crazy. . . . Same old New York. But the ofay faces am different from over there. And the air it—O Gawd, it works in you' flesh and blood like Scotch. O Lawdy, Lawdy! I wants to live to a hundred and finish mah days in New York."

Jake threw himself up as if to catch the air pouring down from the blue sky. . . .

"Harlem! Harlem! Little thicker, little darker and noisier and smellier but Harlem just the same. The niggers done plowed through Hundred and Thirtieth Street. Heading straight foh One Hundred and Twenty-fifth. Spades beyond Eighth Avenue. Going, going, going Harlem! Going up! Nevah befoh I seed so many dickty shines in such swell motorcars. Plenty moh nigger shops. Seventh Avenue done gone high-brown. O Lawdy! Harlem bigger, Harlem better and sweeter."

"Streets and streets! One Hundred and Thirty-second, Thirty-third, Thirty-fourth. It wasn't One Hundred and Thirty-fifth and it wasn't beyond theah. . . . O Lawd! how did I fohgit to remember the street and number. I reeled out there like a drunken man. I been so happy. . . .

"Thirty-fourth, Thirty-second, Thirty-third. . . . Only difference in the name. All the streets am just the same and all the houses like as peas. I could try this one heah or that one there but—Rabbit foot! I didn't even git her name. Oh, Jakie, Jake! What a big Ah-Ah you is.

"I was a fool not to go back right then when I feeled like it. What did I want to tighten up mahself and crow and strut like a crazy cat for? A grand Ah-Ah I is. Feet in mah hands. Take me back to the Baltimore tonight. I ain't gwine to know no peace till I lay these here hands on mah tantalizing brown again."

One Way To Heaven

by Countee Cullen

Constancia Brandon, for whom Mattie worked, was the mirror in which most of social Harlem delighted to gaze and see itself. She was beautiful, possessed money enough to be willful, capricious, and rude whenever she desired to deviate from her usual suave kindness; and she was not totally deficient in brains. Tall and willowy, with a fine ivory face whose emaciation spelled weakness and weariness, she quickly dispelled such false first impressions when she began to talk, with either her eyes or her tongue, in the use of both of which she was uncommonly gifted. Her gray eyes had strange contractile powers, narrowing into the minutest slits of disbelief and boredom, or widening into incredibly lovely globes of interest and amazement. They were not the windows of her soul, but they were the barometers by which one might gauge her interest in what he was saying.

Synthesis seemed to have had no part in her making. She had been born in Boston, and baptized Constance in the Baptist church; but at sixteen she had informed her astounded parents and her equally astounded and amused friends that thenceforth her name was to be Constancia; that she found the religious ecstasies of the Baptist and Methodist faiths too harrowing for her nerves; and that she would attempt to scale the heavenly ramparts by way of the less rugged paths of the Episcopalian persuasion.

From the beginning her manner was grand, and she gave one the impression that the great triumvirate, composed of God, the Cabots, and the Lodges, had with her advent into the world let down the color bar and been reorganized, to include hereafter on an equal footing Constancia Brown. She had never experienced any racial disturbances or misgivings at attributing her equanimity on this score to one English grandfather, one grandfather black as soot, one grandmother the color of coffee and cream in their most felicitous combination, one Creole grandmother, and two sane parents. She was interested in her genealogy only because she wanted to ascertain if there really was somewhere in the medley a Gypsy woman or man whose slowly diminishing blood was responsible for her incessant and overwhelming love of jewelry. From the moment her ears had been pierced they had never been devoid of ornaments; sleeping or waking, she gave evidence of wise and charming investments in bracelets, rings, and pendants.

But her tongue was her chief attraction, ornament, and deterrent. Her linguistic powers, aided by an uncanny mnemonic ability, had brought her high honors at Radcliffe and the headlong devotion of George Brandon. Her schoolmates called her Lady Macbeth, not that she was tragic, but that she never spoke in a monosyllable where she could use a longer word; she never said "buy" when she might use "purchase," and purchased nothing to which she might "subscribe." The first night he met her at an Alpha Phi Alpha fraternity ball George Brandon had pleased her mightily by dubbing her Mrs. Shakespeare.

George Brandon, short, thick-set, light brown, and methodical, was an Oklahoma Brandon whose very fingertips were supposed to smell of oil and money. Constancia, whose lawyer father enjoyed a comfortable if not opulent living, had really lacked for no good thing, and so had been able to meet George Brandon with a disinterestedness and reserve that other young girls of colored Boston had not been able to simulate. She had been amused at his enervated, drawling speech and his doglike devotion to her, but from that first meeting she had harbored kindly feelings for him because he had recognized her verbal literary ability by the sobriquet of Mrs. Shakespeare. It was inevitable, then, that after six months of frantic courting she should have accepted him when he pleaded that if she failed to do so he would be in no fit condition to be graduated from the Harvard Medical College.

"Not for your money, my dear," she had assured him,

"nor for any inherent and invisible pulchritude in yourself, but in order to spare the world an accomplished physician, will I enter the enchanted realms of wedlock with you."

George had been happy to have her, even on the basis of so stilted and unromantic an acceptance. But the small-sized Oklahoma town to which he had taken her had not been able to reconcile itself to Mrs. Shakespeare. The small group of the Negro élite found her insufferable; they never knew what she was talking about. When she was hostess her guests generally left feeling that they had been insulted by her grandiose manners and complicated words; when she was guest her hostess never knew whether her comments on the party were commendable or derogatory. Matters fared no better at the monthly interracial meetings where the races met to exchange ideas and mutual good-will pledges, but not to touch hands. Constancia was elected secretary of the association, and thereafter the minutes were totally unintelligible save to herself, and when read made the bewildered workers for racial adjustment feel guilty of dark and immoral intentions. Mrs. Marshall, the wife of the white Baptist minister, and Mrs. Connelly, the wife of the leading white merchant, resented beyond concealment Constancia's chic vestments, blazing rings, and pendants; nor did they like the composed tone in which she would rise to say, "I unequivocally disagree with Mrs. Marshall," or, "I feel that Mrs. Connelly is in grievous error on this question."

In Oklahoma the Brandons could keep no servants; for Constancia had a strong democratic leaning which would not permit her to speak down to her menials. "I shall speak as I always do," she would say to the vainly expostulating George, "and they must learn to understand me. I do not want to embarrass them by making them self-conscious, by causing them to think that I do not believe that they have as much intelligence as I." And she continued to exhort her unintelligent help to "Come hither," to "Convey this communication to the doctor," or to "Dispatch this missive," until in utter self-defense they rebelled, and in true native fashion quit without giving notice.

Finally, at the repeated prayers of their respective ladies, the Reverend Mr. Marshall and Mr. Connelly, along with several colored members of the interracial committee, intimated to George that for the sake of racial amity it would be better if Constancia no longer kept the minutes of the meetings. And it was in order to placate Constancia for this loss of power and prestige that George brought her to Harlem.

In Harlem, Constancia had found her paradise. The oil wells of Oklahoma were the open-sesame for which the portals of that extensive domain which goes by the name of Harlem society had swung wide to her. Wherever she went she conquered, and her weapons were various and well selected. Her interest in social activities won over the doctors' and lawyers' wives with whom, as Dr. Brandon's wife, she must naturally spend a part of her time; her democratic treatment of actors, writers, and singers made them her devoted slaves, while the very first week she was in New York her astounding vivacity and bewildering language completely floored Mrs. Vanderbilt-Jones of Brooklyn, who sent her an invitation to the Cosmos ball, and who even consented in all her rippling glory of black silk spangled with jet to attend Constancia's first Sunday night at home. For six days Harlem buzzed with the astonishing sight of Mrs. Vanderbilt-Jones in an animated and gracious conversation with Lottie Smith, singer of blues. Constancia had indeed been more than conqueror.

The Brandons purchased a fourteen-room house in what was called by less-moneyed and perhaps slightly envious Harlemites Striver's Row. George, who despite the unceasing emissions from the Oklahoma wells, came of industrious stock and willed to be a capable practicing physician, was relegated to the ground floor, while Constancia ruled supremely over the rest of the house.

She was endowed with taste of a diffusive sort, which communicated itself to the furnishings of her home as well as to her guests. What money could secure she bought, but indiscriminately. A survey of her home found ages and periods and faddistic moments juxtaposed in the most comradely and unhistoric manner, while the contributions of countries were wedded with the strictest disregard for geography.

Constancia never moved an eyelash to corral, but every author who came to her home either brought or sent an autographed copy of his books. Constancia dutifully and painstakingly read them all, after which she would give George an intricate résumé (which he promptly forgot) in order that, should he ever emerge into society, he might converse with intelligence and while talking to Bradley Norris not compliment him on the beauty of a poem which had been written by Lawrence Harper. No artist or singer was permitted to plead fatigue or temperament at

Constancia's *soirées.* He might offend once, but Constancia would remark within ample hearing distance that temperament was the earmark of vulgarity and incapacity. If the erring virtuoso sinned a second time, she blue-penciled him, and remembered him with an elephant's relentlessness. For this reason her innumerable parties never lacked excitement and verve, and there was seldom a week in which the *New York Era* or the *Colonial News* did not carry a portrait of "Harlem's most charming hostess."

Lest it be thought that Constancia was built along strictly frivolous lines, let it be noted in all fairness and in her defense that she found time to belong to sixteen lodges which she never attended, but in which she was never unfinancial, and at whose yearly women's meetings she was always called upon to speak. She was a teacher in the Episcopalian Sunday school, because it convened in the morning and so left her free for her afternoon visits and her Sunday-evening at-homes. She was a member of the Board of the National Negro Uplift Society and a director of the Diminutive Harlem Theater Group; and she yearly donated fifty dollars for the best poem "by any poet" (never would she consent to stipulate "by any colored poet," although a colored poet had always won the award), published during the year in the *Clarion,* the Negro monthly magazine. Added to this, she belonged to two bridge clubs, one sorority, a circulating library, and she gave one hour a week in demonstrating household duties at the Harlem Home for Fallen Girls.

The freemasonry existing between the races in New York neither pleased nor disturbed her. She was equally gracious to an eccentric dancer from the Lafayette Variety Theater and to a slumming matron from Park Avenue, out with fear and trembling to discover just how the other color lived. When at one of her parties it was suggested to her in fiery language by a spirited young Negro, who could neither forget nor forgive, that a celebrated white writer present was out to exploit and ridicule her, she had replied:

"Ridicule me? If he contrives to depict me as I am, he shall have achieved his first artistic creation. If he does less, he shall have ridiculed himself. And besides, don't be so damnably self-conscious or you will be miserable all your life. Now vouchsafe me your attendance and let me introduce you to the ogre who has come to devour us all."

She had then taken the protesting youngster by the

hand, piloted him through her groups of chattering guests, and brought him to a standstill before Walter Derwent.

"My dear Mr. Derwent, I want you to do me a kindness. Here is a young man who is laboring under the apprehension that your frequent visits to Harlem have an ulterior motive, that you look upon us as some strange concoction which you are out to analyze and betray. I wish you would either disabuse him of, or confirm him in, his fears."

And she had left them together, both equally frightened. After leaving them, she had paused to shout into Mrs. Vanderbilt-Jones's deaf and sparkling ear:

"I have just coupled a diminutive god with a sprouting devil." She passed on before Mrs. Vanderbilt-Jones could summon courage enough to demand an explanation of the riddle.

Mattie had been Constancia's maid for over six years, six days out of seven. Being maid meant making herself generally useful, and giving orders to Porter, *l'homme à tout faire,* who was disinclined to see work which was not pointed out to him. Mattie adored Constancia, although she disapproved of her parties and thought her guests exceedingly strange and curiously mannered. Constancia spoke of Mattie as the perfect maid, a jewel of the first water. She had reached this conclusion when, coming home one afternoon, she had interrupted Mattie in the midst of her dusting to inform her:

"Mattie, I have just been psychoanalyzed."

Mattie had said nothing for a moment, but had ceased dusting, and then delved down into her apron pocket, whence she extracted a small pocket dictionary. After turning its pages and scanning the word carefully, she had turned to the fascinated Constancia and, without a ripple stirring her smooth black face, had said:

"Yes, Ma'am. I hope you like it."

Constancia had flown to her, had kissed her, and called her a *rara avis,* which had disturbed Mattie throughout the day because she could not find that in her dictionary.

Miss Cynthie

by Rudolph Fisher

For the first time in her life somebody had called her "madam." She had been standing, bewildered but unafraid, while innumerable redcaps appropriated piece after piece of the baggage arrayed on the platform. Neither her brief seventy years' journey through life nor her long two days' travel northward had dimmed the live brightness of her eyes, which, for all their bewilderment, had accurately selected her own treasures out of the row of luggage and guarded them vigilantly. "These yours, madam?"

The biggest redcap of all was smiling at her. He looked for all the world like Doc Crinshaw's oldest son back home. Her little brown face relaxed; she smiled back at him.

"They got to be. You all done took all the others."

He laughed aloud. Then—"Carry 'em in for you?"

She contemplated his bulk. "Reckon you can manage it —puny little feller like you?"

Thereupon they were friends. Still grinning broadly, he surrounded himself with her impedimenta, the enormous brown extension-case on one shoulder, the big straw suitcase in the opposite hand, the carpetbag under one arm. She herself held fast to the umbrella. "Always like to have sump'm in my hand when I walk. Can't never tell when you'll run across a snake."

"There aren't any snakes in the city."

"There's snakes everywhere, chile."

They began the tedious hike up the interminable platform. She was small and quick. Her carriage was surprisingly erect, her gait astonishingly spry. She said:

"You liked to took my breath back yonder, boy, callin' me madam. Back home everybody call me Miss Cynthie. Even their chillun. Black folks, white folks too. Miss Cynthie. Well, when you come up with that madam o' yourn, I say to myself, 'Now, I wonder who that chile's a-grinnin' at? Madam stands for mist'ess o' the house, and I sho' ain' mist'ess o' nothin' in this hyeh New York.' "

"Well, you see, we call everybody madam."

"Everybody?—Hm." The bright eyes twinkled. "Seem like that's worry me some—if I was a man."

He acknowledged his slip and observed, "I see this isn't your first trip to New York."

"First trip any place, son. First time I been over fifty mile from Waxhaw. Only travelin' I've done is in my head. Ain' seen many places, but I's seen a passel o' people. Reckon places is pretty much alike after people been in 'em awhile."

"Yes, ma'am. I guess that's right."

"You ain' no reg'lar bag-toter, is you?"

"Ma'am?"

"You talk too good."

"Well, I only do this in vacationtime. I'm still in school."

"You is. What you aimin' to be?"

"I'm studying medicine."

"You is?" She beamed. "Aimin' to be a doctor, huh? Thank the Lord for that. That's what I always wanted my David to be. My grandchile hyeh in New York. He's to meet me hyeh now."

"I bet you'll have a great time."

"Mussn't bet, chile. That's sinful. I tole him 'fore he left home, I say, 'Son, you the only one o' the chillun what's got a chance to amount to sump'm. Don't th'ow it away. Be a preacher or a doctor. Work yo' way up and don' stop short. If the Lord don' see fit for you to doctor the soul, then doctor the body. If you don' get to be a reg'lar doctor, be a tooth-doctor. If you jes' can't make that, be a foot-doctor. And if you don't get that fur, be a undertaker. That's the least you must be. That ain' so bad. Keep you acquainted with the house of the Lord. Always mind the house o' the Lord—whatever you do, do like a church steeple: aim high and go straight.' "

"Did he get to be a doctor?"

"Don' b'lieve he did. Too late startin', I reckon. But he's done succeeded at sump'm. Mus' be at least a undertaker, 'cause he started sendin' the homefolks money, and he come home las' year dressed like Judge Pettiford's boy what went off to school in Virginia. Wouldn't tell none of us 'zackly what he was doin', but he said he wouldn' never be happy till I come and see for myself. So hyeh I is." Something softened her voice. "His mammy died befo' he knowed her. But he was always sech a good child—" The something was apprehension. "Hope he *is* a undertaker."

They were mounting a flight of steep stairs leading to an exit-gate, about which clustered a few people still hoping to catch sight of arriving friends. Among these a tall young brown-skinned man in a light gray suit suddenly waved his panama and yelled, "Hey, Miss Cynthie!"

Miss Cynthie stopped, looked up, and waved back with a delighted umbrella. The redcap's eyes lifted too. His lower jaw sagged.

"Is that your grandson?"

"It sho' is," she said and distanced him for the rest of the climb. The grandson, with an abandonment that superbly ignored onlookers, folded the little woman in an exultant, smothering embrace. As soon as she could, she pushed him off with breathless mock impatience.

"Go 'way, you fool, you. Aimin' to squeeze my soul out my body befo' I can get a look at this place?" She shook herself into the semblance of composure. "Well. You don't look hungry, anyhow."

"Ho-ho! Miss Cynthie in New York! Can y' imagine this? Come on. I'm parked on Eighth Avenue."

The redcap delivered the outlandish luggage into a robin's-egg-blue open Packard with scarlet wheels, accepted the grandson's dollar and smile, and stood watching the car roar away up Eighth Avenue.

Another redcap came up. "Got a break, hey, boy?"

"Dave Tappen himself—can you beat that?"

"The old lady hasn't seen the station yet—starin' at him."

"That's not the half of it, bozo. That's Dave Tappen's grandmother. And what do you s'pose she hopes?"

"What?"

"She hopes that Dave has turned out to be a successful undertaker!"

"Undertaker? Undertaker!"

They stared at each other a gaping moment, then doubled up with laughter.

"Look—through there—that's the Chrysler Building. Oh, hallelujah! I meant to bring you up Broadway—"

"David—"

"Ma'am?"

"This hyeh wagon yourn?"

"Nobody else's. Sweet buggy, ain't it?"

"David—you ain't turned out to be one of them moonshiners, is you?"

"Moonshiners—Moon—Ho! No indeed, Miss Cynthie. I got a better racket 'n that."

"Better which?"

"Game. Business. Pickup."

"Tell me, David. What is yo' racket?"

"Can't spill it yet, Miss Cynthie. Rather show you. Tomorrow night you'll know the worst. Can you make out till tomorrow night?"

"David, you know I always wanted you to be a doctor, even if 'twasn' nothin' but a foot-doctor. The very leas' I wanted you to be was a undertaker."

"Undertaker! Oh, Miss Cynthie!—with my sunny disposition?"

"Then you ain' even a undertaker?"

"Listen, Miss Cynthie. Just forget 'bout what I am for a while. Just till tomorrow night. I want you to see for yourself. Tellin' you will spoil it. Now stop askin', you hear? —because I'm not answerin'—I'm surprisin' you. And don't expect anybody you meet to tell you. It'll mess up the whole works. Understand? Now give the big city a break. There's the elevated train going up Columbus Avenue. Ain't that hot stuff?"

Miss Cynthie looked. "Humph!" she said. "Tain' half high as that trestle two mile from Waxhaw."

She thoroughly enjoyed the ride up Central Park West. The stagger lights, the extent of the park, the high, close, kingly buildings, remarkable because their stoves cooled them in summer as well as heated them in winter, all drew nods of mild interest. But what gave her special delight was not these: it was that David's car so effortlessly sped past the headlong drove of vehicles racing northward.

They stopped for a red light; when they started again their machine leaped forward with a triumphant eagerness that drew from her an unsuppressed, "Hot you, David! That's it."

He grinned appreciatively. "Why, you're a regular New Yorker already."

"New York nothin'! I done the same thing fifty years ago—befo' I knowed they was a New York."

"What!"

"Deed so. Didn' I use to tell you 'bout my young mare, Betty? Chile, I'd hitch Betty up to yo' grandpa's buggy and pass anything on the road. Betty never knowed what another horse's dust smelt like. No 'n deedy. Shuh, boy, this ain' nothin' new to me. Why that broke-down Fo'd yo uncle Jake's got ain' nothin'—nothin' but a sorry mess. Done got so slow I jes' won' ride in it—I declare I'd rather walk. But this hyeh thing, now, this is right nice." She settled back in complete, complacent comfort, and they sped on, swift and silent.

Suddenly she sat erect with abrupt discovery.

"David—well—bless my soul!"

"What's the matter, Miss Cynthie?"

Then he saw what had caught her attention. They were traveling up Seventh Avenue now, and something was miraculously different. Not the road; that was as broad as ever, wide, white, gleaming in the sun. Not the houses; they were lofty still, lordly, disdainful, supercilious. Not the cars; they continued to race impatiently onward, innumerable, precipitate, tumultuous. Something else, something at once obvious and subtle, insistent, pervasive, compelling.

"David—this mus' be Harlem!"

"Good Lor', Miss Cynthie—!"

"Don' use the name of the Lord in vain, David."

"But I mean—gee!—you're no fun at all. You get everything before a guy can tell you."

"You got plenty to tell me, David. But don' nobody need to tell me this. Look a yonder."

Not just a change of complexion. A completely dissimilar atmosphere. Sidewalks teeming with leisurely strollers, at once strangely dark and bright. Boys in white trousers, berets, and green shirts, with slickened black heads and proud swagger. Bareheaded girls in crisp organdy dresses, purple, canary, gay scarlet. And laughter, abandoned strong Negro laughter, some falling full on the ear, some not heard at all, yet sensed—the warm life-breath of the tireless carnival to which Harlem's heart quickens in summer.

"This is it," admitted David. "Get a good eyeful. Here's One Hundred and Twenty-fifth Street—regular little Broadway. And here's the Alhambra, and up ahead we'll pass the Lafayette."

"What's them?"

"Theaters."

"Theaters? Theaters. Humph! Look, David—is that a colored folks church?" They were passing a fine gray-stone edifice.

"That? Oh. Sure it is. So's this one on this side."

"No! Well, ain' that fine? Splendid big church like that for colored folks."

Taking Lis cue from this, her first tribute to the city, he said, "You ain't seen nothing yet. Wait a minute."

They swung left through a side street and turned right on a boulevard. "What do you think o' that?" And he pointed to the quarter-million-dollar St. Mark's.

"That a colored church, too?"

" 'Tain' no white one. And they built it themselves, you know. Nobody's hand-me-down gift."

She hea ed a great happy sigh. "Oh, yes, it was a gift, David. It was a gift from on high." Then, "Look a hyeh —which a one you belong to?"

"Me? Why, I don't belong to any—that is, none o' these. Mine's over in another section. Y'see, mine's Baptist. These are all Methodist. See?"

"M-m. Uh-huh. I see."

They circled a square and slipped into a quiet narrow street overlooking a park, stopping before the tallest of the apartment houses in the single commanding row.

Alighting, Miss Cynthie gave this imposing structure one sidewise, upward glance, and said, "Y'all live like bees in a hive, don't y'?—I boun' the women does all the work, too." A moment later, "So this is a elevator? Feel like I'm glory-bound sho' nuff."

Along a tiled corridor and into David's apartment. Rooms leading into rooms. Luxurious couches, easy chairs, a brown-walnut grand piano, gay-shaded floor lamps, paneled walls, deep rugs, treacherous glass-wood floors—and a smiling golden-skinned girl in a gingham housedress, approaching with outstretched hands.

"This is Ruth, Miss Cynthie."

"Miss Cynthie!" said Ruth.

They clasped hands. "Been wantin' to see David's girl ever since he first wrote us 'bout her."

"Come—here's your room this way. Here's the bath. Get out of your things and get comfy. You must be worn out with the trip."

"Worn out? Worn out? Shuh. How you gon' get worn out on a train? Now if 'twas a horse, maybe, or Jake's no-

count Fo'd—but a train—didn' but one thing bother me
on that train."

"What?"

"When the man made them beds down, I jes' couldn'
manage to undress same as at home. Why, s'posin' sump'm
bus' the train open—where'd you be? Naked as a jaybird
in dewberry time."

David took in her things and left her to get comfortable. He returned, and Ruth, despite his reassuring embrace, whispered:

"Dave, you can't fool old folks—why don't you go
ahead and tell her about yourself? Think of the shock
she's going to get—at her age."

David shook his head. "She'll get over the shock if she's
there looking on. If we just told her, she'd never understand. We've got to railroad her into it. Then she'll be
happy."

"She's nice. But she's got the same ideas as all old folks
—"

"Yea—but with her you can change 'em. Specially if everything is really all right. I know her. She's for church
and all, but she believes in good times too, if they're right.
Why, when I was a kid—" He broke off. "Listen!"

Miss Cynthie's voice came quite distinctly to them, singing a jaunty little rhyme:

Oh I danced with the gal with the hole in her
    stockin',
And her toe kep' a-kickin' and her heel kep'
    a-knockin'—

Come up, Jesse, and get a drink o' gin,
'Cause you near to the heaven as you'll ever get ag'in.

"She taught me that when I wasn't knee-high to a
cricket," David said.

Miss Cynthie still sang softly and merrily:

Then I danced with the gal with the dimple in her
    cheek,
And if she'd 'a' kep' a-smilin', I'd 'a' danced for a
    week—

"God forgive me," prayed Miss Cynthie as she discovered David's purpose the following night. She let him and
Ruth lead her, like an early Christian martyr, into the La-

fayette Theater. The blinding glare of the lobby produced
a merciful self-anesthesia, and she entered the sudden dimness of the interior as involuntarily as in a dream. . . .

Attendants outdid each other for Mr. Dave Tappen. She
heard him tell them, "Fix us up till we go on," and found
herself sitting between Ruth and David in the front row of
a lower box. A miraculous device of the devil, a motion
picture that talked, was just ending. At her feet the orchestra was assembling. The motion picture faded out amid a
scattered round of applause. Lights blazed and the orchestra burst into an ungodly rumpus.

She looked out over the seated multitude, scanning row
upon row of illumined faces, black faces, white faces, yellow, tan, brown; bald heads, bobbed heads, kinky and
straight heads; and upon every countenance, expectancy
—scowling expectancy in this case, smiling in that, complacent here, amused there, commentative elsewhere, but
everywhere suspense, abeyance, anticipation.

Half a dozen people were ushered down the nearer aisle
to reserved seats in the second row. Some of them caught
sight of David and Ruth and waved to them. The chairs
immediately behind them in the box were being shifted.
"Hello, Tap!" Miss Cynthie saw David turn, rise, and
shake hands with two men. One of them was large, bald
and pink, emanating good cheer; the other short, thin, sal-
low with thick black hair and a sour mien. Ruth also acknowledged their greeting. "This is my grandmother,"
David said proudly. "Miss Cynthie, meet my managers,
Lou and Lee Goldman." "Pleased to meet you," managed
Miss Cynthie. "Great lad, this boy of yours," said Lou
Goldman. "Great little partner he's got, too," added Lee.
They also settled back expectantly.

"Here we go!"

The curtain rose to reveal a cottonfield at dawn. Pickers
in blue denim overalls, bandannas, and wide-brimmed
straws, or in gingham aprons and sunbonnets, were singing
as they worked. Their voices, from clearest soprano to
richest bass, blended in low concordances, first simply
humming a series of harmonies, until, gradually, came
words, like figures forming in mist. As the sound grew, the
mist cleared, the words came round and full, and the sun
rose, bringing light as if in answer to the song. The chorus
swelled, the radiance grew, the two, as if emanating from
a single source, fused their crescendos, till at last they

achieved a joint transcendence of tonal and visual brightness.

"Swell opener," said Lee Goldman.

"Ripe," agreed Lou.

David and Ruth arose. "Stay here and enjoy the show,
Miss Cynthie. You'll see us again in a minute."

"Go to it, kids," said Lou Goldman.

"Yea—burn 'em up," said Lee.

Miss Cynthie hardly noted that she had been left, so absorbed was she in the spectacle. To her, the theater had
always been the antithesis of the church. As the one was
the refuge of righteousness, so the other was the strong-
hold of transgression. But this first scene awakened memories, captured and held her attention by offering a blend of
truth and novelty. Having thus baited her interest, the
show now proceeded to play it like the trout through swift
flowing waters of wickedness. Resist as it might, her mind
was caught and drawn into the impious subsequences.

The very music that had just rounded out so majesti-
cally now distorted itself into ragtime. The singers came
forward and turned to dancers; boys, a crazy, swaying
background, threw up their arms and kicked their legs in a
rhythmic jamboree; girls, an agile, brazen foreground,
caught their skirts up to their hips and displayed their cop-
per calves, knees, thighs, in shameless, incredible steps.
Miss Cynthie turned dismayed eyes upon the audience, to
discover that mob of sinners devouring it all with fond satisfaction. Then the dancers separated and with final aban-
don flung themselves off the stage in both directions.

Lee Goldman commented through the applause, "They
work easy, them babies."

"Yea," said Lou. "Savin' the hot stuff for later."

Two black-faced cotton-pickers appropriated the scene,
indulging in dialogue that their hearers found uproarious.

"Ah'm tired."

"Ah'm hongry."

"Dis job jes' wears me out."

"Starves me to death."

"Ah'm so tired—you know what Ah'd like to do?"

"What?"

"Ah'd like to go to sleep and dream I was sleepin'."

"What good dat do?"

"Den I could wake up and still be 'sleep."

"Well y'know what Ah'd like to do?"

"No. What?"

"Ah'd like to swaller me a hog and a hen."

"What good dat do?"

"Den Ah'd always be full o' ham and eggs."

"Ham? Shuh. Don't you know a hog has to be smoked 'fo he's a ham?"

"Well, if I swaller him, he'll have a smoke all around him, won' he?"

Presently Miss Cynthie was smiling like everyone else, but her smile soon fled. For the comics departed, and the dancing girls returned, this time in scant travesties of their earlier voluminous costumes—tiny sunbonnets perched jauntily on one side of their glistening bobs, bandannas reduced to scarlet neck-ribbons, waists mere brassieres, skirts mere gingham sashes.

And now Miss Cynthie's whole body stiffened with a new and surpassing shock; her bright eyes first widened with unbelief, then slowly grew dull with misery. In the midst of a sudden great volley of applause her grandson had broken through that bevy of agile wantons and begun to sing.

He too was dressed as a cotton-picker, but a Beau Brummell among cotton pickers; his hat bore a pleated green band, his bandanna was silk, his overalls blue satin, his shoes black patent leather. His eyes flashed, his teeth gleamed, his body swayed, his arms waved, his words came fast and clear. As he sang, his companions danced a concerted tap, uniformly wild, ecstatic. When he stopped singing, he himself began to dance, and without sacrificing crispness of execution, seemed to absorb into himself every measure of the energy which the girls, now merely standing off and swaying, had relinquished.

"Look at that boy go," said Lee Goldman.

"He ain't started yet," said Lou.

But surrounding comment, Dave's virtuosity, the eager enthusiasm of the audience were all alike lost on Miss Cynthie. She sat with stricken eyes watching this boy whom she'd raised from a babe, taught right from wrong, brought up in the church, and endowed with her prayers, this child whom she had dreamed of seeing a preacher, a regular doctor, a tooth-doctor, a foot-doctor, at the very least an undertaker—sat watching him disport himself for the benefit of a sin-sick, flesh-hungry mob of lost souls, not one of whom knew or cared to know the loving-kindness of God; sat watching a David she'd never foreseen, turned tool of the devil, disciple of lust, unholy prince among sinners.

For a long time she sat there watching with wretched

eyes, saw portrayed on the stage David's arrival in Harlem, his escape from "old friends" who tried to dupe him;
saw him working as a trap-drummer in a nightclub, where
he fell in love with Ruth, a dancer; not the gentle Ruth
Miss Cynthie knew, but a wild and shameless young savage who danced like seven devils—in only a girdle and
breastplates; saw the two of them join in a song-and-dance
act that eventually made them Broadway headliners, an
act presented *in toto* as the pre-finale of this show. And
not any of the melodies, not any of the sketches, not all
the comic philosophy of the tired-and-hungry duo, gave
her figure a moment's relaxation or brightened the dull defeat in her staring eyes. She sat apart, alone in the box, the
symbol, the epitome of supreme failure. Let the rest of the
theater be riotous, clamoring for more and more of Dave
Tappen, "Tap," the greatest tapster of all time, idol of uptown and downtown New York. For her, they were laud-
ing simply an exhibition of sin which centered about her
David.

"This'll run a year on Broadway," said Lee Goldman.

"Then we'll take it to Paris."

Encores and curtains with Ruth, and at last David came
out on the stage alone. The clamor dwindled. And now he
did something quite unfamiliar to even the most consistent
of his followers. Softly, delicately, he began to tap a rou-
tine designed to fit a particular song. When he had estab-
lished the rhythm, he began to sing the song:

Oh I danced with the gal with the hole in her
    stockin',
And her toe kep' a-kickin' and her heel kep'
    a-knockin'—

Come up, Jesse, and get a drink o' gin,
'Cause you near to the heaven as you'll ever get
    ag'in—

As he danced and sang this song, frequently smiling
across at Miss Cynthie, a visible change transformed her.
She leaned forward incredulously, listened intently, then
settled back in limp wonder. Her bewildered eyes turned
on the crowd, on those serried rows of shriftless sinners.
And she found in their faces now an overwhelmingly curious thing: a grin, a universal grin, a gleeful and sinless
grin such as not the nakedest chorus in the performance
had produced. In a few seconds, with her own song, David

had dwarfed into unimportance, wiped off their faces, swept out of their minds every trace of what had seemed to be sin; had reduced it all to mere trivial detail and revealed these revelers as a crowd of children, enjoying the guileless antics of another child. And Miss Cynthie whispered,

"Bless my soul! They didn' mean nothin' . . . They jes' didn' see no harm in it—"

Then I danced with the gal with the dimple in her cheek,
And if she'd 'a' kep' a-smilin', I'd 'a' danced for a week—
Come up, Jesse—

The crowd laughed, clapped their hands, whistled. Someone threw David a bright yellow flower. "From Broadway!"

He caught the flower. A hush fell. He said:

"I'm really happy tonight, folks. Y'see this flower? Means success, don't it? Well, listen. The one who is really responsible for my success is here tonight with me. Now what do you think o' that?"

The hush deepened.

"Y'know folks, I'm sump'm like Adam—I never had no mother. But I've got a grandmother. Down home everybody calls her Miss Cynthie. And everybody loves her. Take that song I just did for you. Miss Cynthie taught me that when I wasn't knee-high to a cricket. But that wasn't all she taught me. Far back as I can remember, she used to always say one thing: Son, do like a church steeple—aim high and go straight. And for doin' it"—he grinned, contemplating the flower—"I get this."

He strode across to the edge of the stage that touched Miss Cynthie's box. He held up the flower.

"So y'see, folks, this isn't mine. It's really Miss Cynthie's." He leaned over to hand it to her. Miss Cynthie's last trace of doubt was swept away. She drew a deep breath of revelation; her bewilderment vanished, her redoubtable composure returned, her eyes lighted up; and no one but David, still holding the flower toward her, heard her sharply whispered reprimand:

"Keep it, you fool. Where's yo' manners—givin' 'way what somebody give you?"

David grinned:

"Take it, tyro. What you tryin' to do—crab my act?"

Thereupon Miss Cynthie, smiling at him with bright, meaningful eyes, leaned over without rising from her chair, jerked a tiny twig off the stem of the flower, then sat decisively back, resolutely folding her arms, with only a leaf in her hand.

"This'll do me," she said.

The finale didn't matter. People filed out of the theater. Miss Cynthie sat awaiting her children, her foot absently patting time to the orchestra's jazz recessional. Perhaps she was thinking, "God moves in a mysterious way," but her lips were unquestionably forming the words:

> danced with the gal—hole in her stockin'—
> —toe kep' a-kickin'—heel kep' a-knockin'.

Jack In The Pot

by Dorothy West

It was unbelievable. Week after week she had come on
Wednesday afternoon to this smelly, third-run neighborhood movie house, paid her dime, received her "Beano"
card, and gone inside to wait through an indifferent feature until the house light came on, and a too jovial white
man wheeled a board onto the stage and busily fished in a
bowl for numbers.

Today, it had happened. As the too jovial white man
called each number, she found a corresponding one on her
card. When he called the seventh number and explained
dramatically that whoever had punched five numbers in a
row had won the jackpot of fifty-five dollars, she listened
in smiling disbelief that there was that much money in his
pocket. It was then that the woman beside her leaned toward her and said excitedly, "Look, lady, you got it!"

She did not remember going down the aisle. When it
was over, she tottered dazedly to her seat, and sat in a
dreamy stupor, scarcely able to believe her good fortune.

The drawing continued, the last dollar was given away,
the theater darkened, and the afternoon crowd filed out.
The little gray woman, collecting her wits, followed them.

She revived in the sharp air. She had fifty-five dollars in
her purse. It was wonderful to think about.

She reached her own intersection and paused before
Mr. Spiro's general market. Here she regularly shopped,

settling part of her bill fortnightly out of her relief check. When Mr. Spiro put in inferior stock because most of his customers were poor-paying reliefers, she had wanted to shop elsewhere. But she could never get paid up.

Excitement smote her. She would go in, settle her account, and say good-bye to Mr. Spiro forever. Resolutely she turned into the market.

Mr. Spiro, broad and unkempt, began to boom heartily from behind the counter. "Hello, Mrs. Edmunds."

She lowered her eyes and asked diffidently, "How much is my bill, Mr. Spiro?"

He recoiled in horror. "Do I worry about your bill, Mrs. Edmunds? Don't you pay something when you get your relief check? Ain't you one of my best customers?"

"I'd like to settle," said Mrs. Edmunds breathlessly.

Mr. Spiro eyed her shrewdly. His voice was soft and insinuating. "You got cash, Mrs. Edmunds? You hit the number? Every other week you give me something on account. This week you want to settle. Am I losing your trade? Ain't I always treated you right?"

"Sure, Mr. Spiro," she answered nervously.

"See," he said triumphantly, "it's like I said. You're one of my best customers. Worrying about your bill when I ain't even worrying. I was telling your investigator"—he paused significantly—"when Mr. Edmunds gets a job, I know I'll get the balance. Mr. Edmunds got himself a job maybe?"

She was stiff with fright. "No, I'd have told you right off, and her, too. I ain't one to cheat on relief. I was only saying how I wished I could settle. I wasn't saying that I was."

"Well, then, what you want for supper?" Mr. Spiro asked soothingly.

"Loaf of bread," she answered gratefully, "two pork chops, one kinda thick, can of spaghetti, little can of milk."

The purchases were itemized. Mrs. Edmunds said good night and left the store. She felt sick and ashamed, for she had turned tail in the moment that was to have been her triumph over tyranny.

A little boy came toward her in the familiar rags of the neighborhood children. Suddenly Mrs. Edmunds could bear no longer the intolerable weight of her mean provisions.

"Little boy," she said.

"Ma'am?" He stopped and stared at her.

"Here." She held out the bag to him. "Take it home to your mamma. It's food. It's clean."

He blinked, then snatched the bag from her hands, and turned and ran very fast in the direction from which he had come.

Mrs. Edmunds felt better at once. Now she could buy a really good supper. She walked ten blocks to a better neighborhood and the cold did not bother her. Her misshapen shoes were winged.

She pushed inside a resplendent store and marched to the meat counter. A porterhouse steak caught her eye. She could not look past it. It was big and thick and beautiful.

The clerk leaned toward her. "Steak, moddom?"

"That one."

It was glorious not to care about the cost of things. She bought mushrooms, fresh peas, cauliflower, tomatoes, a pound of good coffee, a pint of real cream, a dozen dinner rolls, and a maple walnut layer cake.

The winter stars were pricking the sky when she entered the dimly lit hall of the old-law tenement in which she lived. The dank smell smote her instantly after the long walk in the brisk, clear air. The Smith boy's dog had dirtied the hall again. Mr. Johnson, the janitor, was mournfully mopping up.

"Evenin' Mis' Edmunds, ma'am," he said plaintively.

"Evening," Mrs. Edmunds said coldly. Suddenly she hated Mr. Johnson. He was so humble.

Five young children shared the uninhabitable basement with him. They were always half sick and he was always neglecting his duties to tend them. The tenants were continually deciding to report him to the agent, and then at the last moment deciding not to.

"I'll be up to-morrow to see 'bout them windows, Mis' Edmunds, ma'am. My baby kep' frettin' today, and I been so busy doctorin'."

"Those children need a mother," said Mrs. Edmunds severely. "You ought to get married again."

"My wife ain' daid," cried Mr. Johnson, shocked out of his servility. "She's in that T. B. home. Been there two years and about on the road to health.

"Well," said Mrs. Edmunds inconclusively, and then added briskly, "I been waiting weeks and weeks for them window strips. Winter's half over. If the place was kept warm—"

"Yes'm, Mis' Edmunds," he said hastily, his bloodshot eyes imploring. "It's that ol' furnace. I done tol' the agent

time and again, but they ain' fixin' to fix up this house
'long as you all is relief folks."

The steak was sizzling on the stove when Mr. Edmunds'
key turned in the lock of the tiny three-room flat. His step
dragged down the hall. Mrs. Edmunds knew what that
meant: "No man wanted." Two years ago Mr. Edmunds
had begun, doggedly, to canvas the city for work, leaving
home soon after breakfast and rarely returning before supper.

Once he had had a little stationery store. After losing it,
he had spent his small savings, and sold or pawned every
decent article of furniture and clothing before applying for
relief. Even so, there had been a long investigation while
he and his wife slowly starved. Fear had been implanted
in Mrs. Edmunds. Thereafter she was never wholly unafraid. Mr. Edmunds had had to stand by and watch his
wife starve. He never got over being ashamed.

Mr. Edmunds stood in the kitchen doorway, holding his
rain-streaked hat in his knotted hand. He was forty-nine,
and he looked like an old man.

"I'm back," he said. "Cooking supper."

It was not a question. He seemed unaware of the intoxicating odors.

She smiled at him brightly.

"Smell good?"

He shook suddenly with the cold that was still in him.
"Smells like always to me."

Her face fell in disappointment, but she said gently,
"You oughtn't to be walking 'round in this kind of
weather."

"I was looking for work," he said fiercely. "Work's not
going to come knocking."

"Things'll pick up in the spring," she said soothingly.

"Not for me," he answered gloomily. "Look how I look.
Like a bum. I wouldn't hire me, myself."

"What you want me to do about it?" she asked furiously.

"Nothing," he said with wry humor, "unless you can
make money, and make me just about fifty dollars."

She caught her breath, and stared at his shabbiness. She
had seen him look like this so long that she had forgotten
that clothes would make a difference.

She nodded toward the stove. "That steak and all.
Guess you think I got a fortune. Well, I won a little old
measly dollar at the movies."

His face lightened, and his eyes grew soft with affection.

"You shouldn't have bought a steak," he said. "Wish you'd bought yourself something you been wanting. Like gloves. Good warm gloves. Hurts my heart when I see you with cold hands."

She was ashamed, and wished she knew how to cross the room to kiss him. "Go wash," she said gruffly. "Steak's 'most too done already."

It was a wonderful dinner. Both of them had been starved for fresh meat. Mrs. Edmunds' face was flushed, and there was color in her lips, as if the good blood of the meat had filtered through her skin.

Over coffee and cake they talked contentedly. Mrs. Edmunds wanted to tell the truth about the money, and waited for an opening.

"We'll move out of this hole some day soon," said Mr. Edmunds. "Things won't be like this always." He was full and warm and confident.

"If I had fifty dollars," Mrs. Edmunds began cautiously, "I believe I'd move tomorrow. Pay up these people what I owe, and get me a fit place to live in."

"Fifty dollars would be a drop in the bucket. You got to have something coming in steady."

He had hurt her again. "Fifty dollars is more than you got," she said meanly.

"It's more than you got, too," he said mildly. "Look at it like this. If you had fifty dollars and made a change, them relief folks would worry you like a pack of wolves. But say f'instance, you had fifty dollars, and I had a job, we could walk out of here without a howdy-do to anybody."

It would have been anticlimactic to tell him about the money. She got up. "I'll do the dishes. You sit still."

He noticed no change in her and went on earnestly, "Lord's bound to put something in my way soon. We don't live human. I never see a paper 'cept when I pick one up in the subway. I ain't had a cigarette in three years. We ain't got a radio. We don't have no company. All the pleasure you get is a ten-cent movie one day a week. I don't even get that."

Presently Mrs. Edmunds ventured, "You think the investigator would notice if we got a little radio for the bedroom?"

"Somebody got one to give away?" His face was eager.

"Maybe."

"Well, seeing how she could check with the party what give it to you, I think it would be all right."

"Well, ne' mind—" Her voice petered out.

It was his turn to try. "Want to play me a game of cards?"

He had not asked her for months. She cleared her throat.

"I'll play a hand or two."

He stretched luxuriously. "I feel so good. Feeling like this, bet I'll land something tomorrow."

She said very gently, "The investigator comes tomorrow."

He smiled quickly to hide his disappointment. "Clean forgot. It don't matter. That meal was so good it'll carry me straight through Friday."

She opened her mouth to tell him about the jackpot, to promise him as many meals as there was money. Suddenly someone upstairs pounded on the radiator for heat. In a moment someone downstairs pounded. Presently their side of the house resounded. It was maddening. Mrs. Edmunds was bitterly aware that her hands and feet were like ice.

" 'Tisn't no use," she cried wildly to the walls. She burst into tears.

Her husband crossed quickly to her. He kissed her cheek. "I'm going to make all this up to you. You'll see."

By half-past eight they were in bed. By quarter to nine Mrs. Edmunds was quietly sleeping. Mr. Edmunds lay staring at the ceiling. It kept coming closer.

Mrs. Edmunds waked first and decided to go again to the grand market. She dressed and went out into the street. An ambulance stood in front of the door. In a minute an interne emerged from the basement, carrying a bundled child. Mr. Johnson followed, his eyes more bleary and bloodshot than ever.

Mrs. Edmunds rushed up to him. "The baby?" she asked anxiously.

His face worked pitifully. "Yes, ma'am, Mis' Edmunds. Pneumonia. I heard you folks knockin' for heat last night but my hands was too full. I ain't forgot about them windows, though. I'll be up tomorrow bright and early."

Mr. Edmunds stood in the kitchen door. "I smell meat in the morning?" he asked incredulously. He sat down, and she spread the feast, kidneys and omelet, hot buttered rolls and strawberry jam. "You mind," he said happily, "explaining this mystery? Was that dollar of yours made out of elastic?"

"It wasn't a dollar like I said. It was five. I wanted to surprise you."

She did not look at him and her voice was breathless. She had decided to wait until after the investigator's visit to tell him the whole truth about the money. Otherwise they might both be nervous and betray themselves by their guilty knowledge.

"We got chicken for dinner," she added shyly.

"Lord, I don't know when I had a piece of chicken."

They ate, and the morning passed glowingly. With Mr. Edmunds' help, Mrs. Edmunds moved the furniture and gave the flat a thorough cleaning. She liked for the investigator to find her busy.

The afternoon waned. The Edmundses sat in the living room, and there was nothing to do. They were hungry but dared not start dinner. With activity suspended, they became aware of the penetrating cold and rattling windows. Mr. Edmunds began to have that wild look of waiting for the investigator.

Mrs. Edmunds suddenly had an idea. She would go and get a newspaper and a package of cigarettes for him.

At the corner she ran into Mr. Johnson. Rather he ran into her, for he turned the corner with his head down, and his gait as unsteady as if he had been drinking.

"That you, Mr. Johnson?" she said sharply.

He raised his head, and she saw that he was not drunk.

"Yes, ma'am, Mis' Edmunds."

"The baby—is she worse?"

Tears welled out of his eyes. "The Lord done took her."

Tears stood in her own eyes. "God knows I'm sorry to hear that. Let me know if there's anything I can do."

"Thank you, Mis' Edmunds, ma'am. But ain't nothin' nobody can do. I been pricin' funerals. I can get one for fifty dollars. But I been to my brother, and he ain't got it. I been everywhere. Couldn't raise no more than ten dollars." He was suddenly embarrassed. "I know all you tenants is on relief. I wasn't fixin' to ask you all."

"Fifty dollars," she said strainedly, "is a lot of money."

"God'd have to pass a miracle for me to raise it. Guess the city'll have to bury her. You reckon they'll let me take flowers?"

"You being the father, I guess they would," she said weakly.

When she returned home the flat was a little warmer. She entered the living room. Her husband's face brightened.

"You bought a paper!"

She held out the cigarettes. "You smoke this kind?" she asked lifelessly.

He jumped up and crossed to her. "I declare I don't know how to thank you! Wish that investigator'd come. I sure want to taste them."

"Go ahead and smoke," she cried fiercely. "It's none of her business. We got our rights same as working people."

She turned into the bedroom. She was utterly spent. Too much had happened in the last twenty-four hours.

"Guess I'll stretch out for a bit. I'm not going to sleep. If I do drop off, listen out for the investigator. The bell needs fixing. She might have to knock."

At half-past five Mr. Edmunds put down the newspaper and tiptoed to the bedroom door. His wife was still asleep. He stood for a moment in indecision, then decided it was long past the hour when the investigator usually called, and went down the hall to the kitchen. He wanted to prepare supper as a surprise. He opened the window, took the foodstuffs out of the crate that in winter served as icebox, and set them on the table.

The doorbell tinkled faintly.

He went to the door and opened it. The investigator stepped inside. She was small and young and white.

"Good evening, miss," he said.

"I'm sorry to call so late," she apologized. "I've been busy all day with an evicted family."

"You come on up front, miss," he said. "I'll wake up my wife. She wasn't feeling so well and went to lie down."

She saw the light from the kitchen, and the dark rooms beyond.

"Don't wake Mrs. Edmunds," she said kindly, "if she isn't well. I'll just sit in the kitchen for a minute with you."

He looked down at her, but her open, honest face did not disarm him. He braced himself for whatever was to follow.

"Go right on in, miss," he said. "Sit down, miss."

He stood facing her with a furrow between his brows, and his arms folded. There was an awkward pause. She cast about for something to say, and saw the table.

"I interrupted your dinner preparations."

His voice and his face hardened for the blow.

"I was getting dinner for my wife. It's chicken."

"It looks like a nice one," she said pleasantly.

He was baffled. "We ain't had chicken once in three years."

"I understand," she said sincerely. "Sometimes I spend my whole salary on something I want very much."

"You ain't much like an investigator," he said in surprise. "One we had before you woulda raised Ned." He sat down suddenly, his defenses down. "Miss, I been wanting to ask you this for a long time. You ever have any men's clothes?"

Her voice was distressed. "Every once in a while. But with so many people needing assistance, we can only give them to our employables. But I'll keep your request in mind."

He did not answer. He just sat staring at the floor, presenting an adjustment problem. There was nothing else to say to him.

She rose. "I'll be going now, Mr. Edmunds."

"I'll tell my wife you was here, miss."

A voice called from the bedroom. "Is that you talking?"

"It's the investigator lady," he said. "She's just going."

Mrs. Edmunds came hurrying down the hall, the sleep in her face and tousled hair.

"I was just lying down, ma'am. I didn't mean to go to sleep. My husband should've called me."

"I didn't want him to wake you."

"And he kept you sitting in the kitchen."

She glanced inside to assure herself that it was sufficiently spotless for the fine clothes of the investigator. She saw the laden table, and felt so ill that water welled into her mouth.

"The investigator lady knows about the chicken," Mr. Edmunds said quickly. "She—"

"It was only five dollars," his wife interrupted, wringing her hands.

"Five dollars for a chicken?" The investigator was shocked and incredulous.

"She didn't buy that chicken out of none of your relief money," Mr. Edmunds said defiantly. "It was money she won at a movie."

"It was only five dollars," Mrs. Edmunds repeated tearfully.

"We ain't trying to hide nothing," Mr. Edmunds snarled. He was cornered and fighting. "If you'd asked me how we come by the chicken, I'd have told you."

"For God's sake, ma'am, don't cut us off," Mrs. Edmunds moaned. "I'll never go to another movie. It was only ten cents. I didn't know I was doing wrong." She burst into tears.

The investigator stood tense. They had both been screaming at her. She was tired and so irritated that she wanted to scream back.

"Mrs. Edmunds," she said sharply, "get hold of yourself. I'm not going to cut you off. You won five dollars at a movie and you bought some food. That's fine. I wish all my families could win five dollars for food."

She turned and tore out of the flat. They heard her stumbling and sobbing down the stairs.

"You feel like eating?" Mrs. Edmunds asked dully.

"I guess we're both hungry. That's why we got so upset."

"Maybe we'd better eat, then."

"Let me fix it."

"No." She entered the kitchen. "I kinda want to see you just sitting and smoking a cigarette."

He sat down and reached in his pocket with some eagerness. "I ain't had one yet." He lit a cigarette, inhaled, and felt better immediately.

"You think," she said bleakly, "she'll write that up in our case?"

"I don't know, dear."

"You think they'll close our case if she does?"

"I don't know that neither, dear."

She clutched the sink for support. "My God, what would we do?"

The smoke curled around him luxuriously. "Don't think about it till it happens."

"I got to think about it. The rent, the gas, the light, the food."

"They wouldn't hardly close our case for five dollars."

"Maybe they'd think it was more."

"You could prove it by the movie manager."

She went numb all over. Then suddenly she got mad about it.

It was nine o'clock when they sat down in the living room. The heat came up grudgingly. Mrs. Edmunds wrapped herself in her sweater and read the funnies. Mr. Edmunds was happily inhaling his second cigarette. They were both replete and in good humor.

The window rattled and Mr. Edmunds looked around at it lazily. "Been about two months since you asked Mr. Johnson for weatherstrips."

The paper shook in her hand. She did not look up. "He promised to fix it this morning, but his baby died."

"His baby! You don't say!"

She kept her eyes glued to the paper. "Pneumonia."

His voice filled with sympathy. "Believe I'll go down and sit with him awhile."

"He's not there," she said hastily. "I met him when I was going to the store. He said he'd be out all evening."

"I bet the poor man's trying to raise some money."

She let the paper fall in her lap, and clasped her hands to keep them from trembling. She lied again, as she had been lying steadily in the past twenty-four hours, as she had not lied before in all her life.

"He didn't say nothing to me about raising money."

"Wasn't no need to. Where would you get the first five cents to give him?"

"I guess," she cried jealously, "you want me to give him the rest of my money."

"No," he said. "I want you to spend what little's left on yourself. Me, I wish I had fifty dollars to give him."

"As poor as you are?" she asked angrily. "That's easy to say when you haven't got it."

"I look at it this way," he said simply. "I think how I'd feel in his shoes."

"You got your own troubles," she argued heatedly. "The Johnson baby is better off dead. You'd be a fool to put fifty dollars in the ground. I'd spend my fifty dollars on the living."

" 'Tain't no use to work yourself up," he said. "You ain't got fifty dollars, and neither have I. We'll be quarreling in a minute over make-believe money. Let's go to bed."

Mrs. Edmunds waked at seven and tried to lie quietly by her husband's side, but lying still was torture. She dressed and went into the kitchen, and felt too listless to make her coffee. She sat down at the table and dropped her head on her folded arms. No tears came. There was only the burning in her throat and behind her eyes.

She sat in this manner for half an hour. Suddenly she heard a man's slow tread outside her front door. Terror gripped her. The steps moved on down the hall, but for a moment her knees were water. When she could control her trembling, she stood up and knew that she had to get out of the house. It could not contain her and Mr. Johnson.

It was a raw day, and her feet and hands were beginning to grow numb. She felt sorry for herself. Other people were hurrying past in overshoes and heavy gloves.

There were fifty-one dollars in her purse. It was her right to do what she pleased with them.

In a downtown department store she rode the escalator to the dress department. She walked up and down the rows of lovely garments, stopping to finger critically, standing back to admire.

A salesgirl came toward her, looking straight at her with soft, expectant eyes.

"Do you wish to be waited on, madam?"

Mrs. Edmunds opened her mouth to say "Yes," but the word would not come. She stared at the girl stupidly. "I was just looking," she said.

In the shoe department, she saw a pair of comfort shoes and sat down timidly in a fine leather chair.

A salesman lounged toward her. "Something in shoes?"

"Yes, sir. That comfort shoe."

"Size?" His voice was bored.

"I don't know," she said.

"I'll have to measure you," he said reproachfully. He sat down on a stool and held out his hand.

She dragged her eyes up to his face. "How much you say those shoes cost?"

"I didn't say. Eight dollars."

She rose with acute relief. "I ain't got that much with me."

She retreated unsteadily. Something was making her knees weak and her head light.

Her legs steadied. She went quickly to the down escalator. She reached the third floor and was briskly crossing to the next down escalator when she saw the little dresses. A banner screamed that they were selling at the sacrifice price of one dollar. She decided to examine them.

She searched carefully. There were pinks and blues and yellows. She was looking for white.

Boldly she beckoned a salesgirl. "I'll take this, miss, she said.

All the way home she was excited and close to tears. She was in a fever to see Mr. Johnson. She would let the regret come later. A child lay dead and waiting burial.

She turned her corner at a run. Going down the rickety basement stairs, she prayed that Mr. Johnson was on the premises.

She pounded on his door and he opened it. The agony in his face told her instantly that he had been unable to borrow the money. She tried to speak, and her tongue tripped over her eagerness.

Fear took hold of her and rattled her teeth. "Mr. Johnson, what about the funeral?"

"I give the baby to the student doctors."

"Oh, my God, Mr. Johnson! Oh, my God!"

"I bought her some flowers."

She turned and went blindly up the stairs. Drooping in the front doorway was a frost-nipped bunch of white flowers. She dragged herself up to her flat. Once she stopped to hide the package under her coat. She would never look at that little white dress again. The ten five-dollar bills were ten five-pound stones in her purse. They almost hurled her backward.

She turned the key in her lock. Mr. Edmunds stood at the door. He looked rested and confident.

"I been waiting for you. I just started to go."

"You had any breakfast?" she asked tonelessly.

"I made some coffee. It was all I wanted."

"I shoulda made some oatmeal before I went out."

"You have on the big pot time I come home. Bet I'll land something good," he boasted. "You brought good luck in this house. We ain't seen the last of it." He pecked her cheek and went out, hurrying as if he were late for work.

She plodded into the bedroom. The steam was coming up fine. She sank down on the side of the bed and unbuttoned her coat. The package fell on her lap. She took the ten five-dollar bills and pushed them between a fold of the package. It was burial money. She could never use it for anything else. She hid the package under the mattress.

In Darkness
And Confusion

by Ann Petry

William Jones took a sip of coffee and then put his cup down on the kitchen table. It didn't taste right and he was annoyed because he always looked forward to eating breakfast. He usually got out of bed as soon as he woke up and hurried into the kitchen. Then he would take a long time heating the corn bread left over from dinner the night before, letting the coffee brew until it was strong and clear, frying bacon and scrambling eggs. He would eat very slowly—savoring the early-morning quiet and the just-rightness of the food he'd fixed.

There was no question about early morning being the best part of the day, he thought. But this Saturday morning in July it was too hot in the apartment. There were too many nagging worries that kept drifting through his mind. In the heat he couldn't think clearly—so that all of them pressed in against him, weighed him down.

He pushed his plate away from him. The eggs had cooked too long; much as he liked corn bread it tasted like sand this morning––grainy and coarse inside his throat. He couldn't help wondering if it scratched the inside of his stomach in the same way.

Pink was moving around in the bedroom. He cocked his head on one side, listening to her. He could tell exactly

66

what she was doing, as though he were in there with her. The soft heavy sound of her stockinged feet as she walked over to the dresser. The dresser drawer being pulled out. That meant she was getting a clean slip. Then the thud of her two hundred pounds landing in the rocker by the window. She was sitting down to comb her hair. Untwisting the small braids she'd made the night before. She would unwind them one by one, putting the hairpins in her mouth as she went along. Now she was brushing it, for he could hear the creak of the rocker; she was rocking back and forth, humming under her breath as she brushed.

He decided that as soon as she came into the kitchen he would go back to the bedroom, get dressed, and go to work. For his mind was already on the mailbox. He didn't feel like talking to Pink. There simply had to be a letter from Sam today. There had to be.

He was thinking about it so hard that he didn't hear Pink walk toward the kitchen.

When he looked up she was standing in the doorway. She was a short, enormously fat woman. The only garment she had on was a bright pink slip that magnified the size of her body. The skin on her arms and shoulders and chest was startlingly black against the pink material. In spite of the brisk brushing she had given her hair, it stood up stiffly all over her head in short wiry lengths, as though she wore a turban of some rough dark-gray material.

He got up from the table quickly when he saw her. "Hot, ain't it?" he said, and patted her arm as he went past her toward the bedroom.

She looked at the food on his plate. "You didn't want no breakfast?" she asked.

"Too hot," he said over his shoulder.

He closed the bedroom door behind him gently. If she saw the door was shut, she'd know that he was kind of low in his mind this morning and that he didn't feel like talking. At first he moved about with energy—getting a clean work shirt, giving his shoes a hasty brushing, hunting for a pair of clean socks. Then he stood still in the middle of the room, holding his dark work pants in his hand while he listened to the rush and roar of water running in the bathtub.

Annie May was up and taking a bath. And he wondered if that meant she was going to work. Days when she went to work she used a hot comb on her hair before she ate her breakfast, so that before he left the house in the morning it was filled with the smell of hot irons sizzling against hair grease.

He frowned. Something had to be done about Annie May. Here she was only eighteen years old and staying out practically all night long. He hadn't said anything to Pink about it, but Annie May crept into the house at three and four and five in the morning. He would hear her key go in the latch and then the telltale click as the lock drew back. She would shut the door very softly and turn the bolt. She'd stand there awhile, waiting to see if they woke up. Then she'd take her shoes off and pad down the hall in her stockinged feet.

When she turned the light on in the bathroom, he could see the clock on the dresser. This morning it was four-thirty when she came in. Pink, lying beside him, went on peacefully snoring. He was glad that she didn't wake up easy. It would only worry her to know that Annie May was carrying on like that.

Annie May put her hands on her hips and threw her head back and laughed whenever he tried to tell her she had to come home earlier. The smoky smell of the hot irons started seeping into the bedroom and he finished dressing quickly.

He stopped in the kitchen on his way out. "Got to get to the store early today," he explained. He was sure Pink knew he was hurrying downstairs to look in the mailbox. But she nodded and held her face up for his kiss. When he brushed his lips against her forehead he saw that her face was wet with perspiration. He thought with all that weight she must feel the heat something awful.

Annie May nodded at him without speaking. She was hastily swallowing a cup of coffee. Her dark thin hands made a pattern against the thick white cup she was holding. She had pulled her hair out so straight with the hot combs that, he thought, it was like a shiny skullcap fitted tight to her head. He was surprised to see that her lips were heavily coated with lipstick. When she was going to work she didn't use any, and he wondered why she was up so early if she wasn't working. He could see the red outline of her mouth on the cup.

He hadn't intended to say anything. It was the sight of the lipstick on the cup that forced the words out. "You ain't workin' today?"

"No," she said lazily. "Think I'll go shopping." She winked at Pink, and it infuriated him.

"How you expect to keep a job when you don't show up half the time?" he asked.

"I can always get another one." She lifted the coffee cup to her mouth with both hands and her eyes laughed at him over the rim of the cup.

"What time did you come home last night?" he asked abruptly.

She stared out of the window at the blank brick wall that faced the kitchen. "I dunno," she said finally. "It wasn't late."

He didn't know what to say. Probably she was out dancing somewhere. Or maybe she wasn't. He was fairly certain that she wasn't. Yet he couldn't let Pink know what he was thinking. He shifted his feet uneasily and watched Annie May swallow the coffee. She was drinking it fast.

"You know you ain't too big to get your butt whipped," he said finally.

She looked at him out of the corner of her eyes. And he saw a deep smoldering sullenness in her face that startled him. He was conscious that Pink was watching both of them with a growing apprehension.

Then Annie May giggled. "You and who else?" she said lightly. Pink roared with laughter. And Annie May laughed with her.

He banged the kitchen door hard as he went out. Striding down the outside hall, he could still hear them laughing. And even though he knew Pink's laughter was due to relief because nothing unpleasant had happened, he was angry. Lately every time Annie May looked at him there was open, jeering laughter in her eyes, as though she dared him to say anything to her. Almost as though she thought he was a fool for working so hard.

She had been a nice little girl when she first came to live with them six years ago. He groped in his mind for words to describe what he thought Annie May had become. A Jezebel, he decided grimly. That was it.

And he didn't want Pink to know what Annie May was really like. Because Annie May's mother, Lottie, had been Pink's sister. And when Lottie died, Pink took Annie May. Right away she started finding excuses for anything she did that was wrong. If he scolded Annie May he had to listen to a sharp lecture from Pink. It always started off the same way: "Don't care what she done, William. You ain't goin' to lay a finger on her. She ain't got no father and mother except us. . . ."

The quick spurt of anger and irritation at Annie May had sent him hurrying down the first flight of stairs. But he slowed his pace on the next flight because the hallways were so dark that he knew if he wasn't careful he'd walk over a step. As he trudged down the long flights of stairs he began to think about Pink. And the hot irritation in him disappeared as it usually did when he thought about her. She was so fat she couldn't keep on climbing all these steep stairs. They would have to find another place to live —on a first floor where it would be easier for her. They'd lived on this top floor for years, and all the time Pink kept getting heavier and heavier. Every time she went to the clinic the doctor said the stairs were bad for her. So they'd start looking for another apartment and then because the top floors cost less, why, they stayed where they were. And—

Then he stopped thinking about Pink because he had reached the first floor. He walked over to the mailboxes and took a deep breath. Today there'd be a letter. He knew it. There had to be. It had been too long a time since they had had a letter from Sam. The last ones that came he'd said the same thing. Over and over. Like a refrain. "Ma, I can't stand this much longer." And then the letters just stopped.

As he stood there, looking at the mailbox, half afraid to open it for fear there would be no letter, he thought back to the night Sam graduated from high school. It was a warm June night. He and Pink got all dressed up in their best clothes. And he kept thinking me and Pink have got as far as we can go. But Sam—he made up his mind Sam wasn't going to earn his living with a mop and a broom. He was going to earn it wearing a starched white collar, and a shine on his shoes and a crease in his pants.

After he finished high school Sam got a job redcapping at Grand Central. He started saving his money because he was going to go on to Lincoln—a college in Pennsylvania. It looked like it was no time at all before he was twenty-one. And in the army. Pink cried when he left. Her huge body shook with her sobbing. He remembered that he had only felt queer and lost. There was this war and all the young men were being drafted. But why Sam—why did he have to go?

It was always in the back of his mind. Next thing Sam was in a camp in Georgia. He and Pink never talked about his being in Georgia. The closest they ever came to it was one night when she said, "I hope he gets used to it quick down there. Bein' born right here in New York there's lots he won't understand."

Then Sam's letters stopped coming. He'd come home from work and say to Pink casually, "Sam write today?" She'd shake her head without saying anything.

The days crawled past. And finally she burst out. "What you keep askin' for? You think I wouldn't tell you?" And she started crying.

He put his arm around her and patted her shoulder. She leaned hard against him. "Oh, Lord," she said. "He's my baby. What they done to him?"

Her crying like that tore him in little pieces. His mind kept going around in circles. Around and around. He couldn't think what to do. Finally one night after work he sat down at the kitchen table and wrote Sam a letter. He had written very few letters in his life because Pink had always done it for him. And now standing in front of the mailbox he could even remember the feel of the pencil in his hand; how the paper looked—blank and challenging—lying there in front of him; that the kitchen clock was ticking and it kept getting louder and louder. It was hot that night, too, and he held the pencil so tight that the inside of his hand was covered with sweat.

He had sat and thought a long time. Then he wrote: "Is you all right? Your Pa." It was the best he could do. He licked the envelope and addressed it with the feeling that Sam would understand.

He fumbled for his key ring, found the mailbox key, and opened the box quickly. It was empty. Even though he could see it was empty he felt around inside it. Then he closed the box and walked toward the street door.

The brilliant sunlight outside made him blink after the darkness of the hall. Even now, so early in the morning, it was hot in the street. And he thought it was going to be a hard day to get through, what with the heat and its being Saturday and all. Lately he couldn't seem to think about anything but Sam. Even at the drugstore where he worked as a porter, he would catch himself leaning on the broom or pausing in his mopping to wonder what had happened to him.

The man who owned the store would say to him sharply, "Boy, what the hell's the matter with you? Can't you keep your mind on what you're doing?" And he would go on washing windows, or mopping the floor, or sweeping the sidewalk. But his thoughts, somehow, no matter what he was doing, drifted back to Sam.

As he walked toward the drugstore he looked at the houses on both sides of the street. He knew this street as he knew the creases in the old felt hat he wore the year round. No matter how you looked at it, it wasn't a good street to live on. It was a long cross-town street. Almost half of it on one side consisted of the backs of the three theaters on One Hundred Twenty-fifth Street—a long blank wall of gray brick. There were few trees on the street. Even these were a source of danger, for at night shadowy, vague shapes emerged from the street's darkness, lurking near the trees, dodging behind them. He had never been accosted by any of those disembodied figures, but the very stealth of their movements revealed a dishonest intent that frightened him. So when he came home at night he walked an extra block or more in order to go through One Hundred Twenty-fifth Street and enter the street from Eighth Avenue.

Early in the morning like this, the street slept. Window shades were drawn down tight against the morning sun. The few people he passed were walking briskly on their way to work. But in those houses where the people still slept, the window shades would go up about noon, and radios would blast music all up and down the street. The bold-eyed women who lived in these houses would lounge in the open windows and call to each other back and forth across the street.

Sometimes when he was on his way home to lunch they would call out to him as he went past, "Come on in, Poppa!" And he would stare straight ahead and start walking faster.

When Sam turned sixteen it seemed to him the street was unbearable. After lunch he and Sam went through this block together—Sam to school and he on his way back to the drugstore. He'd seen Sam stare at the lounging women in the windows. His face was expressionless, but his eyes were curious.

"I catch you goin' near one of them women and I'll beat you up and down the block," he'd said grimly.

Sam didn't answer him. Instead he looked down at him with a strangely adult look, for even at sixteen Sam had been a good five inches taller than he. After that when they passed through the block, Sam looked straight ahead. And William got the uncomfortable feeling that he had already explored the possibilities that the block offered. Yet he couldn't be sure. And he couldn't bring himself to ask him. Instead he walked along beside him, thinking desperately, We gotta move. I'll talk to Pink. We gotta move this time for sure.

That Sunday after Pink came home from church they looked for a new place. They went in and out of apartment houses along Seventh Avenue and Eighth Avenue, One Hundred Thirty-fifth Street, One Hundred Forty-fifth Street. Most of the apartments they didn't even look at. They just asked the super how much the rents were.

It was late when they headed for home. He had irritably agreed with Pink that they'd better stay where they were. Twenty-two dollars a month was all they could afford.

"It ain't a fit place to live, though," he said. They were walking down Seventh Avenue. The street looked wide to him, and he thought with distaste of their apartment. The rooms weren't big enough for a man to move around in without bumping into something. Sometimes he thought that was why Annie May spent so much time away from home. Even at thirteen she couldn't stand being cooped up like that in such a small amount of space.

And Pink said, "You want to live on Park Avenue? With a doorman bowin' you in and out. 'Good mornin', Mr. William Jones. Does the weather suit you this mornin'?' " Her voice was sharp, like the crack of a whip.

That was five years ago. And now again they ought to move on account of Pink not being able to stand the stairs any more. He decided that Monday night after work he'd start looking for a place.

It was even hotter in the drugstore than it was in the street. He forced himself to go inside and put on a limp work coat. Then broom in hand he went to stand in the doorway. He waved to the superintendent of the building on the corner. And watched him as he lugged garbage cans out of the areaway and rolled them to the curb. Now, that's the kind of work he didn't want Sam to have to do. He tried to decide why that was. It wasn't just because Sam was his boy and it was hard work. He searched his mind for the reason. It didn't pay enough for a man to live on decently. That was it. He wanted Sam to have a job where he could make enough to have good clothes and a nice home.

Sam's being in the army wasn't so bad, he thought. It was his being in Georgia that was bad. They didn't treat colored people right down there. Everybody knew that. If he could figure out some way to get him farther north Pink wouldn't have to worry about him so much.

The very sound of the word "Georgia" did something to

him inside. His mother had been born there. She had
talked about it a lot and painted such vivid pictures of it
that he felt he knew the place—the heat, the smell of the
earth, how cotton looked. And something more. The way
her mouth had folded together whenever she had said,
"They hate niggers down there. Don't you never none of
you children go down there."

That was years ago, yet even now, standing here on
Fifth Avenue, remembering the way she said it turned his
skin clammy cold in spite of the heat. And of all the
places in the world, Sam had to go to Georgia. Sam, who
was born right here in New York, who had finished high
school here—they had to put him in the army and send
him to Georgia.

He tightened his grip on the broom and started sweeping the sidewalk in long, even strokes. Gradually the
rhythm of the motion stilled the agitation in him. The regular back-and-forth motion was so pleasant that he kept
on sweeping long after the sidewalk was clean. When Mr.
Yudkin, who owned the store, arrived at eight-thirty he
was still outside with the broom. Even now he didn't feel
much like talking, so he only nodded in response to the
druggist's brisk, "Good morning! Hot today!"

William followed him into the store and began polishing
the big mirror in back of the soda fountain. He watched
the man out of the corner of his eye as he washed his hands
in the back room and exchanged his suit coat for a crisp
white laboratory coat. And he thought maybe when the
war is over Sam ought to study to be a druggist instead of
a doctor or a lawyer.

As the morning wore along, customers came in in a
steady stream. They got Bromo-Seltzers, cigarettes, aspirin,
cough medicine, baby bottles. He delivered two prescrip-
tions that cost five dollars. And the cash register rang so
often it almost played a tune. Listening to it he said to
himself, yes, Sam ought to be a druggist. It's clean work
and it pays good.

A little after eleven o'clock three young girls came in.
"Cokes," they said, and climbed up on the stools in front of
the fountain. William was placing new stock on the shelves
and he studied them from the top of the stepladder. As far
as he could see, they looked exactly alike. All three of
them. And like Annie May. Too thin. Too much lipstick.
Their dresses were too short and too tight. Their hair was
piled on top of their heads in slicked set curls.

"Aw, I quit that job," one of them said. "I wouldn't get up that early in the morning for nothing in the world."

That was like Annie May, too. She was always changing jobs. Because she could never get to work on time. If she was due at a place at nine she got there at ten. If at ten, then she arrived about eleven. He knew, too, that she didn't earn enough money to pay for all the cheap, bright-colored dresses she was forever buying.

Her girl friends looked just like her and just like these girls. He'd seen her coming out of the movie houses on One Hundred Twenty-fifth Street with two or three of them. They were all chewing gum and they nudged each other and talked too loud and laughed too loud. They stared hard at every man who went past them.

Mr. Yudkin looked up at him sharply, and he shifted his glance away from the girls and began putting big bottles of Father John's medicine neatly on the shelf in front of him. As he stacked the bottles up he wondered if Annie May would have been different if she'd stayed in high school. She had stopped going when she was sixteen. He had spoken to Pink about it. "She oughtn't to stop school. She's too young," he'd said.

And because Annie May was Pink's sister's child all Pink had done had been to shake her head comfortably. "She's tired of going to school. Poor little thing. Leave her alone."

So he hadn't said anything more. Pink always took up for her. And he and Pink didn't fuss at each other like some folks do. He didn't say anything to Pink about it, but he took the afternoon off from work to go to see the principal of the school. He had to wait two hours to see her. And he studied the pictures on the walls in the outer office, and looked down at his shoes while he tried to put into words what he'd say—and how he wanted to say it.

The principal was a large-bosomed white woman. She listened to him long enough to learn that he was Annie May's uncle. "Ah, yes, Mr. Jones," she said. "Now in my opinion—"

And he was buried under a flow of words, a mountain of words, that went on and on. Her voice was high-pitched and loud, and she kept talking until he lost all sense of what she was saying. There was one phrase she kept using that sort of jumped at him out of the mass of words—"a slow learner."

He left her office feeling confused and embarrassed. If he could only have found the words he could have explained that Annie May was bright as a dollar. She wasn't any "slow learner." Before he knew it he was out in the street, conscious only that he'd lost a whole afternoon's pay and he never had got to say what he'd come for. And he was boiling mad with himself. All he'd wanted was to ask the principal to help him persuade Annie May to finish school. But he'd never got the words together.

When he hung up his soiled work coat in the broom closet at eight o'clock that night he felt as though he'd been sweeping floors, dusting fixtures, cleaning fountains, and running errands since the beginning of time itself. He looked at himself in the cracked mirror that hung on the door of the closet. There was no question about it; he'd grown older-looking since Sam went in the army. His hair was turning a frizzled gray at the temples. His jawbones showed up sharper. There was a stoop in his shoulders.

"Guess I'll get a haircut," he said softly. He didn't really need one. But on a Saturday night the barbershop would be crowded. He'd have to wait a long time before Al got around to him. It would be good to listen to the talk that went on—the arguments that would get started and never really end. For a little while all the nagging worry about Sam would be pushed so far back in his mind, he wouldn't be aware of it.

The instant he entered the barbershop he could feel himself begin to relax inside. All the chairs were full. There were a lot of customers waiting. He waved a greeting to the barbers. "Hot, ain't it?" he said and mopped his forehead.

He stood there a minute, listening to the hum of conversation, before he picked out a place to sit. Some of the talk, he knew, would be violent, and he always avoided those discussions because he didn't like violence—even when it was only talk. Scraps of talk drifted past him.

"White folks got us by the balls—"

"Well, I dunno. It ain't just white folks. There's poor white folks gettin' their guts squeezed out, too—"

"Sure. But they're white. They can stand it better."

"Sadie had two dollars on 546 yesterday and it came out and—"

"You're wrong, man. Ain't no two ways about it. This country's set up so that—"

"Only thing to do, if you ask me, is shoot all them crackers and start out new—"

He finally settled himself in one of the chairs in the corner—not too far from the window and right in the middle

of a group of regular customers who were arguing hotly
about the war. It was a good seat. By looking in the long
mirror in front of the barbers he could see the length of
the shop.

Almost immediately he joined in the conversation.
"Them Japs ain't got a chance—" he started. And he was
feeling good. He'd come in at just the right time. He took
a deep breath before he went on. Most every time he
started talking about the Japs the others listened with deep
respect. Because he knew more about them than the other
customers. Pink worked for some navy people and she
told him what they said.

He looked along the line of waiting customers, watching
their reaction to his words. Pretty soon they'd all be listening to him. And then he stopped talking abruptly. A soldier was sitting in the far corner of the shop, staring down
at his shoes. Why, that's Scummy, he thought. He's at the
same camp where Sam is. He forgot what he was about to
say. He got up and walked over to Scummy. He swallowed all the questions about Sam that trembled on his
lips.

"Hiya, son," he said. "Sure is good to see you."

As he shook hands with the boy, he looked him over
carefully. He's changed, he thought. He was older. There
was something about his eyes that was different than before. He didn't seem to want to talk. After that first quick
look at William he kept his eyes down, staring at his
shoes.

Finally William couldn't hold the question back any
longer. It came out fast. "How's Sam?"

Scummy picked up a newspaper from the chair beside
him. "He's all right," he mumbled. There was a long silence. Then he raised his head and looked directly at William. "Was the las' time I seen him." He put a curious emphasis on the word "las'."

William was conscious of a trembling that started in his
stomach. It went all through his body. He was aware that
conversation in the barbershop had stopped. There was a
cone of silence in which he could hear the scraping noise
of the razors—a harsh sound, loud in the silence. Al was
putting thick oil on a customer's hair and he turned and
looked with the hair-oil bottle still in his hand, tilted up
over the customer's head. The men sitting in the tilted-
back barber's chairs twisted their necks around—awk-
wardly, slowly—so they could look at Scummy.

"What you mean—the las' time?" William asked

sharply. The words beat against his ears. He wished the
men in the barbershop would start talking again, for he
kept hearing his own words. "What you mean—the las'
time?" Just as though he were saying them over and over
again. Something had gone wrong with his breathing, too.
He couldn't seem to get enough air in through his nose.

Scummy got up. There was something about him that
William couldn't give a name to. It made the trembling in
his stomach worse.

"The las' time I seen him he was OK." Scummy's voice
made a snarling noise in the barbershop.

One part of William's mind said, yes, that's it. It's hate
that makes him look different. It's hate in his eyes. You
can see it. It's in his voice, and you can hear it. He's filled
with it.

"Since I seen him las'," he went on slowly, "he got shot
by a white MP. Because he wouldn't go to the nigger end
of a bus. He had a bullet put through his guts. He took
the MP's gun away from him and shot the bastard in the
shoulder." He put the newspaper down and started toward
the door; when he reached it he turned around. "They
courtmartialed him," he said softly. "He got twenty years
at hard labor. The notice was posted in the camp the day I
left." Then he walked out of the shop. He didn't look
back.

There was no sound in the barbershop as William
watched him go down the street. Even the razors had
stopped. Al was still holding the hair-oil bottle over the
head of his customer. The heavy oil was falling on the face
of the man sitting in the chair. It was coming down slowly
—one drop at a time.

The men in the shop looked at William and then looked
away. He thought, I mustn't tell Pink. She mustn't ever get
to know. I can go down to the mailbox early in the morning and I can get somebody else to look in it in the afternoon, so if a notice comes I can tear it up.

The barbers started cutting hair again. There was the
murmur of conversation in the shop. Customers got up
out of the tilted-back chairs. Someone said to him, "You
can take my place."

He nodded and walked over to the empty chair. His
legs were weak and shaky. He couldn't seem to think at
all. His mind kept dodging away from the thought of Sam
in prison. Instead the familiar detail of Sam's growing up
kept creeping into his thoughts. All the time the boy was
in grammar school he made good marks. Time went so

fast it seemed like it was just overnight and he was in long pants. And then in high school.

He made the basketball team in high school. The whole school was proud of him, for his picture had been in one of the white papers. They got two papers that day. Pink cut the pictures out and stuck one in the mirror of the dresser in their bedroom. She gave him one to carry in his wallet.

While Al cut his hair he stared at himself in the mirror until he felt as though his eyes were crossed. First he thought, maybe it isn't true. Maybe Scummy was joking. But a man who was joking didn't look like Scummy looked. He wondered if Scummy was AWOL. That would be bad. He told himself sternly that he mustn't think about Sam here in the barbershop—wait until he got home.

He was suddenly angry with Annie May. She was just plain no good. Why couldn't something have happened to her? Why did it have to be Sam? Then he was ashamed. He tried to find an excuse for having wanted harm to come to her. It looked like all his life he'd wanted a little something for himself and Pink and then when Sam came along he forgot about those things. He wanted Sam to have all the things that he and Pink couldn't get. It got to be too late for them to have them. But Sam—again he told himself not to think about him. To wait until he got home and in bed.

Al took the cloth from around his neck, and he got up out of the chair. Then he was out on the street, heading toward home. The heat that came from the pavement seeped through the soles of his shoes. He had forgotten how hot it was. He forced himself to wonder what it would be like to live in the country. Sometimes on hot nights like this, after he got home from work, he went to sit in the park. It was always cooler there. It would probably be cool in the country. But then it might be cold in winter—even colder than the city.

The instant he got in the house he took off his shoes and his shirt. The heat in the apartment was like a blanket —it made his skin itch and crawl in a thousand places. He went into the living room, where he leaned out of the window, trying to cool off. Not yet, he told himself. He mustn't think about it yet.

He leaned farther out of the window, to get away from the innumerable odors that came from the boxlike rooms in back of him. They cut off his breath, and he focused his mind on them. There was the greasy smell of cabbage and collard greens, smell of old wood and soapsuds and disinfectant, a lingering smell of gas from the kitchen stove, and over it all Annie May's perfume.

Then he turned his attention to the street. Up and down as far as he could see, folks were sitting on the stoops. Not talking. Just sitting. Somewhere up the street a baby wailed. A woman's voice rose sharply as she told it to shut up.

Pink wouldn't be home until late. The white folks she worked for were having a dinner party tonight. And no matter how late she got home on Saturday night she always stopped on Eighth Avenue to shop for her Sunday dinner. She never trusted him to do it. It's a good thing, he thought. If she ever took a look at me tonight she'd know there was something wrong.

A key clicked in the lock, and he drew back from the window. He was sitting on the couch when Annie May came in the room.

"You're home early, ain't you?" he asked.

"Oh, I'm going out again," she said.

"You shouldn't stay out so late like you did last night," he said mildly. He hadn't really meant to say it. But what with Sam—

"What you think I'm going to do? Sit here every night and make small talk with you?" Her voice was defiant. Loud.

"No," he said, and then added, "but nice girls ain't runnin' around the streets at four o'clock in the mornin'." Now that he'd started he couldn't seem to stop. "Oh, I know what time you come home. And it ain't right. If you don't stop it you can get some other place to stay."

"It's OK with me," she said lightly. She chewed the gum in her mouth so it made a cracking noise. "I don't know what Auntie Pink married a little runt like you for, anyhow. It wouldn't bother me a bit if I never saw you again." She walked toward the hall. "I'm going away for the week end," she added over her shoulder. "And I'll move out on Monday."

"What you mean for the week end?" he asked sharply. "Where you goin'?"

"None of your damn business," she said, and slammed the bathroom door hard.

The sharp sound of the door closing hurt his ears so that he winced, wondering why he had grown so sensitive to sounds in the last few hours. What'd she have to say that for, anyway, he asked himself. Five feet five wasn't so short for a man. He was taller than Pink, anyhow. Yet compared to Sam, he supposed he was a runt, for Sam had just kept on growing until he was six feet tall. At the thought he got up from the chair quickly, undressed, and got in bed. He lay there trying to still the trembling in his stomach; trying even now not to think about Sam, because it would be best to wait until Pink was in bed and sound asleep so that no expression on his face, no least little motion, would betray his agitation.

When he heard Pink come up the stairs just before midnight he closed his eyes. All of him was listening to her. He could hear her panting outside on the landing. There was a long pause before she put her key in the door. It took her all that time to get her breath back. She's getting old, he thought. I mustn't ever let her know about Sam.

She came into the bedroom, and he pretended to be asleep. He made himself breathe slowly. Evenly. Thinking I can get through tomorrow all right. I won't get up much before she goes to church. She'll be so busy getting dressed she won't notice me.

She went out of the room and he heard the soft murmur of her voice talking to Annie May. "Don't you pay no attention, honey. He don't mean a word of it. I know menfolks. They's always tired and out of sorts by the time Saturdays come around."

"But I'm not going to stay here any more."

"Yes, you is. You think I'm goin' to let my sister's child be turned out? You goin' to be right here."

They lowered their voices. There was laughter. Pink's deep and rich and slow. Annie May's high-pitched and nervous. Pink said, "You looks lovely, honey. Now, have a good time."

The front door closed. This time Annie May didn't slam it. He turned over on his back, making the springs creak. Instantly Pink came into the bedroom to look at him. He lay still, with his eyes closed, holding his breath for fear she would want to talk to him about what he'd said to Annie May and would wake him up. After she moved away from the door he opened his eyes.

There must be some meaning in back of what had happened to Sam. Maybe it was some kind of judgment from the Lord, he thought. Perhaps he shouldn't have stopped going to church. His only concession to Sunday was to put on his best suit. He wore it just that one day, and Pink pressed the pants late on Saturday night. But in the last few years it got so that every time he went to church he wanted to stand up and yell, "You Goddamn fools! How much more you goin' to take?"

He'd get to thinking about the street they lived on, and the sight of the minister with his clean white collar turned hind side to and the sound of his buttery voice were too much. One Sunday he'd actually gotten on his feet, for the minister was talking about the streets of gold up in heaven; the words were right on the tip of his tongue when Pink reached out and pinched his behind sharply. He yelped and sat down. Someone in back of him giggled. In spite of himself a slow smile had spread over his face. He stayed quiet through the rest of the service, but after that he didn't go to church at all.

This street where he and Pink lived was like the one where his mother had lived. It looked like he and Pink ought to have gotten further than his mother had. She had scrubbed floors, washed, and ironed in the white folks' kitchens. They were doing practically the same thing. That was another reason he stopped going to church. He couldn't figure out why these things had to stay the same, and if the Lord didn't intend it like that, why didn't He change it?

He began thinking about Sam again, so he shifted his attention to the sounds Pink was making in the kitchen. She was getting the rolls ready for tomorrow. Scrubbing the sweet potatoes. Washing the greens. Cutting up the chicken. Then the thump of the iron. Hot as it was, she was pressing his pants. He resisted the impulse to get up and tell her not to do it.

A little later, when she turned the light on in the bathroom, he knew she was getting ready for bed. And he held his eyes tightly shut, made his body rigidly still. As long as he could make her think he was sound asleep she wouldn't take a real good look at him. One real good look and she'd know there was something wrong. The bed sagged under her weight as she knelt down to say her prayers. Then she was lying down beside him. She sighed under her breath as her head hit the pillow.

He must have slept part of the time, but in the morning it seemed to him that he had looked up at the ceiling most of the night. He couldn't remember actually going to sleep.

When he finally got up, Pink was dressed and ready for church. He sat down in a chair in the living room away from the window, so the light wouldn't shine on his face. As he looked at her he wished that he could find relief from the confusion of his thoughts by taking part in the singing and the shouting that would go on in church. But he couldn't. And Pink never said anything about his not going to church. Only sometimes like today, when she was ready to go, she looked at him a little wistfully.

She had on her Sunday dress. It was made of a printed material—big red and black poppies splashed on a cream-colored background. He wouldn't let himself look right into her eyes, and in order that she wouldn't notice the evasiveness of his glance he stared at the dress. It fit snugly over her best corset, and the corset in turn constricted her thighs and tightly encased the rolls of flesh around her waist. She didn't move away, and he couldn't keep on inspecting the dress, so he shifted his gaze up to the wide cream-colored straw hat she was wearing far back on her head. Next he noticed that she was easing her feet by standing on the outer edges of the high-heeled patent-leather pumps she wore.

He reached out and patted her arm. "You look nice," he said, picking up the comic section of the paper.

She stood there looking at him while she pulled a pair of white cotton gloves over her roughened hands. "Is you all right, honey?" she asked.

"Course," he said, holding the paper up in front of his face.

"You shouldn't talk so mean to Annie May," she said gently.

"Yeah, I know," he said, and hoped she understood that he was apologizing. He didn't dare lower the paper while she was standing there looking at him so intently. Why doesn't she go, he thought.

"There's grits and eggs for breakfast."

"OK." He tried to make his voice sound as though he were so absorbed in what he was reading that he couldn't give her all of his attention. She walked toward the door, and he lowered the paper to watch her, thinking that her legs looked too small for her body under the vastness of the printed dress, that womenfolks sure were funny—she's got that great big pocketbook swinging on her arm and hardly anything in it. Sam used to love to tease her about the size of the handbags she carried.

When she closed the outside door and started down the stairs, the heat in the little room struck him in the face. He almost called her back so that he wouldn't be there by himself—left alone to brood over Sam. He decided that when she came home from church he would make love to her. Even in the heat the softness of her body, the smoothness of her skin, would comfort him.

He pulled his chair up close to the open window. Now he could let himself go. He could begin to figure out something to do about Sam. There's gotta be something, he thought. But his mind wouldn't stay put. It kept going back to the time Sam graduated from high school. Nineteen seventy-five his dark-blue suit had cost. He and Pink had figured and figured and finally they'd managed it. Sam had looked good in the suit; he was so tall and his shoulders were so broad it looked like a tailormade suit on him. When he got his diploma everybody went wild—he'd played center on the basketball team, and a lot of folks recognized him.

The trembling in his stomach got worse as he thought about Sam. He was aware that it had never stopped since Scummy had said those words "the las' time." It had gone on all last night until now there was a tautness and a tension in him that left him feeling as though his eardrums were strained wide open, listening for sounds. They must be a foot wide open, he thought. Open and pulsing with the strain of being open. Even his nostrils were stretched open like that. He could feel them. And a weight behind his eyes.

He went to sleep sitting there in the chair. When he woke up his whole body was wet with sweat. It musta got hotter while I slept, he thought. He was conscious of an ache in his jawbones. It's from holding 'em shut so tight. Even his tongue—he'd been holding it so still in his mouth it felt like it was glued there.

Attracted by the sound of voices, he looked out of the window. Across the way a man and a woman were arguing. Their voices rose and fell on the hot, still air. He could look directly into the room where they were standing, and he saw that they were half undressed.

The woman slapped the man across the face. The sound was like a pistol shot, and for an instant William felt his jaw relax. It seemed to him that the whole block grew quiet and waited. He waited with it. The man grabbed his belt and lashed out at the woman. He watched the belt rise and fall against her brown skin. The woman screamed with the regularity of clockwork. The street came alive again. There was the sound of voices, the rattle of dishes. A baby whined. The woman's voice became a murmur of pain in the background.

"I gotta get me some beer," he said aloud. It would cool

him off. It would help him to think. He dressed quickly, telling himself that Pink wouldn't be home for hours yet and by that time the beer smell would be gone from his breath.

The street outside was full of kids playing tag. They were all dressed up in their Sunday clothes. Red socks, blue socks, danced in front of him all the way to the corner. The sight of them piled up the quivering in his stomach. Sam used to play in this block on Sunday afternoons. As he walked along, women thrust their heads out of the opened windows, calling to the children. It seemed to him that all the voices were Pink's voice saying, "You, Sammie, stop that runnin' in your good cloes!"

He was so glad to get away from the sight of the children that he ignored the heat inside the barroom of the hotel on the corner and determinedly edged his way past girls in sheer summer dresses and men in loud plaid jackets and tight-legged cream-colored pants until he finally reached the long bar.

There was such a sense of hot excitement in the place that he turned to look around him. Men with slicked, straightened hair were staring through half-closed eyes at the girls lined up at the bar. One man sitting at a table close by kept running his hand up and down the bare arm of the girl leaning against him. Up and down. Down and up. William winced and looked away. The jukebox was going full blast, filling the room with high, raw music that beat about his ears in a queer mixture of violence and love and hate and terror. He stared at the brilliantly colored moving lights on the front of the jukebox as he listened to it, wishing that he had stayed at home, for the music made the room hotter.

"Make it a beer," he said to the bartender.

The beer glass was cold. He held it in his hand, savoring the chill of it, before he raised it to his lips. He drank it down fast. Immediately he felt the air grow cooler. The smell of beer and whisky that hung in the room lifted.

"Fill it up again," he said. He still had that awful trembling in his stomach, but he felt as though he were really beginning to think. Really think. He found he was arguing with himself.

"Sam mighta been like this. Spendin' Sunday afternoons whorin'."

"But he was part of me and part of Pink. He had a chance—"

"Yeah. A chance to live in one of them hell-hole flats. A chance to get himself a woman to beat."

"He woulda finished college and got a good job. Mebbe been a druggist or a doctor or a lawyer—"

"Yeah. Or mebbe got himself a stable of women to rent out on the block—"

He licked the suds from his lips. The man at the table nearby had stopped stroking the girl's arm. He was kissing her—forcing her closer and closer to him.

"Yeah," William jeered at himself. "That coulda been Sam on a hot Sunday afternoon—"

As he stood there arguing with himself he thought it was getting warmer in the bar. The lights were dimmer. I better go home, he thought. I gotta live with this thing some time. Drinking beer in this place ain't going to help any. He looked out toward the lobby of the hotel, attracted by the sound of voices. A white cop was arguing with a frowzy-looking girl who had obviously had too much to drink.

"I got a right in here. I'm mindin' my own business," she said with one eye on the bar.

"Aw, go chase yourself." The cop gave her a push toward the door. She stumbled against a chair.

William watched her in amusement. "Better than a movie," he told himself.

She straightened up and tugged at her girdle. "You white son of a bitch," she said.

The cop's face turned a furious red. He walked toward the woman, waving his nightstick. It was then that William saw the soldier. Tall. Straight. Creases in his khaki pants. An overseas cap cocked over one eye. Looks like Sam looked that one time he was home on furlough, he thought.

The soldier grabbed the cop's arm and twisted the nightstick out of his hand. He threw it half the length of the small lobby. It rattled along the floor and came to a dead stop under a chair.

"Now what'd he want to do that for?" William said softly. He knew that night after night the cop had to come back to this hotel. He's the law, he thought, and he can't let— Then he stopped thinking about him, for the cop raised his arm. The soldier aimed a blow at the cop's chin. The cop ducked and reached for his gun. The soldier turned to run.

It's happening too fast, William thought. It's like one of those horserace reels they run over fast at the movies.

Then he froze inside. The quivering in his stomach got worse. The soldier was heading toward the door. Running. His foot was on the threshold when the cop fired. The soldier dropped. He folded up as neatly as the brown-paper bags Pink brought home from the store, emptied, and then carefully put in the kitchen cupboard.

The noise of the shot stayed in his eardrums. He couldn't get it out. "Jesus Christ!" he said. Then again, "Jesus Christ!" The beer glass was warm. He put it down on the bar with such violence some of the beer slopped over on his shirt. He stared at the wet place, thinking Pink would be mad as hell. Him out drinking in a bar on Sunday. There was a stillness in which he was conscious of the stink of the beer, the heat in the room, and he could still hear the sound of the shot. Somebody dropped a glass, and the tinkle of it hurt his ears.

Then everybody was moving toward the lobby. The doors between the bar and the lobby slammed shut. High, excited talk broke out.

The tall, thin black man standing next to him said, "That ties it. It ain't even safe here where we live. Not no more. I'm goin' to get me a white bastard of a cop and nail his hide to a street sign."

"Is the soldier dead?" someone asked.

"He wasn't movin' none," came the answer.

They pushed hard against the doors leading to the lobby. The doors stayed shut.

He stood still, watching them. The anger that went through him was so great that he had to hold on to the bar to keep from falling. He felt as though he were going to burst wide open. It was like having seen Sam killed before his eyes. Then he heard the whine of an ambulance siren. His eardrums seemed to be waiting to pick it up.

"Come on, what you waitin' for?" he snarled the words at the people milling around the lobby doors. "Come on!" he repeated, running toward the street.

The crowd followed him to the One Hundred Twenty-sixth Street entrance of the hotel. He got there in time to see a stretcher bearing a limp khaki-clad figure disappear inside the ambulance in front of the door. The ambulance pulled away fast, and he stared after it stupidly.

He hadn't known what he was going to do, but he felt cheated. Let down. He noticed that it was beginning to get dark. More and more people were coming into the street. He wondered where they'd come from and how they'd heard about the shooting so quickly. Every time he looked around there were more of them. Curious, eager voices kept asking, "What happened? What happened?" The answer was always the same. Hard. Angry. "A white cop shot a soldier."

Someone said, "Come on to the hospital. Find out what happened to him."

In front of the hotel he had been in the front of the crowd. Now there were so many people in back of him and in front of him that when they started toward the hospital, he moved along with them. He hadn't decided to go —the forward movement picked him up and moved him along without any intention on his part. He got the feeling that he had lost his identity as a person with a free will of his own. It frightened him at first. Then he began to feel powerful. He was surrounded by hundreds of people like himself. They were all together. They could do anything.

As the crowd moved slowly down Eighth Avenue, he saw that there were cops lined up on both sides of the street. Mounted cops kept coming out of the side streets, shouting, "Break it up! Keep moving. Keep moving."

The cops were scared of them. He could tell. Their faces were dead white in the semidarkness. He started saying the words over separately to himself. Dead. White. He laughed. White cops. White MP's. They got us coming and going, he thought. He laughed again. Dead. White. The words were funny said separately like that. He stopped laughing suddenly because a part of his mind repeated: twenty years, twenty years.

He licked his lips. It was hot as all hell tonight. He imagined what it would be like to be drinking swallow after swallow of ice-cold beer. His throat worked and he swallowed audibly.

The big black man walking beside him turned and looked down at him. "You all right, brother?" he asked curiously.

"Yeah," he nodded. "It's them sons of bitches of cops. They're scared of us." He shuddered. The heat was terrible. The tide of hate quivering in his stomach made him hotter. "Wish I had some beer," he said.

The man seemed to understand not only what he had said but all the things he had left unsaid. For he nodded and smiled. And William thought this was an extraordinary night. It was as though, standing so close together, so many of them like this—as though they knew each other's thoughts. It was a wonderful thing.

The crowd carried him along. Smoothly. Easily. He

wasn't really walking. Just gliding. He was aware that the shuffling feet of the crowd made a muffled rhythm on the concrete sidewalk. It was slow, inevitable. An ominous sound, like a funeral march. With the regularity of a drumbeat. No. It's more like a pulse beat, he thought. It isn't a loud noise. It just keeps repeating over and over. But not that regular, because it builds up to something. It keeps building up.

The mounted cops rode their horses into the crowd. Trying to break it up into smaller groups. Then the rhythm was broken. Seconds later it started again. Each time the tempo was a little faster. He found he was breathing the same way. Faster and faster. As though he were running. There were more and more cops. All of them white. They had moved the colored cops out.

"They done that before," he muttered.

"What?" said the man next to him.

"They moved the colored cops out," he said.

He heard the man repeat it to someone standing beside him. It became part of the slow shuffling rhythm on the sidewalk. "They moved the colored cops." He heard it go back and back through the crowd until it was only a whisper of hate on the still, hot air. "They moved the colored cops."

As the crowd shuffled back and forth in front of the hospital, he caught snatches of conversation. "The soldier was dead when they put him in the ambulance." "Always tryin' to fool us." "Christ! Just let me get my hands on one of them cops."

He was thinking about the hospital and he didn't take part in any of the conversations. Even now across the long span of years he could remember the helpless, awful rage that had sent him hurrying home from this same hospital. Not saying anything. Getting home by some kind of instinct.

Pink had come to this hospital when she had had her last child. He could hear again the cold contempt in the voice of the nurse as she listened to Pink's loud grieving. "You people have too many children anyway," she said.

It left him speechless. He had his hat in his hand and he remembered how he wished afterward that he'd put it on in front of her to show her what he thought of her. As it was, all the bitter answers that finally surged into his throat seemed to choke him. No words would come out. So he stared at her lean, spare body. He let his eyes stay a long time on her flat breasts. White uniform. White shoes. White stockings. White skin.

Then he mumbled, "It's too bad your eyes ain't white, too." And turned on his heel and walked out.

It wasn't any kind of answer. She probably didn't even know what he was talking about. The baby dead, and all he could think of was to tell her her eyes ought to be white. White shoes, white stockings, white uniform, white skin, and blues eyes.

Staring at the hospital, he saw with satisfaction that frightened faces were appearing at the windows. Some of the lights went out. He began to feel that this night was the first time he'd ever really been alive. Tonight everything was going to be changed. There was a growing, swelling sense of power in him. He felt the same thing in the people around him.

The cops were aware of it, too, he thought. They were out in full force. Mounties, patrolmen, emergency squads. Radio cars that looked like oversize bugs crawled through the side streets. Waited near the curbs. Their white tops stood out in the darkness. "White folks riding in white cars." He wasn't aware that he had said it aloud until he heard the words go through the crowd. "White folks in white cars." The laughter that followed the words had a rough, raw rhythm. It repeated the pattern of the shuffling feet.

Someone said, "They got him at the station house. He ain't here." And the crowd started moving toward One Hundred Twenty-third Street.

Great God in the morning, William thought, everybody's out here. There were girls in thin summer dresses, boys in long coats and tight-legged pants, old women dragging kids along by the hand. A man on crutches jerked himself past to the rhythm of the shuffling feet. A blind man tapped his way through the center of the crowd, and it divided into two separate streams as it swept by him. At every street corner William noticed someone stopped to help the blind man up over the curb.

The street in front of the police station was so packed with people that he couldn't get near it. As far as he could see they weren't doing anything. They were simply standing there. Waiting for something to happen. He recognized a few of them: the woman with the loose, rolling eyes who sold shopping bags on One Hundred Twenty-fifth Street; the lucky-number peddler—the man with the white parrot on his shoulder; three sisters of the Heavenly Rest for All movement—barefooted women in loose white robes.

Then, for no reason that he could discover, everybody moved toward One Hundred Twenty-fifth Street. The motion of the crowd was slower now because it kept increasing in size as people coming from late church services were drawn into it. It was easy to identify them, he thought. The women wore white gloves. The kids were all slicked up. Despite the more gradual movement he was still being carried along effortlessly, easily. When someone in front of him barred his way, he pushed against the person irritably, frowning in annoyance because the smooth forward flow of his progress had been stopped.

It was Pink who stood in front of him. He stopped frowning when he recognized her. She had a brown-paper bag tucked under her arm, and he knew she had stopped at the corner store to get the big bottle of cream soda she always brought home on Sundays. The sight of it made him envious, for it meant that this Sunday had been going along in an orderly, normal fashion for her while he— She was staring at him so hard he was suddenly horribly conscious of the smell of the beer that had spilled on his shirt. He knew she had smelled it, too, by the tighter grip she took on her pocketbook.

"What you doing out here in this mob? A Sunday evening and you drinking beer," she said grimly.

For a moment he couldn't answer her. All he could think of was Sam. He almost said, "I saw Sam shot this afternoon," and he swallowed hard.

"This afternoon I saw a white cop kill a colored soldier," he said. "In the bar where I was drinking beer. I saw it. That's why I'm here. The glass of beer I was drinking went on my clothes. The cop shot him in the back. That's why I'm here."

He paused for a moment, took a deep breath. This was how it ought to be, he decided. She had to know sometime and this was the right place to tell her. In this semidarkness, in this confusion of noises, with the low, harsh rhythm of the footsteps sounding against the noise of the horses' hoofs.

His voice thickened. "I saw Scummy yesterday," he went on. "He told me Sam's doing time at hard labor. That's why we ain't heard from him. A white MP shot him when he wouldn't go to the nigger end of a bus. Sam shot the MP. They gave him twenty years at hard labor."

He knew he hadn't made it clear how to him the soldier in the bar was Sam; that it was like seeing his own son shot before his very eyes. I don't even know whether the soldier was dead, he thought. What made me tell her about Sam out here in the street like this, anyway? He realized with a sense of shock that he really didn't care that he had told her. He felt strong, powerful, aloof. All the time he'd been talking he wouldn't look right at her. Now, suddenly, he was looking at her as though she were a total stranger. He was coldly wondering what she'd do. He was prepared for anything.

But he wasn't prepared for the wail that came from her throat. The sound hung in the hot air. It made the awful quivering in his stomach worse. It echoed and re-echoed the length of the street. Somewhere in the distance a horse whinnied. A woman standing way back in the crowd groaned as though the sorrow and the anguish in that cry were more than she could bear.

Pink stood there for a moment. Silent. Brooding. Then she lifted the big bottle of soda high in the air. She threw it with all her might. It made a wide arc and landed in the exact center of the plate-glass window of a furniture store. The glass crashed in with a sound like a gunshot.

A sigh went up from the crowd. They surged toward the broken window. Pink followed close behind. When she reached the window, all the glass had been broken in. Reaching far inside, she grabbed a small footstool and then turned to hurl it through the window of the dress shop next door. He kept close behind her, watching her as she seized a new missile from each store window that she broke.

Plate-glass windows were being smashed all up and down One Hundred Twenty-fifth Street—on both sides of the street. The violent, explosive sound fed the sense of power in him. Pink had started this. He was proud of her, for she had shown herself to be a fit mate for a man of his type. He stayed as close to her as he could. So in spite of the crashing, splintering sounds and the swarming, violent activity around him, he knew the exact moment when she lost her big straw hat; when she took off the high-heeled patent-leather shoes and flung them away, striding swiftly along in her stockinged feet. That her dress was hanging crooked on her.

He was right in back of her when she stopped in front of a hat store. She carefully appraised all the hats inside the broken window. Finally she reached out, selected a small hat covered with purple violets, and fastened it securely on her head.

"Woman's got good sense," a man said.

"Man, oh, man! Let me get in there," said a rawboned woman who thrust her way forward through the jam of people to seize two hats from the window.

A roar of approval went up from the crowd. From then on when a window was smashed it was bare of merchandise when the people streamed past it. White folks owned these stores. They'd lose and lose and lose, he thought with satisfaction. The words "twenty years" re-echoed in his mind. I'll be an old man, he thought. Then: I may be dead before Sam gets out of prison.

The feeling of great power and strength left him. He was so confused by its loss that he decided this thing happening in the street wasn't real. It was so dark, there were so many people shouting and running about, that he almost convinced himself he was having a nightmare. He was aware that his hearing had now grown so acute he could pick up the tiniest sounds: the quickened breathing and the soft, gloating laughter of the crowd; even the sound of his own heart beating. He could hear these things under the noise of the breaking glass, under the shouts that were coming from both sides of the street. They forced him to face the fact that this was no dream but a reality from which he couldn't escape. The quivering in his stomach kept increasing as he walked along.

Pink was striding through the crowd just ahead of him. He studied her to see if she, too, was feeling as he did. But the outrage that ran through her had made her younger. She was tireless. Most of the time she was leading the crowd. It was all he could do to keep up with her, and finally he gave up the attempt—it made him too tired.

He stopped to watch a girl who was standing in a store window, clutching a clothes model tightly around the waist. "What's she want that for?" he said aloud. For the model had been stripped of clothing by the passing crowd, and he thought its pinkish torso was faintly obscene in its resemblance to a female figure.

The girl was young and thin. Her back was turned toward him, and there was something so ferocious about the way her dark hands gripped the naked model that he resisted the onward movement of the crowd to stare in fascination. The girl turned around. Her nervous hands were tight around the dummy's waist. It was Annie May.

"Ah, no!" he said, and let his breath come out with a sigh.

Her hands crept around the throat of the model and she sent it hurtling through the air above the heads of the

crowd. It landed short of a window across the street. The
legs shattered. The head rolled toward the curb. The waist
snapped neatly in two. Only the torso remained whole and
in one piece.

Annie May stood in the empty window and laughed
with the crowd when someone kicked the torso into the
street. He stood there, staring at her. He felt that now for
the first time he understood her. She had never had anything but badly paying jobs—working for young white
women who probably despised her. She was like Sam on
that bus in Georgia. She didn't want just the nigger end of
things, and here in Harlem there wasn't anything else for
her. All along she'd been trying the only way she knew
how to squeeze out of life a little something for herself.

He tried to get closer to the window where she was
standing. He had to tell her that he understood. And the
crowd, tired of the obstruction that he had made by standing still, swept him up and carried him past. He stopped
thinking and let himself be carried along on a vast wave
of feeling. There was so much plate glass on the sidewalk
that it made a grinding noise under the feet of the hurrying crowd. It was a dull, harsh sound that set his teeth
on edge and quickened the trembling of his stomach.

Now all the store windows that he passed were broken.
The people hurrying by him carried tables, lamps, shoe-
boxes, clothing. A woman next to him held a wedding
cake in her hands—it went up in tiers of white frosting
with a small bride and groom mounted at the top. Her
hands were bleeding, and he began to look closely at the
people nearest him. Most of them, too, had cuts on their
hands and legs. Then he saw there was blood on the sidewalk in front of the windows; blood dripping down the
jagged edges of the broken windows. And he wanted
desperately to go home.

He was conscious that the rhythm of the crowd had
changed. It was faster, and it had taken on an ugly note.
The cops were using their nightsticks. Police wagons drew
up to the curbs. When they pulled away, they were full of
men and women who carried loot from the stores in their
hands.

The police cars slipping through the streets were joined
by other cars with loudspeakers on top. The voices coming
through the loudspeakers were harsh. They added to the
noise and the confusion. He tried to listen to what the
voices were saying. But the words had no meaning for

him. He caught one phrase over and over: "Good people of Harlem." It made him feel sick.

He repeated the words "of Harlem." We don't belong anywhere, he thought. There ain't no room for us anywhere. There wasn't no room for Sam in a bus in Georgia. There ain't no room for us here in New York. There ain't no place but top floors. The top-floor black people. And he laughed, and the sound stuck in his throat.

After that he snatched a suit from the window of a men's clothing store. It was a summer suit. The material felt crisp and cool. He walked away with it under his arm. He'd never owned a suit like that. He simply sweated out the summer in the same dark pants he wore in winter. Even while he stroked the material, a part of his mind sneered—you got summer pants; Sam's got twenty years.

He was surprised to find that he was almost at Lenox Avenue, for he hadn't remembered crossing Seventh. At the corner the cops were shoving a group of young boys and girls into a police wagon. He paused to watch. Annie May was in the middle of the group. She had a yellow-fox jacket dangling from one hand.

"Annie May!" he shouted. "Annie May!" The crowd pushed him along faster and faster. She hadn't seen him. He let himself be carried forward by the movement of the crowd. He had to find Pink and tell her that the cops had taken Annie May.

He peered into the dimness of the street ahead of him, looking for her; then he elbowed his way toward the curb so that he could see the other side of the street. He forgot about finding Pink, for directly opposite him was the music store that he passed every night coming home from work. Young boys and girls were always lounging on the sidewalk in front of it. They danced a few steps while they listened to the records being played inside the shop. All the records sounded the same—a terribly magnified woman's voice bleating out a blues song in a voice that sounded to him like that of an animal in heat—an old animal, tired and beaten, but with an insinuating know-how left in her. The white men who went past the store smiled as their eyes lingered on the young girls swaying to the music.

"White folks got us comin' and goin'. Backwards and forwards," he muttered. He fought his way out of the crowd and walked toward a no-parking sign that stood in front of the store. He rolled it up over the curb. It was heavy, and the effort made him pant. It took all his strength to send it crashing through the glass on the door.

Almost immediately an old woman and a young man slipped inside the narrow shop. He followed them. He watched them smash the records that lined the shelves. He hadn't thought of actually breaking the records, but once he started he found the crisp, snapping noise pleasant. The feeling of power began to return. He didn't like these records, so they had to be destroyed.

When they left the music store there wasn't a whole record left. The old woman came out of the store last. As he hurried off up the street he could have sworn he smelled the sharp, acrid smell of smoke. He turned and looked back. He was right. A thin wisp of smoke was coming through the store door. The old woman had long since disappeared in the crowd.

Farther up the street he looked back again. The fire in the record shop was burning merrily. It was making a glow that lit up that part of the street. There was a new rhythm now. It was faster and faster. Even the voices coming from the loudspeakers had taken on the urgency of speed.

Fire trucks roared up the street. He threw his head back and laughed when he saw them. That's right, he thought. Burn the whole damn place down. It was wonderful. Then he frowned. "Twenty years at hard labor." The words came back to him. He was a fool. Fire wouldn't wipe that out. There wasn't anything that would wipe it out.

He remembered then that he had to find Pink. To tell her about Annie May. He overtook her in the next block. She's got more stuff, he thought. She had a table lamp in one hand, a large enamel kettle in the other. The lightweight summer coat draped across her shoulders was so small it barely covered her enormous arms. She was watching a group of boys assault the steel gates in front of a liquor store. She frowned at them so ferociously he wondered what she was going to do. Hating liquor the way she did, he half expected her to cuff the boys and send them on their way up the street.

She turned and looked at the crowd in back of her. When she saw him she beckoned to him. "Hold these," she said. He took the lamp, the kettle, and the coat she held out to him, and he saw that her face was wet with perspiration. The print dress was darkly stained with it.

She fastened the hat with the purple flowers securely on her head. Then she walked over to the gate. "Git out the way," she said to the boys. Bracing herself in front of the gate, she started tugging at it. The gate resisted. She pulled at it with a sudden access of such furious strength that he was frightened. Watching her, he got the feeling that the resistance of the gate had transformed it in her mind. It was no longer a gate—it had become the world that had taken her son, and she was wreaking vengeance on it.

The gate began to bend and sway under her assault. Then it was down. She stood there for a moment, staring at her hands—big drops of blood oozed slowly over the palms. Then she turned to the crowd that had stopped to watch.

"Come on, you niggers," she said. Her eyes were little and evil and triumphant. "Come on and drink up the white man's liquor." As she strode off up the street, the beflowered hat dangled precariously from the back of her head.

When he caught up with her she was moaning, talking to herself in husky whispers. She stopped when she saw him and put her hand on his arm.

"It's hot, ain't it?" she said, panting.

In the midst of all this violence, the sheer commonplaceness of her question startled him. He looked at her closely. The rage that had been in her was gone, leaving her completely exhausted. She was breathing too fast in uneven gasps that shook her body. Rivulets of sweat streamed down her face. It was as though her triumph over the metal gate had finished her. The gate won anyway, he thought.

"Let's go home, Pink," he said. He had to shout to make his voice carry over the roar of the crowd, the sound of breaking glass.

He realized she didn't have the strength to speak, for she only nodded in reply to his suggestion. Once we get home she'll be all right, he thought. It was suddenly urgent that they get home, where it was quiet, where he could think, where he could take something to still the tremors in his stomach. He tried to get her to walk a little faster, but she kept slowing down until, when they entered their own street, it seemed to him they were barely moving.

In the middle of the block she stood still. "I can't make it," she said. "I'm too tired."

Even as he put his arm around her she started going down. He tried to hold her up, but her great weight was too much for him. She went down slowly, inevitably, like a great ship capsizing. Until all of her huge body was crumpled on the sidewalk.

"Pink," he said. "Pink. You gotta get up," he said it over and over again.

She didn't answer. He leaned over and touched her gently. Almost immediately afterward he straightened up. All his life, moments of despair and frustration had left him speechless—strangled by the words that rose in his throat. This time the words poured out.

He sent his voice raging into the darkness and the awful confusion of noises. "The sons of bitches," he shouted. "The sons of bitches."

So Softly Smiling

by Chester Himes

To Roy Johnny Squires, a lieutenant in the U. S. Army, who for six months had seen much of life and too much of death, through the blinding glare of desert heat, it felt unreal being home in Harlem for thirty days. North African warfare had left its mark on him—it kept raging through his brain like a red inferno that would never cease, tautening his muscles and jerking his reflexes and keeping his eyes constantly on the alert. For hours he had been tramping the familiar streets, scanning the familiar faces; and even now, at two in the morning, it did not mean a thing. His nerves were sticking out like wires.

It was too un-dead, un-wounded, bloodless, entire—too human. That was it—too human again after the bombings and the shellings and the snipings, the charges with twenty and the arrivals with twelve; the egg-sized balls of heat that grew like mushrooms at the base of the brain. It was too filled with something, too much like just lying down and crying like a baby. A drink was in line; a drink was most needed.

He pushed into a tony after-hours spot on 125th Street and headed toward the bar.

"Make mine rye," he said to the bartender.

And then, halfway turning, he saw her. He was startled. He had left her in the dull, dawn khamsins where only her face had stood between him and a death that was never

99

two feet off. Those purely feminine features with a tawny skin like an African veld at sunset, so smooth you forever wanted to touch it, crowned by blue-black hair that rolled up from her forehead in great curling billows like low storm clouds. That mouth, wide enough for a man to really kiss, and the color of crushed rosebuds. He could not be mistaken.

She was sitting by herself over against the wall at a low, lounge table, as if waiting for someone. The pianist was playing Chopin's *Fantasie,* and she was lost in listening; maybe trying to catch something that the music promised but never gave. He swung slowly from the bar and sauntered over, magnetized, and stood across the table, looking down at her. Not disrespectfully, not recklessly; but with all the homage in the world.

"You're as beautiful as I knew you'd be," he said.

She turned a widened glance on him, and something new and unexpected, almost unbelievable, came alive in her face, as if she might have seen what the music promised but never gave. Then her long black lashes lowered lacquered fans over the sudden boy-and-girl game in her eyes. After a moment she looked up-from-under into his face and murmured, "I am?" slightly questioning, the corners of her mouth quirking in beginning laughter.

The shaded wall light mellowed her into a painting, lifelike and provocative, with eyes like two candles in a darkened church; and perfume came out of her hair and burnt through him like flame. For a long time now there had only been the girl in the clouds; and he could not help himself. He reached out and drew her to him and kissed her with long and steady pressure.

Behind them, someone gasped; a laugh caught, moved, and died.

But he did not hear. Because her lips were smooth and soft and resilient, like the beginning of life, as he had dreamed they would be; and he kept kissing her until the breath had gone from both of them.

Finally she broke away, gasping, "Why did you do that?"

"I don't know," he confessed, his eyes on hers; and after a moment added, as if thinking aloud, "to get something, I guess."

She waited so long that he thought she would not reply, then she asked, "Did you?"

"Yes."

"I'm glad."

They stood on the brink of something suddenly discovered, something new and big and important, looking at each other until the long, live moment ran out. And then he dropped a bill on the table and took her by the arm and they went outside and turned down Seventh Avenue, silent for the most part, drawing feelings from each other without words, and after a time it began to snow again, but neither of them noticed. Hours later, it seemed, they came to Central Park, and sat on a bench and kissed.

The February daybreak found them still there, two whitened images in the softly sifting snow; and finally she said, "I should have waited for Dorothy, she'll be furious."

"Then—then you're not married?" quickly, as if he had been afraid to ask before.

"No, darling," she teased. "Aren't my kisses adorably inexperienced?"

He kissed her again, then said with an odd solemnity, "They're everything I dreamed that they would be."

They had breakfast at a crowded little lunch counter, but were oblivious of the other people; and when they couldn't stretch the minutes any longer, he said, his intense glance playing over her face, "I have to go back in twenty-nine days, so please don't fall in love with me." Taking a deep breath, he continued, "But don't leave me, please don't leave me; I'm already so much in love with you."

She was looking at him, at his young, gaunt face with too much thinness down the cheeks and too much blankness in the eyes, hiding too much that he had seen that she could now feel hard and constricted inside of him. Looking at him; and at his tall, lithe figure in the jaunty uniform of a commissioned officer, question-marked against the counter and back-grounded against the row of coffee-drinking workers, which, without any effort, had she closed her eyes, she could have seen without its litheness, bloated and wormy and unidentifiable as either black or white in the barren heat of an African desert. But her gaze remained steadily on his face, brown and full-lipped and handsome, and once she opened her mouth as if to speak, and then closed it as if she could not find the handle to the words, and finally, when she replied, it was only to say, "Yes," answering in the affirmative to a number of questions he might have found it hard to ask.

Three days later they taxied to Grand Central Station and boarded a train for some little sleepy town somewhere—it did not matter—and they were married. Miss Mona Morrison, successful poet, who had lived alone on Sugar Hill, became the ordinary wife of a U. S. Army officer.

But it did not seem at all strange that this should be happening to her, or to either of them; the strange thing would have been its not happening.

"Sometimes coming back from a raid in the dawn," he told her that night, emotion fingering the edges of his voice, "I'd look up at the reddening sky and feel that all the earth was consuming itself in fire and only heaven would be left; and I'd want so much to be in love, I'd ache with it."

And she whispered in reply, "If I could be that; if I could be heaven and always have you."

After that, nothing was real. It was fantasy, ecstasy, dread and apprehension. It was glory. They went to live in her apartment, and did not need a thing. Neither people nor food nor sleep. Nor the world. Because there was too much of each other within the hours that they would never have.

And the days passed through this enchanted unreality, wired-together and meteoric. There were twenty-six; then there were twenty-five. But each day was filled to over-flowing and could not hold it all; and always some spilled into the day following.

In twenty-three days; and then twenty-two.

They barricaded themselves behind illusion and fought against it in the manner of two small children playing house.

They were riding down Fifth Avenue atop a bus, and she was saying. "A month is long enough to stay in Harlem. Next month we'll spend with my folks in Springfield, Ohio. You'll love my mother." Laughing, she added. "She's a Seventh Day Adventist, by way of description."

"I've got some remote relatives in Chicago, too, whom we can visit for a time," he said, catching the spirit of the fantasy, "although my parents are both dead."

"And after that we can wander lazily to the coast. Have you ever been to Los Angeles?" she asked.

He shook his head.

"It's good for a month, too. And I'll introduce you to some of the celebs—Ethel Waters and Rochester and Hall Johnson; you'll enjoy Hall, he's a man of many thoughts; and even Lena Horne, although I'll not promise I won't be jealous if she smiles at you.

"Carmel is a lovely place, too," she went on, "After the war—"

He quickly interrupted, "What war?" and they laughed.

"It's funny how you can grow past things so quickly," she observed, surprised. "Ten days ago I was a rather self-centered poet who prided herself on being remote— and now I feel as if that was another life."

"It was," he said. And then quickly, almost fearfully, she vowed, "But I'll never grow past you. When you're gone . . ."

She caught herself, but it was too late.

This was it; he was going back, and she was staying here.

"I used to ask myself," he confessed, " 'What have I got in this war? Let the white people fight their own war—I've got nothing to win.' And then I read where someone said, perhaps it was Walter White or Randolph, that America belonged to the Negro as much as it did to anyone. And I got a funny feeling, maybe it was pride, or ownership—I don't know. Anyway, I enlisted. And then one day the 'old man' called us in and said, 'We're it.' "

He was silent for a time, looking at the passing sights, and when she did not speak, he went on, trying to explain something:

"I-I don't know just when it started, but I got to feeling that I was fighting for the Four Freedoms. Maybe I had to feel it; maybe I had to feel that it was a bigger fight than just to keep the same old thing we've always had. But it got to be big in my mind—bigger than just fighting a war. It got to be more like building, well, building security and peace and freedom for everyone."

"And—and, what I mean," he stumbled on, "is we don't have to hide from it. It's got to be building for freedom and it's got to be so big and wide there'll be room in it for happiness, too."

She said an odd thing. "We're going to have a son." Because she knew that in these things there was this—which no one could take—this going on of life, which gave to everything else purpose, meaning, a future.

"How do you know?" he asked, startled.

"How could we miss?" she countered.

And they were laughing again, so wonderfully happy. But even a song could bring it back, a voice from the radio singing the half-forgotten words: *Leaves are falling and I am recalling* . . . Because this was so young, so alive, so biological; this was for a togetherness throughout eternity.

It was there the night Bill and Louise threw the party for them, although that was one of the happiest days they ever knew. But for a time they forgot about it; they felt almost as if they had it beaten.

All the old bunch was there, you know their names. Louise made mint juleps and they danced a little and flirted with each other's wives and then began a discussion on political interpretations, which ended with Ted telling the story of *Barker Brown*. Then Henry told the one about the two whales and the "cracker" . . . " 'You mean to say you ain't never seen a *cracker?'*, the old whale asked the baby whale . . ." Not to be outdone, Walter told the tale of the ghost of Rufus Jones which came back to earth in the body of a white man and was elected to governor of Mississippi. But the colored folks knew he was old Rufus Jones.

They were having such a wonderful time that Eddie suggested that they do it over again at his flat next month. "How is it with you and Roy, Mona?" he asked.

How was it?

It was on top of them, that is how it was. In thirteen days he was going back to Africa to fight for a democracy he never had; it was reality . . . And then in twelve . . .

The togetherness which was meant to be would be gone . . . In eleven days . . . And then in ten . . . It hung over their heads, staining every moment with a blind, futile desperation, beneath which everything was distorted and magnified out of proportion to its importance, so that now things began to hurt which before would not have mattered, and minor incidents which should have sunk beneath a kiss now grew into catastrophes.

It was that way when he met Earl Henry and Bill Peters who had gone to Chicago university with him. Earl was a cavalry lieutenant, and Pete, sporting the wings of the 99th Pursuit Squadron, said, "I'm an eagle now, sonny."

A reunion was in order, so they found a pleasant little bar on 116th Street.

Roy intended to call Mona from the first, knowing that she would be expecting him home, and would worry. But a slightly tipsy celebrant was monopolizing the house telephone, making up with a girl whom, judging from the phrases which drifted Roy's way, he had promised to take some place and hadn't. Roy got change from the barman so as to use the booth telephone; but the barman served the second round of drinks first—you know how those things happen—and then Pete was telling a joke about an Alabama senator and a Negro minister that was good enough to pass on. When he did stand up and start toward the telephone, Earl caught him by the sleeve, and—

". . . literally forced me to listen," he was telling Mona as the reason he was late.

"And then the third round of drinks was served and I —I proposed a toast to the loveliest woman in all the world."

But in between there had been a moment when he had not thought of her, and this she sensed—this was important.

When she did not smile, he knew that it was there, something pregnant with a hurt; and it was then his words took on the tone of explanation, "I wouldn't, for anything in the world, have stayed if I had thought you would have minded in the least, darling."

Not enough sleep, lack of proper eating, and living each instant on the brink of desperation with the end of their togetherness always there, even on the lips of a kiss, impelled her to say, against her will, "But you could have called, darling, knowing how I would worry—"

"But, sweetheart, I intended to. I had the nickel in my hand—"

"I understand, darling . . ." Pushing from inside of her . . . "I *want* you to be with your friends . . ." Out of the vacuum left by her relief at seeing him . . . "Sometimes I think we have been together too much . . ." Out of the hours pacing the floor with ragged nerves gouging her like rusted nails . . . "But couldn't you have taken a moment to telephone? If I did not love you so, I would not have been so worried."

He began again, "I wanted to, I intended to—" He spread his hands, pleading, "Can't you understand? Won't you believe me? What is it, sweetheart? I—I—"

Pushing and pushing, up through the congested tears in her throat, out between her quivering lips, "If you had wanted to, you would have, Roy, darling. It's because you weren't thinking of me that you didn't; and when you stopped thinking about me, it was not the same anymore. When—when you can forget me in a crowd, it—it isn't what we thought; because it's knowing that I am always in your heart that keeps me p-punching."

They were there, suddenly, a wall of words between them.

"I-I had—" he could not say it again. That live-wire edge of futility building up, and now this wall of words that it had built. But courage was needed, patience, understanding; understanding most of all. And he tried again, smoothing out his exasperation with superhuman will, "Sweetheart, can we talk about it tomorrow? Can we— don't you think we should go to bed tonight? We're both upset. If we could sleep a little in—in—" he paused, and then went on, "I mean, it—it might make a difference, don't you think?"

Without moving, he moved toward her, as if to take her in his arms. And without moving, she moved away.

"Don't you understand what I am saying, Roy?" Pushing and pushing—oh, Dear God, please stop me . . . "Don't you?" . . . Pushing . . .

Her words were like steady shots. Is this how it would feel? A weird relation of thoughts. Could death be worse than this? . . . Echoing in his brain with the shallow faintness of distance: *"Don't you?"*

Now between them the words were gone, engulfing them in unbearable emptiness; and then the upsurge of overwhelming hurt. So tangible he shook great waves of it from his head in a violent reflex gesture, and yet other waves surged over him. They were caught and being carried along, swiftly, blindly; and in her fear, instinctively, she reached out for his hand.

Just that touch, just the touch of hands, and they were safe again; they were in each other's arms and she was crying, "I didn't mean it, darling. Honestly, I didn't mean it."

"I'm a rat," he said hoarsely. "How can you love such a rat as I?"

No, not eventful like the winning of a battle, nor dramatic like the downing of a plane; but to two people in this peopled world, it was a crossing into permanence, a bridging of the gap into immortality, which in the final analysis makes the *human* race the supreme race. For now, togetherness would always be; no matter the war, which had to be fought and won. No matter death, which was but another crossing. There would always be togetherness—always—because they had gotten over.

And suddenly, they began to plan the future.

"We'll buy a farm," he said. "A tiny one just big enough for us. I'll send every cent of my salary home."

"And while you're building us peace and freedom and

security, I'll be building our home," she added. "A ram-
bling, old-fashioned, comfortable house out of old stones. I
will build it with my hands. And—"

And underneath their rainbow, like planes flying low
over the desert, the days moved westward. There were six,
and then there were five.

They caught a bus and went upstate and selected a plot
of four acres and made a deal with the real estate broker-
age; and the next day they consulted an architect in Harlem and pored over blueprints.

"We'll have the nursery here," she said. "It'll catch the
sun all day. And out back—"

"We'll plant an orchard," he supplemented. "Pears and
peaches—"

"And apples—"

"And we'll have a swing."

"Over here will be your den and when you're a famous
attorney you can say—"

"We'll plant flowers," he cut in.

"Of course. Down beside the walk and here in front on
both sides. Floral firecrackers and golden stars and hy-
acinths and—"

"I'll come through Holland on the way home and bring
the tulips back," he said. "Pink and white and . . ."

And then there were none . . .

"I'm simply crazy about you, darling," she was telling
him. "Remember that most. Remember that I love everything you do, the color of your skin, the way you walk,
the way you carry your shoulders so high and bravely; the
way you sometimes say 'not particularly so' and 'I mean;
well, what I mean,' and the little habit you have of dip-
ping your head and running your hand across your hair
when you are thinking . . ."

"And I love the way your eyes look now while you are
talking of it," he said. "I'll be seeing them on those days
when I take off. I'll always remember your eyes, sweetheart."

"I'll never forget anything about you," she declared.
"Never!"

And though they had braced themselves against it from
the very first, when the pickup car pulled to a stop where
they waited at the curb, neither of them was prepared
for sight of it. Until the last moment, until the driver said,
"I'm sorry, sir," they clung to each other, kissing each
other, their eyes locked together, so gallantly, although
their lips were trembling and breaking up beneath.

And then he was inside and the driver shifted gears and the motor sounded and he was moving away from her.

She kept biting her lips to hold back screams, and then motion came into her body and she began to wave, wildly, and the words came out in a gasping rush, "Don't forget the tulips, Roy. Don't forget the tulips, darling."

And through the open window, he was yelling back, "I forgot to tell you, set out the apple trees in April. And if it's a girl—" The rest was drowned in motor roar.

The last he saw of her, as the car was engulfed in traffic, she was standing at the curb, so tiny it seemed from that distance, and so rigid, and finally, so softly smiling.

Who's Passing For Who?

by Langston Hughes

One of the great difficulties about being a member of a minority race is that so many kindhearted, well-meaning bores gather around to help. Usually, to tell the truth, they have nothing to help with, except their company—which is often appallingly dull.

Some members of the Negro race seem very well able to put up with it, though, in these uplifting years. Such was Caleb Johnson, colored social worker, who was always dragging around with him some nondescript white person or two, inviting them to dinner, showing them Harlem, ending up at the Savoy—much to the displeasure of whatever friends of his might be out that evening for fun, not sociology.

Friends are friends and, unfortunately, overearnest uplifters are uplifters—no matter what color they may be. If it were the white race that was ground down instead of Negroes, Caleb Johnson would be one of the first to offer Nordics the sympathy of his utterly inane society, under the impression that somehow he would be doing them a great deal of good.

You see, Caleb, and his white friends, too, were all bores. Or so we, who lived in Harlem's literary bohemia during the "Negro Renaissance" thought. We literary ones considered ourselves too broad-minded to be bothered with questions of color. We liked people of any race who smoked incessantly, drank liberally, wore complexion and morality as loose garments, and made fun of anyone who didn't do likewise. We snubbed and high-hatted any Negro or white luckless enough not to understand Gertrude Stein, Ulysses, Man Ray, the theremin, Jean Toomer, or George Antheil. By the end of the 1920's Caleb was just catching up to Dos Passos. He thought H. G. Wells good.

We met Caleb one night in Small's. He had three assorted white folks in tow. We would have passed him by with but a nod had he not hailed us enthusiastically, risen, and introduced us with great acclaim to his friends who turned out to be schoolteachers from Iowa, a woman and two men. They appeared amazed and delighted to meet all at once two Negro writers and a black painter in the flesh. They invited us to have a drink with them. Money being scarce with us, we deigned to sit down at their table.

The white lady said, "I've never met a Negro writer before."

The two men added, "Neither have we."

"Why, we know any number of *white* writers," we three dark bohemians declared with bored nonchalance.

"But Negro writers are much more rare," said the lady.

"There are plenty in Harlem," we said.

"But not in Iowa," said one of the men, shaking his mop of red hair.

"There are no good *white* writers in Iowa either, are there?" we asked superciliously.

"Oh, yes, Ruth Suckow came from there."

Whereupon we proceeded to light in upon Ruth Suckow as old hat and to annihilate her in favor of Kay Boyle. The way we flung names around seemed to impress both Caleb and his white guests. This, of course, delighted us, though we were too young and too proud to admit it.

The drinks came and everything was going well, all of us drinking, and we three showing off in a high-brow manner, when suddenly at the table just behind us a man got up and knocked down a woman. He was a brownskin man. The woman was blonde. As she rose he knocked her down again. Then the red-haired man from Iowa got up and knocked the colored man down.

He said, "Keep your hands off that white woman."

The man got up and said, "She's not a white woman. She's my wife."

One of the waiters added, "She's not white, sir, she's colored."

Whereupon the man from Iowa looked puzzled, dropped his fists, and said, "I'm sorry."

The colored man said, "What are you doing up here in Harlem anyway, interfering with my family affairs?"

The white man said, "I thought she was a white woman."

The woman who had been on the floor rose and said, "Well, I'm not a white woman, I'm colored, and you leave my husband alone."

Then they both lit in on the gentleman from Iowa. It took all of us and several waiters, too, to separate them. When it was over the manager requested us to kindly pay our bill and get out. He said we were disturbing the peace. So we all left. We went to a fish restaurant down the street. Caleb was terribly apologetic to his white friends. We artists were both mad and amused.

"Why did you say you were sorry," said the colored painter to the visitor from Iowa, "after you'd hit that man —and then found out it wasn't a white woman you were defending, but merely a light-colored woman who looked white?"

"Well," answered the red-haired Iowan, "I didn't mean to be butting in if they were all the same race."

"Don't you think a woman needs defending from a brute, no matter what race she may be?" asked the painter.

"Yes, but I think it's up to you to defend your own women."

"Oh, so you'd divide up a brawl according to races, no matter who was right?"

"Well, I wouldn't say that."

"You mean you wouldn't defend a colored woman whose husband was knocking her down?" asked the poet.

Before the visitor had time to answer, the painter said, "No! You just got mad because you thought a black man was hitting a *white* woman."

"But she *looked* like a white woman," countered the man.

"Maybe she was just passing for colored," I said.

"Like some Negroes pass for white," Caleb interposed.

"Anyhow, I don't like it," said the colored painter, "the way you stopped defending her when you found out she wasn't white."

"No, we don't like it," we all agreed except Caleb.

Caleb said in extenuation, "But Mr. Stubblefield is new to Harlem."

The red-haired white man said, "Yes, it's my first time here."

"Maybe Mr. Stubblefield ought to stay out of Harlem," we observed.

"I agree," Mr. Stubblefield said. "Good night."

He got up then and there and left the café. He stalked as he walked. His red head disappeared into the night.

"Oh, that's too bad," said the white couple who remained. "Stubby's temper just got the best of him. But explain to us, are many colored folks really as fair as that woman?"

"Sure, lots of them have more white blood than colored, and pass for white."

"Do they?" said the lady and gentleman from Iowa.

"You never read Nella Larsen?" we asked.

"She writes novels," Caleb explained. "She's part white herself."

"Read her," we advised. "Also read the *Autobiography of an Ex-colored Man.*" Not that we had read it ourselves —because we paid but little attention to the older colored writers—but we knew it was about passing for white.

We all ordered fish and settled down comfortably to shocking our white friends with tales about how many Negroes there were passing for white all over America. We were determined to *épater le bourgeois* real good via this white couple we had cornered, when the woman leaned over the table in the midst of our dissertations and said, "Listen, gentlemen, you needn't spread the word, but me and my husband aren't white either. We've just been *passing* for white for the last fifteen years."

"What?"

"We're colored, too, just like you," said the husband. "But it's better passing for white because we make more money."

Well, that took the wind out of us. It took the wind out of Caleb, too. He thought all the time he was showing some fine white folks Harlem—and they were as colored as he was!

Caleb almost never cursed. But this time he said, "I'll be damned!"

Then everybody laughed. And laughed! We almost had hysterics. All at once we dropped our professionally self-conscious "Negro" manners, became natural, ate fish, and talked and kidded freely like colored folks do when there are no white folks around. We really had fun then joking about that red-haired guy who mistook a fair colored woman for white. After the fish we went to two or three more night spots and drank until five o'clock in the morning.

Finally we put the light-colored people in a taxi heading downtown. They turned to shout a last good-by. The cab was just about to move off, when the woman called to the driver to stop.

She leaned out the window and said with a grin, "Listen, boys! I hate to confuse you again. But, to tell the truth, my husband and I aren't really colored at all. We're white. We just thought we'd kid you by passing for colored a little while—just as you said Negroes sometimes pass for white."

She laughed as they sped off toward Central Park, waving, "Good-by!"

We didn't say a thing. We just stood there on the corner in Harlem dumbfounded—not knowing now *which* way we'd been fooled. Were they really white—passing for colored? Or colored—passing for white?

Whatever race they were, they had had too much fun at our expense—even if they did pay for the drinks.

Roy's Wound

by James Baldwin

As, in the late afternoon, John approached his home
again, he saw little Sarah, her coat unbuttoned, come
flying out of the house, and run the length of the street
away from him, into the far drugstore. Instantly, he was
frightened; he stopped a moment, wondering what could
justify such hysterical haste. It was true that Sarah was
full of self-importance and made any errand she was to
run seem a matter of life or death; nevertheless, she had
been sent on an errand, and with such speed that her
mother had not had time to make her button up her coat.

Then he felt weary; if something had really happened it
would be very unpleasant upstairs now, and he did not
want to face it. Or perhaps it was simply that his mother
had a headache and had sent Sarah to the store for aspirin. But if this were true, it meant that he would have to
prepare supper, and take care of the children, and be
naked under his father's eye all the evening long. And he
began to walk more slowly.

There were some boys standing on the stoop. They
watched him as he approached, and he tried not to look at
them, and to approximate their swagger. One of them
said, as John mounted the low stone steps and started into
the hall, "Boy, your brother was hurt real bad today."

He looked at them in a kind of dread, not daring to ask
for details; and he observed that they too might have been

in a battle: something hangdog in their looks suggested they had been put to flight. Then he looked down, and saw that there was blood on the threshold, and blood spattered on the tile floor of the vestibule. He looked again at the boys, who had not ceased to watch him, and hurried up the stairs.

The door was half open—for Sarah's return, no doubt; and he walked in, making no sound, feeling a confused impulse to flee. There was no one in the kitchen, though the light was burning—the lights were on all through the house. On the kitchen table stood a shopping bag filled with groceries, and he knew that his Aunt Florence had arrived. The washtub, where his mother had been washing earlier, was open still, and filled the kitchen with a sour smell.

He had seen small, smudged coins of blood on the stairs on his way up, and there were drops of blood on the floor here too.

All this frightened him terribly. He stood in the middle of the kitchen, trying to imagine what had happened, and to prepare himself to walk into the living room, where he could hear his father's voice. Roy had been in trouble before, but this new trouble seemed the beginning of the fulfillment of a prophecy. He took off his coat, dropping it on a chair, and was about to go into the living room when he heard Sarah running up the steps.

He waited, and she burst through the door, carrying a clumsily shaped parcel.

"What happened?" he whispered.

She stared at him in astonishment, and a certain wild joy. He thought again that he really did not like his sister. Catching her breath, she said triumphantly, "Roy got stabbed with a knife!" and rushed into the living room.

Roy got stabbed with a knife. Whatever this meant, it meant that his father would be at his worst tonight. John walked slowly into the living room.

His father and mother, a small basin of water between them, knelt by the sofa where Roy lay, and his father was washing the blood from Roy's forehead. Apparently his mother, whose touch was so much more gentle, had been thrust aside by his father, who now could not bear to have anyone else touch his wounded son. And so she watched, one hand in the water, the other clenched in anguish at her waist, which was circled still by the improvised apron of the morning. Her face, as she watched, was tense with fear and pity. His father muttered sweet, delirious things to Roy, and his hands, when he dipped them again in the basin and wrung out the cloth, were trembling. Aunt Florence, still wearing her hat and carrying her handbag, stood a little removed, looking down at Roy with a troubled face.

His mother looked up as Sarah bounded into the room, reached out for the package, and saw him. She said nothing, but looked at him with a strange, quick intentness, almost as though there were a warning on her tongue which she did not at the moment dare to utter. His Aunt Florence said, "We been wondering where you was, boy. This bad brother of yours done gone out and got hisself hurt."

But John understood from her tone that the fuss was, possibly, a little greater than the danger. Roy was not, after all, going to die. And his heart lifted a little. Then his father turned and looked at him.

"Where you been, boy," he shouted, "all this time? Don't you know you's needed here at home?"

More than his words, his face made John stiffen instantly with fear and malice. His father's face was terrible in anger, but now there was more than anger in his face. John saw now what he had never seen there before, except in his own vindictive fantasies: a kind of wild, weeping terror that made the face seem younger, and yet, in another way, unutterably older, and more cruel. And John knew, in the moment his father's glance swept over him, that he hated John because John was not lying on the sofa, where Roy lay. John could scarcely meet his father's eyes, and yet, briefly, he did, saying nothing; feeling in his heart an odd sensation of triumph, and hoping in his heart that Roy, to bring his father low, would die.

His mother had unwrapped the package, and was opening a bottle of peroxide. "Here," she said, "you better wash it with this now." Her voice, was calm, and dry, her expression closed, as she handed the bottle and the cotton to his father.

"This going to hurt," his father said—in such a different voice, so sad and tender!—turning again to the sofa. "But you just be a little man, and hold still—it ain't going to take long."

John watched, and listened, hating him. Roy began to moan. Aunt Florence moved to the mantelpiece, and put her handbag down near the metal serpent. From the room behind him, John heard the baby begin to whimper.

"John," said his mother, "go and pick her up, like a good boy." Her hands, not trembling, were still busy: she had opened the bottle of iodine, and was cutting up strips of bandage.

John walked into his parents' bedroom, and picked up the squalling baby, who was wet. The moment Ruth felt him lift her up, she stopped crying, and stared at him, wide-eyed and pathetic, as though she knew there was trouble in the house. John laughed at her so-ancient seeming distress—he was very fond of his baby sister—and whispered in her ear, as he started back to the living room, "Now, you let your big brother tell you something, baby. Just as soon as you's able to stand on your feet, you run away from *this* house, run far away." He did not quite know why he said this, or where he wanted her to run, but it made him feel better instantly.

His father was saying, as John came back into the room, "I'm sure going to be having some questions to ask you in a minute, old lady. I'm going to be wanting to know just how come you let this boy go out and get half killed."

"Oh, no, you ain't," said Aunt Florence, "you ain't going to be starting none of that mess this evening. You know right doggone well that Roy don't never ask *nobody* if he can do *nothing*—he just go right ahead and do like he pleases. Elizabeth sure can't put no ball and chain on him. She got her hands full right here in this house, and it ain't her fault if Roy got a head just as hard as his father's."

"You got a awful lot to say, look like for once you could keep from putting your mouth in my business." He said this without looking at her.

"It ain't my fault," she said, "that you was born a fool, and always been a fool, and ain't never going to change. I swear to my Father you'd try the patience of Job."

"I done told you before," he said—he had not ceased working over the moaning Roy, and was preparing now to dab the wound with iodine, "that I didn't want you coming in here and using that gutter language in front of my children."

"Don't you worry about my language, brother," she said, with spirit, "you better start worrying about your *life*. What these children hear ain't going to do them near as much harm as what they *see*."

"What they *see*," his father muttered, "is a poor man trying to serve the Lord. *That's* my life."

"Then I guarantee *you*," she said, "that they going to do

their best to keep it from being *their* life. *You* mark my words."

He turned and looked at her; and intercepted the look that passed between the two women. John's mother, for reasons that were not at all his father's reasons, wanted Aunt Florence to keep still. He looked away, ironically. John watched his mother's mouth tighten bitterly. His father, in silence, began bandaging Roy's forehead.

"It's just the mercy of God," he said, at last, "that this boy didn't lose his eye. Look here."

His mother leaned over and looked into Roy's face with a sad, sympathetic murmur. Yet, John felt, she had seen instantly the extent of the danger to Roy's eye, and to his life, and was beyond that worry now; now she was merely marking time, as it were, and preparing herself for the moment when her husband's anger would turn, full force, against her.

His father now turned to John, who was standing near the French doors with Ruth in his arms.

"You come here, boy," he said, "and see what them white folks done to your brother."

John walked over to the sofa, holding himself as proudly beneath his father's furious eyes as a prince approaching the scaffold.

"Look here," said his father, grasping him roughly by one arm, "look at your brother."

John looked down at Roy; who gazed up at him with almost no expression in his dark eyes. But John knew, by the weary, impatient set of Roy's young mouth, that his brother was asking that none of this be held against him. It wasn't his fault, or John's, Roy's eyes said, that they had such a crazy father.

His father, with the air of one forcing the sinner to look down into the pit which is to be his portion, moved away slightly so that John could see Roy's wound.

Roy had been gashed by a knife, luckily not very sharp, but very jagged, from the center of his forehead where his hair began, downward to the bone just above his left eye: the wound described a kind of crazy half-moon, and ended in a violent fuzzy tail, which was the ruin of Roy's eyebrow. Time would darken the half-moon wound into Roy's dark skin, but nothing would bring together again the so violently divided hairs of his eyebrow. This crazy lift, this question, would remain with him forever, and emphasize forever something mocking and sinister in Roy's face. John felt a sudden impulse to smile, but his father's eyes were on him, and he fought the impulse back. Certainly the wound was now very ugly, and very red, and must, John felt, with a quickened sympathy toward Roy, who had not cried out, have been very painful. He could imagine the sensation caused when Roy staggered into the house, blinded with his blood; but, just the same, he wasn't dead, he wasn't changed, he would be in the streets again the moment he was better.

"You see," came now from his father. "It was white folks, some of them white folks *you* like so much, that tried to cut your brother's throat."

John thought, with immediate anger, and with a curious contempt for his father's inexactness, that only a blind man, however white, could possibly have been aiming at Roy's throat; and his mother said, with a calm insistence:

"And he was trying to cut theirs. Him and them bad boys."

"Yes," said Aunt Florence, "I ain't heard you ask that boy nary a question about how all this happened. Look like you just determined to raise cain any*how*—and make everybody in this house suffer because something done happened to the apple of your eye."

"I done ask you," cried his father, in exasperation, "to stop running your *mouth*. Don't none of this concern you —this is *my* family, and this is *my* house. You want me to slap you side of the head?"

"You slap me," she said placidly, "and I *do* guarantee you, you won't do no more slapping in a hurry."

"Hush now," said his mother, rising, "ain't no need for all this. What's done is done. We ought to be on our knees, thanking the Lord it weren't no worse."

"Amen to that," said Aunt Florence, "*tell* that foolish nigger something."

"You can tell that foolish *son* of yours something," he said to his wife, with venom, having decided, it seemed, to ignore his sister, "him standing there with them big, buck eyes. You can tell him to take this like a warning from the Lord. *This* is what white folks does to niggers, I been telling you, now you see."

"He better take it like a warning?" shrieked Aunt Florence, "*He* better take it? Why, Gabriel, it ain't *him* went halfway across this city to get in a fight with white boys. This boy on the sofa went—*deliberately*—with a whole lot of other boys, all the way to the west side, just *looking* for a fight. I declare, I *do* wonder what goes on in your head."

"You know right well," his mother said, looking directly

at his father, "that Johnny don't travel with the same class of boys as Roy goes with. You done beat Roy too many times, here, in this very room, for going out with them bad boys. Roy got hisself hurt this afternoon because he was out doing something he didn't have no business doing, and that's the end of it. You ought to be thanking your Redeemer he ain't dead."

"And for all the care you take of him," he said, "he might as well be dead. Don't look like you much care whether he lives, or dies."

"*Lord,* have mercy," said Aunt Florence.

"He's my son, too," she said, with heat, "I carried him in my belly for nine months, and I know him just like I know his Daddy, and they's just *exactly* alike. Now. You ain't got no *right* in the world to talk to me like that."

"I reckon you *know,*" he said, choked, and breathing hard, "all about a mother's love. I sure reckon on you telling me how a woman can sit in the house all day, and let her own flesh and blood go out and get half butchered. Don't you *tell* me you don't know no way to stop him— because I remember *my* mother, God rest her soul, and *she'd* have found a way."

"She was my mother, too," said Aunt Florence, "and I recollect, if you don't, you being brought home many a time more dead than alive. She didn't find no way to stop *you.* She wore herself *out,* beating on you, just like you been wearing yourself out, beating on this boy here."

"My, my, *my,*" he said, "you got a lot to say."

"I ain't doing a thing," she said, "but trying to talk some sense into your big, black, hard head. You better stop trying to blame everything on Elizabeth, and look to your own wrong doings."

"Never mind, Florence," his mother said, "it's all over, and done with now."

"I'm out of this house," he shouted, "every day the Lord sends, working to put the food in these children's mouths. Don't you think I got a right to ask the mother of these children to look after them, and see that they don't break their *necks* before I get back *home?*"

"You ain't got but one child," said his mother, "that's liable to go out and break his neck, and that's Roy, and you know it. And I don't know how in the world you expect me to run this house, and look after these children, and keep running around the block after Roy. *No,* I can't stop him, I done told you that, and you can't stop him neither. You don't know *what* to do with this boy, and that's why you all the time trying to fix the blame on somebody. Ain't nobody to *blame*, Gabriel. You just better pray God to stop him before somebody puts another knife in him, and puts him in his *grave*."

They stared at each other a moment in an awful pause, a startled, pleading question in her eyes; then, with all his might, he reached out and slapped her across the face. She crumpled at once, hiding her face with one thin hand, and Aunt Florence moved to hold her up. Sarah watched all this with greedy eyes. Then Roy sat up, and said in a shaking voice:

"Don't you slap my mother. That's my *mother*. You slap her again, you black bastard, and I swear to God I'll kill you."

In the moment that these words filled the room, and hung in the air like the infinitesimal moment of hanging, jagged light which precedes an explosion, John and his father were staring into each other's eyes. John thought for that moment that his father believed that those words had come from him: his eyes were so wild, and depthlessly malevolent, and his mouth was twisted into a snarl of pain. Then, in the absolute silence which followed Roy's words, John saw that his father was not seeing him, was not seeing anything, unless it were a vision. John wanted to turn and flee, as though he had encountered in the jungle some evil beast, crouching and ravenous, with eyes like hell unloosed; and exactly as though, on a road's turning, he found himself staring at certain destruction, he found that he could not move. Then his father turned away from him, and looked down at Roy.

"What did you say?" his father asked.

"I told you," said Roy, "not to touch my mother."

"You cursed me," said his father.

Roy said nothing; neither did he drop his eyes.

"Gabriel," said his mother, "Gabriel. Let us pray."

His father's hands were at his waist, and he took off his belt. Tears were in his eyes.

"Gabriel," cried Aunt Florence, "ain't you done playing the fool for tonight?"

Then his father raised his belt, and it fell with a whistling sound on Roy, who shivered and fell back, his face to the wall, but did not cry out. And the belt was raised again, and again; the air rang with the whistling, and the *crack!* against Roy's flesh. The baby, Ruth, began to scream.

"My Lord, my Lord," his father whispered, *"my Lord, my Lord."*

He raised the belt again, but Aunt Florence caught it from behind, and held it. His mother rushed over to the sofa, and caught Roy in her arms, crying as John had never seen a woman, or anybody, cry before. Roy caught his mother around the neck and held on to her as though he were drowning.

His Aunt Florence and his father faced each other.

"Yes, Lord," Aunt Florence said, "you was born wild, and you's going to die wild. But ain't no need to try to take the whole world with you. You can't change nothing, Gabriel. You ought to know that by now."

Revolt Of
The Angels

by John Henrik Clarke

The two Harlem piano movers who had taken the negative side of the argument were quiet now, waiting for the
defender of the affirmative to gather his thoughts. He was
a big man; seemingly bigger than his two friendly oppo-
nents put together. Because of this, it did not seem unfair
that he had no one to assist him in imparting his point of
view.

For more than an hour the three men had been standing
by their large red truck, waiting between assignments. It
was their custom on these occasions to test each other's
knowledge of the great subjects and issues that influence
the destiny of mankind. The fact that their formal knowledge of these subjects was extremely limited did not deter
their discussions in the slightest.

The two small men waited and stole quick glances at
their large companion. Their faces were aglow with the
signs of assured victory. Finally one turned to the other
and said: "We've got 'im at las', Leroy. We've taken King
Solomon off of his throne. We've made another wise man
bit th' dust."

The speaker's dark face looked as if age had been baked
into it. He kept watching the large man who was collect-

123

ing his thoughts in preparation for stating his side of the argument.

"I knew we'd tame this wise man some day," the other small man said. The note of triumph and mock haughtiness in his voice gave it a distinct play-acting tone. "We got 'im up a creek without a paddle," he went on, laughing a little. "Now, Hawkshaw, lemme see you talk your way out of this trap."

"Don't count your eggs before you buy your chickens," the big man said, straightening up as his loosely hanging stomach spilled over the rim of his belt. "Th' thing to be resolved is whether a man who has been a drunkard most of his life can straighten himself out and become a pillar of respectability an' a credit to his community. You fellas have said this can not be done an' I disagree . . . I know just th' case to prove my point." He exhaled audibly with some of the pompousness of a political orator preparing for a long discourse. Then he spoke again, slowly, measuring his words very carefully at first.

"During th' last part of th' depression years there was a fella here in Harlem named Luther Jackson who had been drunk so long nobody could remember how he looked when he was sober. Luther wasn't a violent man; he didn't bother nobody unless he wanted some likker and they wouldn't give it to him.

"One day when Luther was near th' end of a three week stupor, he wandered into one of Father Divine's restaurants and sat down at th' bes' table. He thought th' restaurant was a bar and th' bes' table in th' house meant nothing to him. Now, fellas, when I say this was the bes' table in th' house, I mean it was th' bes' table you'd see anywhere. In those days most of Father Divine's restaurants set up a special table for Father just in case he came in an' wanted to dine in style. This special table had snow-white linin', th' bes' of silverware, crystal glasses, th' kind you only see in the homes of millionaires, and a fresh bowl of flowers. A picture of Father Divine was in front of th' flowers with a message under it sayin', 'Thank you Father.' It was some kind of deadly sin for anybody but Father Divine and his invited guests to set at this table.

"A big fat angel saw Luther at th' table an' strutted out of th' kitchen blowin' like a mad bull.

" 'Peace, brother,' she said real loud, 'This is Father Divine's table, get up an' get out of here.'

" 'I want some likker,' Luther says, 'an' I want some more t' wash it down.'

" 'Peace, brother,' th' angel says, puffin' an' trying to keep her temper from explodin'. 'This is Father Divine's table, get up an' get out of here.'

" 'I won't go 'till you give me some likker,' Luther says, 'an I don't care who's table this is.'

"Th' angel threw her hands in th' air and looked at th' ceilin' like she expected something over her head to come down an' help her. 'Peace, Father,' she says, 'remove this evil man from your premises.'

" 'I want some likker!' Luther shouted at her an' slammed his hand on th' table, knockin' down some of th' fine silverware. 'A drinkin' man is in th' house. Go away old woman an' send me a bartender.'

"This made th' angel madder than ever. She went back to th' kitchen holdin' her head like she was scared it was goin' t' fly off.

" 'Where's th' bartender in this place?' Luther asked an' stood up lookin' 'round like he was just fixin' to mop up th' place with his madness.

"Th' big angel was standing in th' kitchen door, shoutin', 'Father Divine don't allow no alcohol drinkers in here. No obscenities! No adulteries!'

"Luther slammed his hand on th' table again an' knocked down some more of th' fine silverware. This made th' angel so angry she couldn't speak. She just stood in th' door of th' kitchen swellin' up like a big toad frog.

" 'Gimme some likker and let me get outa here,' Luther says.

"Then th' angel hollered out all of a sudden and frightened Luther so much he almost jumped over the table.

" 'Peace Father!' th' angel was sayin'. 'Give me console, Father, you are wonderful.'

"Father or someone else must have given her console an' some new strength to go with it, because she threw a pot at Luther's head like he was a long lost husband who deserted her with a house full of hungry young'uns.

"The pot bounced off of Luther's head an' he hollered like a wild bull. 'What's goin' on in this place?' Luther was sayin'. 'Where's th' bartender?'

" 'Father Divine don't 'low no alcohol drinkers in here,' th' angel was sayin' again, 'No obscenities! No adulteries.' Before she finished sayin' this she threw another pot at Luther's head.

"Luther ducked and stood up in a chair as a skillet missed his head by an inch. Then he stepped into the middle of th' table. He had knocked down th' flowers and some of th' fine silverware. Now th' angel was hollerin' like judgment day was at hand. You see, fellas, Luther was standin' on Father Divine's picture. She ran out of pots an' began t' throw big spoons an' ladles.

" 'Peace Father, give me strength,' she hollered, 'give me th' strength to move this satan from your premises.'

"Then she jumped toward Luther like a tiger an' knocked 'im off th' table with a rollin' pin. As Luther fell, he turned th' table over. All of th' snow-white table linen was on th' floor. Th' silverware was scattered around th' table and some of it was in Luther's pockets. Most of th' millionaire crystal glasses were broken.

"The fat angel kept screamin', 'Peace! Peace! Peace!' until some more angels joined up with her. They came at Luther with fire in their eyes. They beat him until he got up, then they beat him down again. Still more angels came and joined the war on Luther—black ones, white ones, lean ones, fat ones, an' all th' sizes in between. They kicked him, they scratched him an' spit on him. While all of this was happenin', an angel came up an' started whackin' at Luther with a cleaver.

"Now Luther was screamin' for his life an' tryin' to get to th' door. Th' angels knocked him down 'gain an' he crawled out of th' door hollerin' for a police to save him. He saw a red box on th' side of a building an' opened it, thinkin' it was a police telephone. He pulled down a lever an' let it stay down. Th' angels had followed him into th' streets. Soon, fire trucks started comin' from every direction—patrol wagons from th' riot squads an' th' emergency squads came. Policemen in cars an' on foot came to th' scene like they were being rained down from th' sky. Still th' angry angels kept chargin' at Luther. The commotion tied up traffic for ten blocks.

"It took more than one hundred policemen to rescue Luther from them angry angels. They had hit him every place including under his feet. The policemen had to take him to th' hospital before they could take him to jail. When he was well enough for his trial, th' judge threw th' book at him an' said he was sorry that he did not have a much bigger book. Life in jail changed Luther. He was, indeed, a new man when he came out. He was upright, law abidin' and he refused to drink anything stronger than coffee.

"So, fellas, I give you the case of Luther Jackson as my proof that a man who has been a drunkard most of his life can straighten himself out and become a pillar of respectability an' a credit to his community.

"Now Luther is a foreman of a stevedore group down on th' docks an' he's also an officer in th' union. He sent down south for his wife an' children an' he made a good home for them right here in Harlem. He is a church-goin' man too an' a senior deacon. Nowhere in this land would you find a more peaceful an' law abidin' citizen than Luther Jackson. Since th' day of that fracas with those angry angels to this day, he never again touched another drop of likker."

The opposition had conceded defeat long before the fat man finished the story. A rebuttal was unnecessary.

A Good Long Sidewalk

by William Melvin Kelley

The barbershop was warm enough to make Carlyle Bedlow sleepy, and smelled of fragrant shaving soap. A fat
man sat in the great chair, his stomach swelling beneath
the striped cloth. Standing behind him in a white, hair-
linted tunic which buttoned along one shoulder, Garland,
the barber, clacked his scissors. Garland's hair was well
kept, his sideburns cut off just where his wire eye-glasses
passed back to his ears. "Hello, Carlyle. How you doing?"
He looked over the tops of his glasses. "So you decided to
let me make a living, huh?"

"Yes, sir." Carlyle smiled. He liked Garland.

"Taking advantage of Bronx misery?"

"Sir?"

"I mean when folks is having trouble getting their cars
dug out, you making money shoveling Bronx snow."

"Oh. Yes, sir." Garland was always teasing him because
Carlyle's family had moved recently from Harlem to this
neighborhood in the Bronx. He maintained Carlyle
thought the Bronx was full of hicks.

"Okay. You're next. I'll take some of that snow money
from you." He returned to the fat man's head.

Carlyle leaned his shovel in the corner, stamped his

128

feet, took off his jacket, sat down in a wire-backed chair and picked up a comic book. He had already read it, and put it down to watch the barber shave the fat man's neck with the electric clippers.

The fat man, who had been talking when Carlyle came in, continued: "Can't see why he'd want to do that, can you, Garland? But ain't that just like a nigger!" He was very dark. The skin under his chin was heavily pocked and scarred.

"And just like a white woman too!"

"Man, these cats marry some colored girl when they starting out, just singing in joints and dives. She supports him while he's trying to get ahead. But then he gets a hit record, or a job at the Waldorf and—bingo!—he drops her quick, gets a divorce, and marries some white bitch."

"White chicks know where it's at. They laying in wait for him. When he makes it, they'll cut in on a good thing every time. Anyway, it won't last a year. And you can quote me on that." Garland finished cutting great patches of hair from the man's head and started to shape the back.

A short, light-skinned Negro opened the door and leaned in. "Hello, Garland." He did not close the door and cold wind blasted in around him.

"Say, man, how you doing? You after the boy there. All right?" He continued to work, hardly looking at the head in front of him; he could cut hair blindfolded.

The short man nodded and closed the door behind him. He removed his coat, put his gloves carefully into a pocket, sat down, and stretched. Only then did he take off his hat. His hair was straight and black; he did not seem to need a haircut. "I read in *The Amsterdam* how Mister Cool and his white sweetie finally got shackled."

"Yes, sir. We just talking about that." Garland reached behind him, touched a switch and from an aluminum box, lather billowed into his palm. "Ain't that just like a Negro!"

"And like a white bitch too!" the fat man added. "Don't trim the sideburns, Garland. Just around the ears. I'll trim the sideburns myself."

Garland nodded. "Man, I seen the same thing happen a thousand times. A Negro making more money than a white man starting to act foolish like a white man. Even though he should know better. I guess it ain't really that Negro's fault. All his life he been poor and a nobody." Garland put the lather behind the fat man's ears. "So as soon as he gets some money it's bound to mess up his mind."

"Don't touch the sideburns, Garland." The fat man shifted under the striped sheet. "Yeah, I think you right. And them white bitches is waiting to ambush him."

The short man folded his thin arms across his chest. "Well, don't all a colored man's problems begin with Mister Charlie and Miss Mary?"

"Mostly when Miss Mary wants to make time with her nigger chauffeur or handyman and Mister Charlie finds out about it. He don't blame Miss Mary for it, that's sure." The fat man leaned forward.

Garland stopped shaving, reflecting. "Mostly when you find some white woman being nice to you, nicer than she ought to be. Then watch out!" He started to shave behind the fat man's ears. "Them white women know where it's at."

The short man nodded. "Yeah, but I can't see why no colored man'd want to marry no white chick on purpose like Mister Cool did. Not when there's so many fine spade chicks around."

Garland agreed. "I like my women the way I like my coffee: hot, strong, and black!"

The fat man jerked his head. "I guess he thinks he taking a step up. Now he thinks he better than all the other boots standing on the corner. He's got himself a white recording contract with a big white company, and a booking at a fine, white night club, and a white Cadillac and an apartment on Park Avenue painted all white and a white bitch too. Why, man, he almost white himself . . . except for one thing: he still a nigger!"

They all laughed, slapping their thighs.

It seemed much colder with his hair cut short, his neck shaved clean. Carlyle trudged flat-footed, planting his feet firmly so as not to slip, up the middle of the carless street, through the shadows cast by the snow-clogged trees. He wished he could go home, take off his wet shoes, listen to records, and read the paper that each night his father carried home tucked under his arm. He knew too that the later it got, the angrier his father would be; his father liked to eat as soon as he came home. Besides, his father would want him or his little brother to clear their own driveway and Carlyle had not asked to take the shovel. He decided then, walking along the rutted street, he would not waste his time with small jobs; he would look for a long snow-banked walk of a house set way back from the street.

This is what he finally found, down a solitary side street lit faintly by a single street lamp at the middle of the block; the house, set back on a short hill that surely, in the spring and summer, would be a thick lawn, perhaps bordered with flowers. Snow clung to the empty, blackened branches of a hedge concealing a grotesque iron fence. The house too was grotesque, painted gray, its gables hung with dagger-like icicles.

He hesitated a moment, looking up at the house; there did not seem to be any light burning, and he did not want to wade twenty or thirty feet through shin-deep snow only to find no one at home. Going farther on up the sidewalk, he found a lighted window down the side near the back and he returned to the gate and started up the drifted walk.

The porch was wood and clunked hollow when he stamped the snow from his feet. He climbed the steps gingerly and peered at the names on the door-bell. If there was a man's name, he still might not find work—women living alone or old couples more usually needed someone to clean snow. There was a woman's name—Elizabeth Reuben—and a man's too, but his, which was typed, had been recently crossed out. Carlyle rang the bell.

No longer walking, his feet got cold very quickly and when, after what seemed a long while, the door opened— and then only a crack—he was hopping from one foot to the other.

"Yes? What is it?" He could see a nose and one eye, could hear a woman's voice.

"Miz Reuben?" He slurred the "miss" or "missus" so as not to insult her either way.

"Yes."

"Would you like to have your walk shoveled?" He moved closer and spoke to the nose and eye.

There was a pause while she looked him over, up and down, and inspected the shovel he held in his hand. "No. I'm sorry. I don't think so."

"Well, uh . . ." There was nothing else to say. He thanked her and turned away.

"Wait!" It sounded almost like a scream. And then softer: "Young man, wait."

He turned back and found the door swung wide. The nose and eye had grown to a small, plumpish, white woman of about forty in a pale blue wool dress. She was not exactly what he would have called pretty, but she was by no means a hag. She was just uninteresting looking. Her hair was a dull brown combed into a style that did her no good; her eyes were flat and gray like cardboard. "On second thought, young man, I think it would be nice to have my walk cleaned off. I'm expecting some visitors and it will make it easier for them . . . to find me." She smiled at him. "But come inside; you must be frozen solid walking around in all this snow and cold."

"That's all right, ma'am. I'll start right away." He took a step back and lifted his shovel.

"You do as I say and come in the house this very moment." She was still smiling, but there was enough of a mother's tone in her voice to make him walk past her through the door, which she closed behind him. "Rest your coat and shovel there and follow me. I'm taking you into the kitchen to put something warm into your stomach."

He did as she ordered and walked behind her down the hall, lit by a low-watt bulb in a yellowing shade.

The first thing he noticed was that the kitchen smelled of leaking gas. There was a huge pile of rags and bits of cloth on the table in the center of the room. There were more rags on the window sill and stuffed at the bottom of the back door.

She saw him looking at them. "It's an old house. It gets very drafty." She smiled nervously, wringing her hands. "Now, are you old enough to drink coffee? Or would you rather have hot chocolate?"

He had remained on his feet. She bustled to the table and swept the rags onto the floor with her arm. "Sit down, please." He did. "Now, what would you rather have?"

"Hot chocolate, please."

"Hot chocolate? Good. That's better for you." She headed toward the stove, almost running; it was big and old-fashioned with a shelf for salt and pepper above the burners. "What's your name, dear?"

"Carlyle, ma'am. Carlyle Bedlow."

"Carlyle? Did you know you were named after a famous man?"

"No, ma'am. I was just named after my father. His name's—"

She was laughing, shrilly, unhappily. He had said something funny but did not know what it was. It made him uneasy.

"What, dear? You started to say something. I interrupted you."

"Nothing, ma'am." He was wondering now what he had said, and why she was being so nice, giving him hot chocolate. Maybe she was giving him the hot chocolate so she could talk to him about things he did not understand and laugh at his ignorance. It was just like the men in the barbershop said: Most of a colored man's trouble began with white people. They were always laughing and making fun of Negroes . . .

"Do you like your hot chocolate sweet, Carlyle? I can put some sugar in it for you." Behind her voice he could hear the milk sizzling around the edges of the saucepan, could hear the gas feeding the flame.

"Yes, ma'am. I like it sweet."

The milk sizzled louder still as she poured it across the hot sides into his cup. She brought it and sat across from him on the edge of her chair, waiting for him to taste it. He did so and found it good; with his mind's eye, he followed it down his throat and into his stomach.

"Is it good?" Her gray eyes darted across his face.

"Yes, ma'am."

She smiled and seemed pleased. That puzzled him. If she had him in to laugh at him, why was she so anxious to get him warm, why did she want him to like the hot chocolate? There had to be some other reason, but just then the chocolate was too good to think about it. He took a big swallow.

"Well now, let's get down to business. I've never had to hire anybody to do this before. I used to do it myself when I was younger and . . . then . . . there was a man here who'd do it for me . . . but he's not here any more." She trailed off, caught herself. "How much do you usually get for a stoop and a walk that long?" She smiled at him again. It was a fleeting smile which warmed only the corners of her mouth and left her eyes sad. "I've been very nice to you. I should think you'd charge me less than usual."

So that was it! She wanted him to do her walk for practically nothing! White people were always trying to cheat Negroes. He had heard his father say that, cursing the Jews in Harlem. He just stared at her, hating her.

She waited an instant for him to answer then started to figure out loud. "Well, let's see. That's a long walk and there's the sidewalk and the stoop and the steps and it's very cold and I probably can't get anyone else . . . It's a

question of too little supply and a great deal of demand."
She was talking above him again. "I'd say I'd be getting
off well if I gave you five dollars." She stopped and looked
across at him, helplessly. "Does that sound fair? I really
don't know."

He continued to stare, but now because he could hardly
believe what she said. At the most, he would have charged
only three dollars, and had expected her to offer one.

She filled in the silence. "Yes, five. That sounds right."

He finished his chocolate with a gulp. "But, ma'am, I
wouldn't-a charged you but three. Really!"

"Three? That doesn't sound like enough." She bolted
from the table and advanced on him. "Well, I'll give you
the extra two for being honest. Perhaps you can come
back and do something else for me." She swooped on him,
hugged, and kissed him. The kiss left a wet, cold spot on
his cheek. He lurched away, surprised, knocking the cup
and saucer from the table. The saucer broke in two; the
cup bounced, rolled, lopsided and crazy, under the table.

"No, ma'am." He jumped to his feet. "I'm sorry,
ma'am."

"That's all right. It's all right. I'm sor—That's all right
about the saucer." She scrambled to her knees and began
to pick up the pieces and the cup. Once she had them in
her lap, she sat, staring away at nothing, shaking her head.

Now he knew for certain what she was up to; he remembered what Garland had said: When you find some
white woman being nicer than she ought to be, then watch
out! She wanted to make time with him. He started from
the kitchen. Maybe he could leave before it was too late.

"Wait, young man." She stood up. "I'll pay you now
and you won't have to come inside when you're through."
She pushed by him and hurried down the shadowy hallway. He followed her as before, but kept his distance.

Her purse was hanging on a peg on the coat-rack, next
to his own jacket. She took them both down, handed him
his jacket, averting her eyes, and fumbled in her purse,
produced a wallet, unzipped it, pulled out a bill and
handed it to him.

"But it's a five, ma'am." He could not understand why
she wanted to pay him that much now that he was not
going to make time with her.

She looked at him for the first time, her eyes wet. "I
told you I'd pay you five, didn't I?"

"Yes, ma'am."

"All right. Do a good job. And remember, don't come back."

"Yes, ma'am."

"You let yourself out." She started to the back of the house even before he had finished buttoning his jacket. By the time he opened the door she was far down the hall, and, as he closed it behind him and stepped into the dark, twinkling cold, he could hear her in the kitchen. She was tearing rags.

The next evening the white woman was in the newspaper. A boy trying to deliver a package had found her in the gas-filled kitchen, slumped over a table piled high with rags. Carlyle's father, who saw it first, mentioned it at dinner. "Had a suicide a couple blocks from here." He told who and where.

Carlyle sat staring at his plate.

His father went on: "White folks! Man, if they had to be colored for a day, they'd all kill they-selves. We wouldn't have no race problem then. White folks don't know what hard life is. What's wrong, Junior?"

"She was a nice lady."

His parents and his little brother looked at him.

"You know her, Junior?" His mother put down her fork.

"She was a nice lady, Mama. I shoveled her walk yesterday. She give me five dollars."

"Oh, Junior." His mother sighed.

"Five dollars?" His father leaned forward. "Crazy, huh?"

"Have some respect!" His mother turned on his father angrily.

Carlyle looked at his mother. "Are white people all bad? There's some good ones, ain't there, Mama?"

"Of course, Junior." His mother smiled. "What made you think—"

"Sure, there is, Junior." His father was smiling too. "The dead ones is good."

Some Get Wasted

by Paule Marshall

A shout hurled after him down the rise: "Run, baby.
Run, fool!" and Hezzy knew, the terror snapping the ten-
dons which strung together his muscles, that he had been
caught in a sneak, was separated from his People, alone,
running with his heart jarring inside his narrow chest, his
stomach a stone weight and his life riding on each rise and
plunge of his legs. While far behind, advancing like pieces
of the night broken off, were the Crowns. He couldn't
dare turn to look, couldn't place their voices because of
the wind in his ears, but he knew they were Crowns. They
had to be.

"Run, baby, run. You running real pretty, but we's with
you all the way. . . ."

And he was running pretty. So that he began to feel an
ease and lightness. His feet skimmed the path while his
arms cut away the air around him. But then he had
learned how to run from the master. Him and the Little
People was always hanging around the block watching
Turner and the Big People practice their running. Turner
was always saying, "Dig, you studs, one thing, don't never
let another club catch you in a sneak. Especially you Little
People. Don't never get too far away from the rest of the
guys. In this club when we go down everybody goes together. When we split, everybody splits together. But if
you should get caught in a sneak, haul ass out of there.

136

Run, baby. Your legs is your life then, you can believe that."

Yeah, Turner would dig the way he was running. He would go round the block tomorrow, all cool like nothing had happened and say—ignoring Turner but talking loud enough so's he hear—"Man, dig what happened to me last night after the action in the park. Them dirty Crowns caught me in a sneak, man. Come chasing me all over the fuggen place. But I put down some speed on them babies and burned their eyes."

Even now, their jeers seemed fainter, further away: "Run, baby . . . like we said, you running pretty. . . ." The night was pulling them back, making them part of it again. Man, he could outrun those punks any time, any place. His heart gave a little joyous leap and he sprinted cleanly ahead, the pebbles scattering underfoot.

The day, this night, his flight had begun a week ago. The Little People had gotten the word that something was up and had gone over to the Crib where the Noble Knights, their Big People, hung out. The Crib was the square of bare earth in front of the decaying brownstone where Turner lived.

"The jive is on," Turner said as soon as they were assembled.

And before the words were barely out, Sizzle who lived only to fight, said, "Like I been telling you, man, it's about time. Them Crowns been messing all over us. Pulling sneaks in our turf. Stomping and wasting our Little People like they did Duke. Slapping around our broads when they come outta school . . . Man, I hate them studs. I hate them dirty Crown Buggers."

"Man, cool your role," Turner said. Then: "Like I said, the jive is on. And strong this time. We ain't just goin' down in their turf and stomp the first Crown we see and split, like we always do. This is gonna be organized. We already got word to the Crowns and they're ready. Now dig. Next Monday, Memorial Day, we look. Over in Prospect Park, on the Hill. Time the parade ends and it starts getting dark, time the Crowns show, we lock. Now pick up on the play. . . ."

Hezzy, crowded with his guys on the bottom step of the stoop listened, his stomach dropping as it did on the cyclone in Coney Island. Going down with the Big People at last! Down with the hearts! And on Memorial Day when every club in the city would be gangbusting. The Italian cats in South Brooklyn, them Spanish studs in East Harlem. And on the Hill—Massacre Hill they called it—where many a stud had either built his rep or gotten wasted.

He had heard how three years ago on Easter Sunday when the Noble Knights clashed with the Crusaders on the Hill, Turner had gotten the bullet crease on his forehead and had started his bad rep. Heard how the cat had gone to church packing his zip that morning and gone down to lock with the Crusaders that afternoon.

Hezzy looked up over the other heads at the bullet crease. It was like the cat's skin was so tough the bullet had only been able to graze it. It was like nothing or nobody could waste the cat. You could tell from his eyes. The iris fixed dead-center in the whites and full of dark swirls of colors like a marble and cold, baby. When Turner looked sideways he never shifted his eyes, but turned his head, slow, like time had to wait on him. Man, how them simple chicks goofed behind that look. The stud didn't even have to talk to 'em. Just looked and they was ready to give him some . . .

"Dig, we ain't wearing no club jackets neither," Turner was saying. "Cause they ain't no need to let The Man know who we is. And another thing, it's gonna be dark out there, so watch whose head you busting." The unmoving eyes fixed the Crosstown Noble Knights. "You studs down?"

"We down, man."

"You all down?" His chin flicked toward the Little People at the bottom of the stoop.

"Yeah, we down," Hezzy answered.

"We don't want none of you Little People coming up weak," Turner said.

"Man, I ain't saying we ain't got some punks in the Division, but we leaves them studs home when we bopping."

All around the eyes glanced his way, but he kept his gaze on Turner.

"What's your name again, man?" Turner said and there was a tightness in his voice.

"Hezzy, man," and he touched the turned-down brim of the soiled sailor hat he always wore where his name was emblazoned in black.

"You suppose to be president of the Little People since Duke got wasted?"

"Ain't no suppose, man. I am the president."

"All right, my man, but cool your role, you dig?"

He was all flushed inside. His head felt like it was
twisted behind drinking some wine—and when the meeting was over and he and his little guys were back on their
corner, they pooled their coins for a pint of Thunderbird
and drank in celebration of how bad and cool he had been
in front of the Big People.

Late that night he wandered alone and high through his
turf. And all around him the familiar overflow of life
streamed out of the sagging houses, the rank hallways, the
corner bars, bearing him along like a dark tide. The voices
loud against the night sky became his voice. The violence
brooding over the crap games and racing with the cars became the vertigo inside his head. It was his world, his way
—and that other world beyond suddenly no longer mattered. Rearing back he snatched off his hat, baring his
small tough black child's face. "Hezzy," he shouted, his
rage and arrogance a wine-tinged spume. "Yeah, that's
right, Hezzy. Read about me in the *News* next week, ya
dumb squares."

The night before Memorial Day he wet his bed, and in
the morning awoke in the warm wet rankness of himself,
shaking from a dream he couldn't remember, his eyes en-
crusted with cold. Quickly pulling on his hat, he shoved
his half-brothers from around him.

"Boy, what time you got in here last night?"

He jammed a leg into his trousers.

"You hear me? What time? Always running the
streets . . . But you watch, you gonna get yourself all
messed up one of these days . . . Just don't act right no
more. I mean, you used to would stay round the house
sometime and help me out . . . used to would listen sometime . . . and go to school. . . ."

It was the same old slop, in the same old voice that was
as slack as her body and as lifeless as her eyes. He always
fled it, had to, since something in him always threatened
to give in to it. Even more so this morning. For her voice
recalled something in his dream. It seemed to reach out in
place of her arms to hold him there, to take him, as she
had sometimes done when he was small, into her bed.
Jumping up, he slammed the door on that voice, cutting it
off and almost threw himself down the five flights of stairs.
As he hit the street the sun smacked him hard across the
face and he saw his Little People waiting for him on the
corner.

The parade was half over when Hezzy and his guys fol-

lowing Turner and the Big People some distance ahead
reached Bedford Avenue. Old soldiers, remnants of the
wars, shuffled along like sleep-walkers, their eyes tearing
from the dust and glare. Boy Scouts, white mostly, with
clear eyes and smooth fresh faces, marched under the rippling flags to the blare of "America, America, God shed
his grace on thee . . ." and the majorettes kicked high
their white legs, the flesh under the thighs quivering in the
sunlight. Their batons flashed silver. And the crowd surged
against the barricades with a roar.

"Man, dig the squares," Hezzy said, the smoke flaring
from under the sailor hat.

"They sure out here, ain't they," the boy beside him
said.

"Man! You know, I feel sorry for squares, I tell you the
truth. They just don't know what's happening. I mean, all
they got is this little old jive parade while tonight here we
are gonna be locking with the Crowns up on the
Hill. . . ."

Later, in Prospect Park he watched scornfully from behind his oversized sunglasses as the parade disbanded: the
old soldiers wheezing and fanning under the trees, the Boy
Scouts lowering the heavy flags, the majorettes lolling on
the grass, laughing, their blond hair spread out as if to
dry. "Yeah," he said, "I feel real sorry for squares."

As always whenever they came to Prospect Park they
visited the small amusement area and Hezzy seeing that
they had gotten separated from Turner and the Big People
suddenly let out a whoop and clambered aboard the merry-go-round, his four guys behind him. Startling the other
children there with their bloodcurdling cries, they fu-
·riously goaded their motionless painted mounts, cursing
whenever they grabbed for the ring and missed.

"Man," he said laughing as they leaped off together into
the trampled grass and dust. "You all is nothing but punks
riding some old jive merry-go-round."

"Seems like I seen you on there too, baby."

"How you mean, man? I was just showing you cats how
to do the thing."

Later they sneaked through the zoo, and forcing their
way close to the railing with their cocked elbows, teased
the animals and sounded each other's mother:

"Yoa mother, man."

"Yours, Jim."

Leaning dangerously over the rail, they gently coaxed
the seals out of the water. "Come on up, baby, and do

your number for the Knights. The Noble Knights of Gates Avenue, baby."

They stood almost respectfully in front of the lion cage. "Lemme tell ya, Jim, that's about a bad stud you see in there," Hezzy said. "You try locking with that cat and get yourself all messed up. . . ."

And all the while they ate, downing frankfurters and Pepsis, and when their money was gone, they jostled the Boy Scouts around the stands and stole candy. Full finally, they climbed to a ridge near Massacre Hill and there, beneath a cool fretwork of trees and sun they drank from a pint bottle of wine, folding their small mouths around the mouth of the bottle and taking a long loud suck and then passing it on with a sigh.

The wine coupled with the sun unleashed a wildness in them after a time and they fell upon each other, tussling and rolling all in a heap, savagely kneeing each other and sending the grass and the bits of loosened sod flying up around them. And then just as abruptly they fell apart and lay sprawled and panting under the dome of leaves.

"Man, you seen the new Buick?" one of them said after a long silence. "I sure would like to cop me one of them."

"Cop with what, man? You'll never make enough bread for that."

"Who's talking about buying it, Jim. Ain't no fun behind that, I means to steal me one."

"For what? You can't even drive."

"Don't need to. I just want that number sitting outside my house looking all pretty. . . ."

Hezzy, silent until then, said, shaking his head in sad and gentle reproof. "That's what I mean about you studs. Always talking about stealing cars and robbing stores like that's something. Man, that slop ain't nothing. Any jive stud out here can steal him a car or rob a store. That don't take no heart. You can't build you no real rep behind that weak slop. You got to be out here busting heads and wasting cats, Jim. That's the only way you build you a rep and move up in a club. . . ."

"Well, we out here, ain't we?" one of them said irritably. "Most of the guys in the division didn't even show this morning."

"Them punks!" he cried and sat up. At the thought of them out on the corner drinking and jiving the chicks, having a good time, safe, the wine curdled in his stomach. For a dangerous second he wanted to be with them. "Let's make it," he shouted, leaping up, and feeling for the sec-

tion of lead pipe under his jacket. "Let's find Turner and
the rest of the guys." And as they plunged down the rise,
he looked up and squinting in the sunlight, cried, "Who
needs all this sun and slop anyways. Why don't it get
dark?"

As if acceding to his wish, the sun veered toward Massacre Hill and paused there for a moment as if gathering
its strength for the long descent. Slowly the dusk banked
low to the east began to climb—and all over the park the
marchers departed. The merry-go-round stood empty. The
refreshment stands were boarded up. And the elephants,
sensing the night coming on, began trumpeting in the zoo.

They found their Big People in a small wood on the
other side of Massacre Hill, the guys practicing the latest
dance steps, drinking from a gallon bottle of wine, play-
fully sparring, cursing—just as if they were in the Crib,
although there was an edginess to all they did, a wariness.

Turner, with Sizzle and Big Moose—the baleful Moose
who had done in a Crown when he was Hezzy's age, thirteen, and gotten busted, rehabilitated, paroled and was
back bopping with the cats—was squatting under a tree,
his impassive gaze on the path leading to the Hill.

Hezzy saw the bulge at his pocket. The cat was packing
his burn! And suddenly he felt as safe as the guys back on
the corner drinking and jiving with the chicks. Everything
was cool.

The dusk had begun slowly sifting down through the
trees when Sizzle sprang up—and it was seeing a tightly
coiled wire spring loose. "Them sneaky Crown bastards,"
he cried, almost inarticulate with rage. "They ain't gonna
show. Just like the last time. Remember?" he shouted
down at Turner. "Remember how the pricks sent us word
they was coming down and then didn't show. Punked out.
Every last one of the bastards. Remember?"

Turner nodded, his eyes still fixed on the path.

And Big Moose said petulantly, "I never did go for bopping in Prospect Park no ways. Give me the streets, baby,
so if I got to haul ass I'm running on asphalt. Out here is
too spooky with all these jive trees. I won't even know
where I'm running—and knowing me I'm subject to run
right into The Man and find myself doing one to five for
gangbusting again."

"Man," Turner said laughing, but with his eye still on
the path. "There ain't no need to let everybody know you
punking out."

"I ain't punking out," Moose said. "It's just too dark out

here. How I'm going to know for sure it's a Crown's head
I'm busting and not one of our own guys?"

And Hezzy said, his voice as steady, as chiding as Turner's. "You'll know, man. Just smell the punk's breath before you smash him. Them cheap Crowns drink that thirty
cents a pint slop."

"Who asked you?" Big Moose swung on him.

"Cool, man," Turner caught Moose's arm and turned to
Hezzy. He stared at him with eyes filled with the dusk.
"Moose, man," he said after a time, his gaze still on Hezzy,
"looks like I might have to put you out of the club and
move up my man Hezzy here, especially if the stud fights
as bad as he talks. I might even have to move over,
Jim . . ."

Hezzy returned the dark and steady gaze, the chilling
smile—and again he felt high, soaring.

The Crowns came at the very edge of the day. A dozen
or more small dark forms loping toward them down the
path which led to the hill. They spotted the Noble Knights
and the wind brought their cry: "The Crowns, punks. It's
the Crowns."

There was a moment's recoil among the Noble Knights
and then Turner was on his feet, the others behind him
and their answering shout seemed to jar the trees around
them: "The Noble Knights, muh-fuggers! The Noble
Knights are down!"—and with Turner in the lead and
Sizzle, Big Moose and Hezzy just behind, they charged up
the rise from the other side, up into the descending night
and as they gained the low crest and met the oncoming
Crowns, the darkness reached down and covered them en-
tirely.

The battle was brief as always, lasting no more than two
or three minutes, and disorderly. They thrashed and grap-
pled in the dark, cursing, uncertain whom they were hitting. The cries burst like flares: "The Crowns!" "The
Noble Knights, baby!" The dull red spurt of a gun lit the
darkness and then they were fighting blind again.

In those minutes which seemed like hours a rubber hose
smacked up against Hezzy's head, knocking off his hat and
blinding him with pain for a second. He did not mind the
pain, but the loss of his hat, the wind stinging his exposed
head, terrified and then enraged him. He struck out savagely and something solid gave way beneath the lead pipe
in his hand—and as it did something within him burst
free: a sap which fed his muscles and sent his arm slash-
ing into the surging darkness. Each time someone rushed

him shouting, "The Crowns, punk!" he yelled, "The Noble Knights, baby!" and struck, exulting.

The pipe flew from his hand and he drew his shiv, the blade snatching a dull yellow gleam from somewhere and as he held it at the ready, shouting for a Crown he heard the first whistle then the next, shrill, piercing the heart of the night. For an instant which seemed endless, there was silence on the hill. And it was as if the sound of the whistle had cut off the air in their throats. Their bodies froze in the violent attitudes of the fight—and it was as if they were playing "statues." Knights and Crowns were one suddenly, a stunned, silent, violently cohered mass. Comrades. For the whisper passed among them without regard to friend or foe: "The Man, baby! The Man." Then the darkness exploded into fragments that took on human form and they scattered headlong down the hill.

The ground below was a magnet which drew Hezzy to it and he plunged helpless toward it, bruised and terrified and suddenly alone as the others behind him raced down another path. And then no longer alone as the shout sounded behind him. "There goes one of the punks, I betcha. Let's waste the muh-fugger."

He had been caught in a sneak.

"Run, baby . . . Like we said, you running pretty . . . But we're still with ya. . . ."

And he was, as they said, still running pretty. He was certain of his escape now. The black wall ahead would soon give way, he knew, to a street and neon signs and people and houses with hallways to hide him until he could get back to his turf. Yet a single regret filtered down through the warm night and robbed the flight of its joy. He longed for his hat. Tears of outrage started up. If only he had wasted one of the bastards to make up for his loss. Or shived one of them good. He ran crying for the hat, until overwhelmed by his loss, he wheeled around and for a moment stood cursing them. Then, turning, he ran ahead.

But in that moment they were on him. It was as if they had known all along that he would pause and had held back, saving themselves till that error. Now they came on swiftly, intent, suddenly silent. The distance between them narrowed. The sound of their approach welled out of the night; and out of the silence came a single taunt: "What's the matter, baby, you ain't running so pretty no more?"

His fear suddenly was a cramp which spread swiftly to

all his muscles. His arms tightened. His shoulders. The paralysis reached his legs so that his stride was broken and his feet caught in the ruts of the path. Fear was a phlegm in his throat choking off his air and a film over his eyes which made the black wall of trees ahead of him waver and recede. He stumbled and as he almost went down, their cry crashed in his ears: *The Noble Knights, punk! The Knights are down!*

He turned as if jerked around and over the loud rale of his breathing he listened, unbelieving, to the echo of the words. They called again, "The Knights, muh-fugger!" nearer this time, and the voices clearly those of Turner, Sizzle and Big Moose. And Hezzy's relief was a weakness in his legs and a warmth flooding his chest. The smile that everyone always said was so like his mother's broke amid his tears and he started toward them, hailing them with the shiv he still held, laughing as he wept, shouting, "Hey, you bop-crazy studs, it's . . ."

The gun's report drowned his name. The bullet sent a bright forked light through him and pain discovered the secret places of his body. Yet he still staggered toward them, smiling, but stiffly now, holding out the knife like a gift as they sped by without looking. Even when they were gone and he was dead, a spoor of blood slowly trailed them. As if, despite what they had done, they were still his People. As if, no matter what, he would always follow them. Overhead the black dome of the sky cleared and a few stars glinted. Cold tears in the warm May night.

Now That
Henry Is Gone

by Clayton Riley

Henry fell without a sound, arms loose, he crumpled like cloth and hit the basement floor. There was laughter from the crowded room, from people who thought he was joking, and the woman named Betty Toenail went right on dancing as if she expected him to rise again, grinning and doing The Monkey, the way he had done all night.

"Get up, man," someone called, "quit acting the fool."

The music and Betty continued, hands clapped in time with finger-popping through the smoke and dimness—what a party it was.

For two nights or three—no one was sure—the crowd kept coming, growing larger, shouting louder, on and on it went as few people left and many arrived, pushing into the basement of a Seventh Avenue building near 114th Street where T. J. Jones was superintendent. And T. J. Jones had started it all with a single half-pint of wine. He and Skeeter Davis drank with Brother Randolph-from-the-Bronx who later bought a gallon jug of muscatel and invited John Grimes who told Boo Johnson, so Skeeter D. went back to the liquor store for another and soon came back with Horace Tubbs, Ro Callister, Adam Travis, who all sometimes take a taste. Before the new refreshment could be opened, Pony Brewster was there with Leon Bell and two phonographs they had *found*. Herman Lipscomb got the word—he had LP records and 45's and his partner Charley Taylor who said, "The old-timers are headed around." Including those who didn't need last names: Beazle, Twenty-one, Biggus and Littlus, Junebug, Pill, Fatlip, The Chopper, Deuce, See-me, Roadrunner, DoWrong, Trolleycar, and Quarter-to-Midnight. They were sippers all, so another trip to the store was in order. Skeeter D. and Cousin Randolph conferred, being bankers for the day, and decided to go for broke with gallons and the ladies who returned with them. Deuce said, "Check, here come Sleepy Willa Morris and Lottie Jones, Pearl Booker, Alma Brock, Lessie Fernandez, Mama Wright, Bea Brown, and Betty Toenail, Jr."

Collation in paper cups, cigarettes and some sticks to smoke, the phonograph all the way up when Arthur Morris arrived and said to Betty, "Stack 'em back, baby!" The dancing began. And not to be left out, Miss Q trotted in with Birdlegs and Sweetroll, who went no place without I.I., who stuttered a little and traveled with Miss Jibbs, Sister Sidewalk, Miss Mouse, Lady Fish and Princess Queen.

"Well," says Adam Travis, explaining somewhat later to the Investigator, "I go with the crowd, you see. I'm standing on Lenox and 21st when my main man Ro says, 'Dig, it's on.' So I hat on down there with him and a couple of other cats to check the happenings. If it ain't swinging, you understand, I'm ready to do the bird. But everything is cool, on time and lovely—make yourself to home. Party time! I get a buzz, light stuff though, and step awhile with Lady Fish. She'll hip you to that. Pluck for days and I didn't ask who's buying, I'm in my world, you dig? Henry and me, we didn't run together. Not that he was uncool, just in another bag. I was leaning when he fell, but at least one stud said it was Betty Toenail who did him. Can I ask why you want to know?"

Some of which the Investigator doesn't understand but puts it in the record, saying to the others in the gallery, "Gentlemen, it is my considered opinion that a sordid collusion exists between these witnesses, there is a calculated attempt to confuse us. We have heard the woman called 'Betty Toenail' villified, maligned and repeatedly accused of this heinous act. Yet we are not yet certain what that act was or whether it even took place. Adam," he said to Adam Travis, "We intend to get to the bottom of this."

"That's cool," says Adam.

Henry fell without a sound, arms loose, he crumpled like cloth and hit the basement floor. There was laughter from the crowded room, from people who thought he was joking. . . .

"Get up, man," someone called, "quit acting the fool." It was Beazle, who told the Investigator, "Skeeter D. and Brother Randolph-from-the-Bronx don't know, but I saw them making it down 10th by Central Park, up-tight and looking for a scene. Pill and them are supposed to play bid whist at Henry's crib, laying up the way they do. Skeeter D. and Brother Randolph are on the block or in the life as some folks call it—it's hustling any way you cut it. Some of this, a little of that, you pick up a few bills—enough to keep scuffling. Mostly though, you move as much as you can, looking for a break, a good deal or something. Everybody's chance to cop is lying around somewhere—you move enough, you get yours and relax. So Skeeter and Randolph don't know I'm peeping when they beat some dude for his bread. He's gray so I cool the whole thing. But I dug it. And these two dummies, because they haven't seen a coin for a while, throw a gig and blow that cash treating everybody to some squeeze, down in T. J.'s basement. It was them, not Betty T, who got into it with Henry. Another cat told me that Skeeter D. and Brother Randolph gorilla'd Henry. Can I ask why you want to know?"

People kept coming in all night. Egypt Land and the big man called Bonecrusher were among them, though they aren't known to socialize much. And several more who could only be called "Say, man," or "Listen, girl," or "Look here." A few thieves, a junky trio, here a whore, there a pimp, amateur assassins, bullies, purse-snatchers, car-washers, pool sharks, muggers, stolen property agents, agitators, cowards, signifiers, beggars, and when everyone else was counted, Henry arrived.

Later, when Quarter-to-Midnight was taken to the Great Hall, he would sit beneath a harsh white light and be surrounded by an arena of spectators. Five hundred pale gray faces would surround him. On a stool, rubbing his hands together, Quarter-to-Midnight would wait. Presently—a stir in the assembly, a man in black robes, strolling and smiling, stopping and saying, "You are the individual called Quarter-to-Midnight?"

"Yes, sir, that's what I'm called."

"Why?"

"People like to bug me about being so dark."

"I shall address you as Quarter, henceforth."

"Square business, baby. And you, what's your stick?"

"I am the Investigator. Address me as Mr. Investigator."

"Solid," says Quarter-to-Midnight.

"Quarter, we are assembled here today in order to discern what if any malfeasance may have attended the demise of an individual named Henry Jackson, who was, I am told, a compatriot of yours. Be advised that any information you divulge shall be considered confidential and remain confined to the members of this investigative body and their immediate families. You are to discuss what you say and hear in this chamber with no one. Is that quite clear?"

Some of which Quarter-to-Midnight doesn't understand. "Yes, sir," he replies, "it's all clear."

"Then you may begin your testimony."

While Quarter-to-Midnight speaks, Betty Toenail, Jr., subpoenaed as a material witness, sought as a primary suspect, makes a phone call to a younger brother who, as it turns out, is unable to receive the call but later is given a message by his employer.

Betty Toenail, born in poverty, raised with indifference and hardened by her environment, becomes a prostitute. At fourteen she is a seasoned professional plying the trade in transient hotels, alleys, and subway stations. Her face is embroidered with a number of stitches, the souvenirs she receives from the fists and other weapons of her customers and business rivals. She is arrested many times and counts her years by these events. Picked up on Christmas Eve by a jovial patrolman who promises leniency in exchange for her favors, she complies but spends her holiday in a jail cell nonetheless with a magistrate's words ringing in her ears. "Trust no one. Learn to defend yourself." Years later, standing quietly on a sidewalk near Mount Morris Park, Betty Toenail meets Henry and goes to live with him. It is a fine relationship, lasting through many troubles and she is able to retire from her work when Henry finds steady employment as a waiter. They live in peace, insofar as such a state is possible in that district. The betrayal that separates them is not caused specifically by a human failing. Their first meeting in months occurs at T. J. Jones' basement party.

And Quarter-to-Midnight began.

"It's early, you dig? Three o'clock and I'm loafing on 16th and Seventh. Skeeter D. shows and hips me to the happenings at T. J.'s. Cool. We make it and at first it's a lame set. Nothing but hard-legs. T. J., Skeeter D., Brother Randolph and the crew. Henry was on the scene too."

A moan swept through the assembly and the Investigator cried, "Henry? Did you mention Henry?"

"Henry," replied Quarter-to-Midnight, "was there from the git-go."

"That's from the beginning, gentlemen," a clerk explained.

A moan swept through the assembly and the Investigator cried, "We have been misled. But continue."

"Well," Quarter-to-Midnight went on, "we started tasting. Sides were blowing decent sounds. I start to step with Miss Jibbs, she'll hip you to that. Some youngblood shows and starts to shoot up—I don't play that since my asthma but everybody is cool and the good times roll. I keep a cup of Must-I-Tell and my head starts smoking. All the people hit it pretty soon, The Chopper, See-me—"

"We know who was there," the Investigator interrupted. "Go on."

"The sounds get groovy and boom, baby, Betty T. comes in and takes the floor. The chick's frame goes like honey, in a solo first but before long, boom, baby, dig Deuce. He's velvet, no jive. They get together and start to gig, off-timing and the bit. Never missing step, saying the word, telling the story. Betty's moves were preaching the gospel and Deuce, with ease, testified to everything she said. But then he's an old-time soft-shoe tapper from way back. Before it was over it was rock-house in the joint. Everybody got up. It was something else. Soul got to all those people. Cats who would shiv each other for a bean were laughing together, the broads were behaving like royalty and the set became beautiful. Soul, baby. Love. Even me and Egypt Land, we never make it anywhere without scuffing, but we were pouring pluck together. Are you ready for that? Smiles, jokes, shake a hand, we were all beautiful. Cats couldn't believe it. Then, boom, baby, it was over. We thought Henry was shucking but it wasn't a hype. You dig?"

Henry fell without a sound, arms loose, he crumpled like cloth and hit the basement floor. There was laughter from the crowded room, from people who thought he was joking, and the woman named Betty Toenail went right on dancing as if . . .

This noon, while I was out to lunch, a telephone call came for me. Generally my employer strictly forbids use

of his phone for calls—incoming or outgoing—and it surprised me to have him take a message, then pass it on to
me. It's a small book warehouse, one large room divided
into three sections. If one of us has to contact someone,
send a message, there's a drugstore up the street, where
some of the fellows go to eat. They have several pay
phones.

"Evans," he said, "you had a call. A woman."

"I'm sorry," I told him, "I've asked people not to call
me on the job."

"That's okay. Something about Henry. I couldn't understand her too well, she didn't speak clearly."

I went back to my work certain there had been a mistake or perhaps that's only what I hoped.

A shipment of children's books came in soon after-
wards; one of the new men brought them to me on a skid
and said they were to be put away into the bins. The call
began to bother me. Who could it have been; what
woman? And what about Henry?

Let me tell you, I spent several years on the block, or in
the life as you will. A little of this or that—hustling, I
guess. Maybe you've seen a few of the people or dealt
with some. They stand on streets, eyes wide, waiting, clus-
ters of them like famished birds. A few rush off, into a bar
or somebody's apartment.

I was arrested for petty theft a few years ago and spent
time in prison. When I was released the warden told me,
"Trust no one. Learn to defend yourself." I was fortunate
to get this job; they ask no questions here and I'm treated
well. I wear a shirt and tie to work each day and have several pairs of good shoes. My father used to tell us to keep
clean and stay out of trouble. Betty and the others turned
out badly, but I'm in night school and working steady.
Like my father, who stayed out of trouble all his life, wore
a wing-collar and tie out of the house each day to "go to
business," I'm doing all right. He ran an elevator (changed
clothes in the locker room). I work with books. Things
have gotten better.

But if something actually has happened to Henry—I'll
know tonight.

"Get up, man," someone called, "quit acting the fool."
But Henry never moved and soon the place was empty.
Scattering toward the street, stumbling, gasping; no one
wanted to believe or think about what had happened, what
each had seen. Only Betty stayed behind, still moving to
the music, a little more high than she usually got. And she

waited, looking down at Henry through the smoke, the dimness, not realizing that Betty was alone. Outside, the scrambling quickly began. There were those who went along Seventh—uptown or down—in a trot with their loose change jangling, while some went east toward Lenox and the rest headed for Eighth. Everyone disappeared. Until the investigation.

Unfinished

by LeRoi Jones

Coming into Jocks in Harlem, with friends and the inside redlit-up middle-class faggots (no, homosexuals) scattered discreetly around, sharp in their new shit.

Summer evening, with friends, I said. Their faces float around, and their names. Love, talk, expectation, the leading on. The close light that separates the tribes of life. Where is the spectacular, and the handling of it, and the love of it, and the reward for its being alive and screaming? The love of everything.

Which is calm enough. These faces hanging in the calm, and the low talk and occasional soft ha-ha of a fag.

Then you sprawl and talk about what happened that day, that wild summer 65 uptown, when a lot new blood came in, and there were a lot of closer questioners of day to day making-it in America.

The atmosphere is important. Very important. The tales people will tell even to this day, of shit that simply did not happen. Feet walked by above us. You cd see some through a window. Few people made up biographies for them.

There were snakes and panthers in the town. Tho a lot of funny shit happened. A lot of fools got exposed. A lot of cowards. A lot of maniacs. Reality syndrome. Black people piled in the street. Negroes piled in certain nigger coolout stations.

153

WHITE PHILANTHROPY RUNS AMUCK AGAIN

Sit in a useless evening not even getting drunk. Just
with people and make some remarks. Maybe these dancers
were there that night, and there was nothing to talk about
because you can't talk to dancers about academic shit like
what the world is. So you can suck-sipping ale out the end
of a glass, listen to some vague shit about somebody who
told somebody else off, and not even be there. You could
be in southcarolina murdering the governor, by strangling
him with a wide belt, and your knee cocked in the small
of his back.

People are going about their business. Somebody else
comes in the bar, everybody looks up, the fags respond or
disrespond, or if it's somebody somebody knows, there is a
little more racket, before the half-white juke box takes
over again. And maybe some lightskinned lady with
streaks in her hair will wander in mission unknown.

All settled in time and space, another nothing to add to
hundreds of others. The various freaks up and down the
streets. Like black blondes or niggers with good jobs.
Maybe junkies from southcarolina who came up north to
get deadhooked forever, in the evil smells of dying blackness. But they, at least, are real. These dead junkies. In
their weird outside world. But then another colored man
will stop in the hallways of some shaky white philanthropy
and talk to you like he was practicing to be a traitor.

A multiplicity of failures. But everybody, shit, can claim
something. To have made it! Whatever. From whatever to
where ever the wind blows enough dollars to cool out bad
conscience. Facing us, on the street each day, thousands of
fools and cowards.

So they all join hands and make a fool/coward cartel
that controls the minds of ordinary men. And it is this cartel we work against, to kill them. Drown them in their
blood, so that the mind might again soar to its completion
and a new brightness begin.

We could sit and joke, or if with heavier friends, phi-
losophize about the day, Malcolm's death, the number of
faggots in The Big Apple, being careful not to offend anybody sitting in our immediate party.

And simple bullshit incidents lend a personal form to
time. And all the facts we want are carried back with the
specific context of their happening.

Red bar faces. The room tilted under the ground, just a

few steps down. The gaiety of pretension. These creeps
won't even get like in the Harlem Club, and tear the windows out. These are cool Knee Grows who have a few
pesos in their pockets (earned by letting whitey pass gas in
their noses). There is a cruel frustration drifts through
places like that . . . places filled with young & old black
boushies. . . . And you could think about white invisible
things being dragged back and forth across the ceiling.
Maybe they are talismans of white magic, secret, hideous,
ofay mojos, their god waves back and forth over black
people's heads, making them long to be white men. It's too
horrible to think about shit like that.

This kind of thing can be entertaining or no. But it's always intimidating.

A guy came into this bar, probably just stopped raining
outside. Very light sprinkle. And this guy comes in hooked
up in these weird kind of metal crutches, where they have
metal straps around the legs. A kind of big brown cat,
bulky even strapped and crippled up like he was. He was
making some kind of noise when he came into the place.
Or it was some kind of rumble accompanied him in, limp-
ing like he was on those metal rods. He must been at the
bar 10 seconds before he pulls himself over near our table.
Metal niggers slid out of his way. I was not even looking.

But it wasn't me anyway. I'm here writing, this never
happened to this person. It was somebody else.

At the table sitting watching him approach the friends
of the world, all happy at being that. No, these shitty
dancers, with lyrical eyelashes, and little tiny walks if
they're technically male, just barely women. The women,
the same, only it's not as spectacular to be women invert
like it is for men. The burden of balls.

Oh the weird smiles that exist in life. Too much. To
think about right now, but if you ever get a chance think
about that shit. How many different kinds of smiles there
are, and what they infer or imply or telegraph.

When the cripple cat came up to the table he says some
shit, to one of the guys. Like he had seen him the other
night on television. And the guy who had been congratu-
lated for being on television gave a sort of pseudo-humble
hero smile (which is not a rare variety actually).

Yes, yes, yes, (addressing the people in invisible
dreams) Yes, yes, that is my work, yes, oh wow, groove
somebody recognized he and set up the guillotine trap. A
long terrorized scream, and the blade, bloody already
comed whistling down. Trying to smile at people is experi-

mentation or cliché. I have a standard good natural tooth viewer I use most times in such occasions. But was that me at the table. The one who speaks now. The heart that feeds me my life.

But this is a story now. There are facts in it anyway, for the careful.

This was a funny looking guy, he needed to stop smiling so you could get a good look at his face. But that's probably why he kept smiling . . . a really fucking sinister smile . . . now that I think about it. Or maybe not sinister, but insinuating, dangerous by default.

And keeps talking and talking, ordering drinks. He began doing this the minute he got up to the table. And fairly loud getting louder with each click of my machine. He was very loud by now. And laughing. But the laughter was decoration for something colder than you ever ran into.

Yeh I saw you on television, and you gave em hell boy. L the minute I saw that program I wanted to call up the station and tell them crackers how much I agreed with what you were saying. Hand. Hand. Pats—shakes. Smiles. Crackers. Hunkies. All the words. I was watching. L was watching like he does, close up and steady, big deep eyes to see. And seeing, can you act my man, the question hung in the world hot as sun. But sunshine is cool, ain't it? It grows the shit from in my heart. It makes the earth magic start. It's cool, and beauty, ba-by. Ba-by. Everything is all right. Up tight. Out of sight. Went on and on, warm lights glows walk box walk. Be lady fair sister sliding down bars, Through Wars, and smoke of dead niggers, negroes, coons, woogies, etcetera, killing each other. Killing Each Other. Selves. Selves. Killing each Other.

I heard your thing, can you dig mine. You a success in the West, aint that a mess. Up in your ches' Polluted Stream. Dead fish, animals still to evolve. A fluke, like black and white together in the same head or bed, it makes no never mind.

He came at me, H had tied my hands behind me, got me in the face. It was bad, and blood came out.

> Where. TimeGap
> keys. Senseless
> Strung Gulls low
> over the sea. That
> was another
> incident in the
> spanish lowlands
> with Hannibal's
> mulattoes, still
> passing for White.
> But yall cain'
> fight.

Correction. The above is bullshit twisted from another time.

What happened. He was bleeding his twisted love. Like the story, and the image of piles of dead fish being broken in half by a jew to feed niggers at the seashore. Shure Rastus. We miss understand, by 3 and one half inches.

Bleed is it bleed bleed bleed. Love, they want white love and there's nothing like that in the world. There's no white peace either (Oh you mis understand . . . we sd *Peach* . . . simple colored monarch. "Arrest Him For Sodomy . . . He Fucked Melville." I'm in jail listening to the cripple now. He moaning inside he loves you so. Stand up L. He wants to touch you his mouth is close, with Vat 69 breath stinging your pause. He got pause thass why he teach moles to shit outta airplanes.

He was going to hit L. He loved him so much. He was going to hit. Him. Why he was screaming inside. Inside. Where the true song rages forever like the very sun. Inside he was screaming it was me not you you just said it but it was me I live and am hurt by the motherfucking world so deeply, much deeper than you what the fuck do you know what the motherfucking shit do you know frail ass motherfucker i'm a cripple hurt motherfucker you ever feel 10 thousand passion tender notes eat your face for time.

He raged now, dropping his crutches on the floor. Inside flowed on out. It was out fire down below, all in the street, fags look out, the cripple, a giant of a man, a motherfucker. . . . WATCH OUT L. . . . WATCH

And L, cool, said brother, what you in to?

The cat came back from outside. He had another drink he came back over. Aw I aint into shit man. I used to sing my ass off though. He began singing. Something about love naturally. A song faggotass Tony Bennett used to sing. But this cat was singing about an actual kindgom, of kings and queens. And he disappeared smiling into the night.

The Other Side
Of Christmas

by Ray J. Meaddough

Whack! The gun spoke harshly, crashing through his mind like the echoes kicking back and forth about the garden. David lunged from the startling line, taking the lead as the runners moved into the far turn. He ruthlessly crushed the surge of strength, the warmth that poured through his body, for he would need it later. He came off the far turn into the backstretch and settled down to a rhythmic ground-eating gait, and the sheer boredom of ten more laps around the garden.

"Hum, baby, hum—boy!"

"Go, Able!"

"Move out, Able ba-by!"

The students started that low growling soar of encouragement, deep and throaty in its power, which raised the goose pimples on his body. Some journalism student, displeased with David as a name, had nicknamed him F918Able, after a jet fighter. The name stuck. But he was not fooled by the distance he had in front of the pack. He refused the body urge to pour speed into the race and remained flat-footed into the near turn, mind wandering from the repetition. Track had been good to him, Able felt. It put F918Able on the sports pages of the country.

159

Of course the student council, the debating team, et cetera, all that was good, but track got him the notice. And it was track that got him elected as the queen's escort for the prom and the opening ceremonies at the educational park. The mayor and the governor would both be there, claiming credit; and if he impressed them, why, there might be a spot in city or state government for a bright young man.

They held up the seven sign; seven laps to go. His body began to complain, minor distress signs which would relent shortly with second wind, but which would get much worse before it was over.

Of course, Hairston didn't approve of all this. Hairston was a Muslim, or a Black Nationalist, or an Atheist, or a Snickite; Able couldn't distinguish between all those hate groups.

"Reputation? Praise? Headlines?" Hairston said. "Shee-it, can you eat it? How much they *paying* you to run?"

"Well you don't get paid, actually. See—"

"Don't get paid? Shee-it!"

"No, you get expenses and money for books and tuition—"

"Lemme see now, Madison Square Garden seats what —forty–fifty thousand? At three dollars a head, that's a hundred and fifty G's. And maybe they rent it for twenty–twenty-five thousand. So that leaves a hundred and twenty-five G's to split between five schools, which is—" he paused for a moment, "Shee-it! I'd run dead last till they came offa some bread!"

He listened unconvinced and unimpressed to Able's tortured explanation of athletics in the colleges. "Man," he said admiringly, "them motherfuckers really got you believing that shit huh? It's like it was in Africa, they took them Bibles over to Africa and got them people believing the *word*, and starving to death! Damn! Motherfuckers talk a bird out a tree!"

Able grunted, going into the backstretch. Motherfuck this, motherfuck that, here mother, there mother, everywhere mother-mother. It was disgusting. Hairston's probably out right now raising a riot somewhere. Gonna be another Ras the Exhorter: "Kill the motherfuckers!"

The harsh grudging pain began to seep into his legs, his chest began to heave, and he was forced to run with his arms at his side to prevent a cramp later, when the pumping would be needed most. Able wished he had a monster like Dick Gregory to take over the unpleasant parts of running. The heavy, dank atmosphere and the smoke began to be oppressive, almost physically holding him back. He wished it was over; that he was on Amsterdam Avenue and One Hundred and Forty-fifth Street looking west across the Hudson, feeling cold fresh air chastise his ears and cleanse his lungs. Or looking east, down the arcade of lights, across Harlem to the Harlem River.

They held up the five sign; the half-mile was two minutes flat; he was on schedule. His panting increased, his hips felt sore. Able forced his mind away from the race, elsewhere, anywhere.

And then there was Brenda, the queen. If any other girl had been elected, he would be worried that something or someone would spoil the operation. But Brenda was a straight white chick. She was on the NAACP College Council with him, and she'd done her share of picket lines too. Of course, Cassandra didn't like her. Sandy said she was just too too . . . *too,* whatever that was. Besides, Sandy had hinted that she would like very much to be asked to the prom. Hint hell! Sandy was as coy as a karate chop. The election had gotten him off the hook with Sandy, and if he could swing something with Brenda, who was a real doll, all that was gravy. Sandy was good-looking too, but he was always faintly embarrassed by that *au naturel* hairdo, and the symbolisms attached to it. He often had the urge to tell Sandy to straighten her hair out in this respect.

It was the pitch that brought him back. The crowd had developed a sound-pattern—pitched, keyed, constant— which had become a background for his thinking. But there was a new element now, a new hysteria which meant something was happening. Able ached to turn around, to see, to assess the threat, but suppressed it. The only thing you saw when you turned around was another runner catching up. But he knew; it was the redhead.

"Watch the redhead," the coach said, "he has a strong kick finish. Watch the redhead."

Which was why he broke for the lead and kept it constant. Make the redhead use his kick to catch up, and the race would begin in the stretch. Faintly, very faintly, he could hear a different pattern, a different rhythm, closing rapidly. The gun nearly threw him off-stride, blasting his head and ears with a brassy ring: *Gun Lap!* Able lurched into the far turn, his mouth as dry as talcum on a baby's butt, his legs lurching, beginning to question orders.

The pattern grew louder behind him; God he was tired, caught up in the middle of the backstretch, started to pass, thought better of it, held back for the homestretch. It was the redhead, hair flaming, teeth bared, tired but confident. But the redhead wasn't supposed to be this close, not *this* fast. I *have* to have this race to make the papers, back and front, maybe even the centerfold. His own teeth bared with effort, and it was a while before he recognized the low gutteral panting in his ears as his own.

Able put his head down, cleared his throat and began to pump into the near turn. He forced himself up on his toes and began to sprint into the stretch. But the redhead was ahead of him—had passed him on the turn—and led by inches.

No! No! It was all wrong! Everything he had worked for going, as the words rose unbidden to his mind: *My God! Why hast Thou forsaken me?*

He threw himself into the sprint, like a physical catharsis, and he began to ascend. His mind retreated from the physical scene, observing his legs as if through a stroboscope. His eyes closed dreamily and he began to soar, aloft, away, aware vaguely of his feet touching the ground, of things passing, of kaleidoscopic impressions on his eyelids, of multicolor flashes of light—reds, greens, purples —of a pervasive blackness inviting him to tarry, rest a while. He lurched suddenly, feeling unsteady, and opened his eyes. The tape was in front of him and he lunged for it, unsure that he could ever run or walk such distance again. It broke on his chest; he began to slow down, legs running in a perfunctory manner as if they knew nothing else, while the pain, running last, demanded recognition.

Two men grabbed him, held him upright while he went through a series of dry heaves, puking what liquids were left in his bowels upward and down through his nose. Able released them, walking upright, praying that he wouldn't faint on national TV. His legs had joined the freedom movement, defying orders and quarreling among themselves as to which would collapse first. He made it to the winner's stand as the PA system clicked into action.

"The results of the Metropolitan mile run: Winner: David Giles, Empire College. Time: 3:54.6, a new college record. A new meet record. A new track record. A new national indoor record." Cheerleaders grabbed their megaphones and yelled, "F! 918!" And the crowd roared, "Able! Able!-Able!" He bowed, smiled, tottered over to the interview stand, and stayed upright—legs shuddering viciously—all the way to the dressing room. But he couldn't move thereafter for forty minutes.

Sandy didn't get uptown from the Garden until six thirty. Her subway ride was uneventful, except to turn on one white mother who was leering and working up courage to make a play. As a matter of fact, she had a thing going with the Eighth Avenue monster which she had christened Deux Ex Machina, and thoroughly enjoyed its metal mutterings as it negotiated the S-curve into One Hundred and Twenty-fifth Street. The street was alive with lights, white, colored, blinking, bubbling, and people hustled or hurried, depending on their financial capability at the time, to utilize the late hours of the Christmas rush. The merchants, in honor of the season, played jazz. They honored all seasons in the same manner, and the people responded out of irreverence, or necessity, or perhaps from a shrewd sense of reality. Sandy picked out parts of Ramsy Lewis's Christmas music, siphoned off the other noises real and musical, and studied it for a minute. It would be from George's, on Eighth Avenue and One Hundred and Twenty-sixth Street. She left the noise and the excitement regretfully, for these were people who could touch and be touched, and turned toward home and the projects. She paused outside of George's for a moment, listening to the sounds and the music. She began an impromptu Boogaloo, swaying in a gentle, sophisticated motion which was at once exciting and artistic. The postman, out for a late pickup, jumped over beside her, and began short deft rhythms of his own. They turned each other on, reading and anticipating moves, dancing more and more together without the slightest hint of a future.

Two little heartbreakers jumped into what was now an area, maintaining the movement with a few awkward deviations of their own. The music was clean and the beat pronounced; George's tweeters and woofers were exact, unlike the record joints up and down Eighth Avenue, with scratchy needles, bad records and worse fidelity. George's had cross-over networks and floating turntables, and the music could be enjoyed without blasting. The girls began to understand the movements, shaking and twisting as if unsure of proper nuances, yet intuitively clear that these tactics had future applications, and they drew speculative glances from the younger predators in the crowd.

A wino moved in to discover the reason for the street crowd. He watched carefully, as carefully as a full load would permit, and attempted a few steps of his own, putting his trousers in mortal peril. He stopped, shrugged, grinned in resignation and staggered down the street yelling, "Merry Christmas," at the top of his lungs.

Sandy did a half-pirouette, dancing beautifully with the crowd clapping—egging her on. Even George was clapping, clapping, smiling in the window, and she stopped, nauseated, feeling like a whore. His was the smile of the classic pimp, selling Negroes to Negroes, and making a profit on what, in fact, he never had in stock. She did a step or two more, turned it over to the kids, and walked sadly into the project.

"MAMA! MAMA! Did you see me on television? I waved at you," Sandy yelled, fending off the puppy who had launched an all-out assault on her toes.

"No, didn't see nothin' of you," Mama answered. "Saw that mile run, what's that boy's name? Able? He sure do run. Didn't he use ta come around once or twice?"

"Yeah, no more though. Hung up on this white girl at school."

Mama maintained a discreet silence while Sandy played briefly with the puppy, rose abruptly and went into the bedroom.

"That's 'cause he's just like you, Lancelot. Yes he is."

The puppy barked, perplexed. "That's 'cause he just doesn't know what to *do* with a white girl, so he *yaps* at her, runs around a couple of times, and *yaps* at her again."

Her watch said seven thirty and she hurried into her schedule in order to be ready on time. Mama had laid out all of her things. She bathed, toweled dry, struggled into her gown, seated herself daintily in front of the vanity. The mirror had long since been broken. Sandy had done it herself, in a fit of pique, and the two images were an eighth of an inch out of alignment.

"Let's see, just the base," to smooth out complexion and hide blemishes. Well, there weren't many blemishes, but it made the color rich and flat. "Then eyeshadow, just a touch," she cautioned herself; as an invitation, not a bomb. She stopped suddenly, "That pampered liberal bitch! The only thing she wants to liberate is a black do-hicky and everybody knows it *too!*" Again she stopped, with the eyebrow pencil in her hand, "She doesn't even want him! He's just something 'interesting,' a thrill." And again with the lipstick, "Her and that condescending smile. Huh! A good man and a cold glass of water would kill her!" She paused again, staring pensively into the mirror, "Maybe it's me, maybe my mouth is just a touch too wide, or too full. Maybe I should get a perm and one of those wild new hairdos." She grabbed a magazine on the bed and thumbed madly through the pages looking for hairdos. "Uh-uh, that's for old women, oops, sorry Mama," although Mama was nowhere near. "Maybe the *au naturel* bouffant and the arty earrings and the sandals are all a game, fooling yourself into being what isn't, or what should be, or what won't be. Jokes my mother taught me," she whispered, sniffing.

"Well, that's me," she sniffed again, "Cassandra Burke, Afro-American, everyb-body's playgirl, and stop crying, you dumb kid, you make me sick." The mirror with the crack could have been replaced long ago, but there were times like this when she felt a strange affinity; when she felt very close to the mirror image, to Sandy with the crack in her being.

The doorbell rang. Her date?

"Sandy!"

"Be right there," she screeched.

Brenda is gonna hurt Able," Sandy pronounced, definitely. "She's gonna swallow him whole like hominy grits. And she won't even bother to chew." She slipped into her pumps and dashed madly for the door, the puppy yapping wildly behind.

At that precise moment in the evening, which, from a bird's-eye point of view, was an elaborate synchronization of nothing, Brenda was waking from a short nap.

"Come," Mother repeated, "it's eight thirty already, eat something."

Brenda yawned deliciously. The potpourri on the headboard was delicately intoxicating, and she had a fleeting notion to stay there and never move. She threw herself out of bed, ran to her bathroom and doused her face in cold, cold water. Refreshed and alert, she threw on a bathrobe and went to the dining room, reminding herself to eat precious little or she would never, never, never fit into that dress. Dinner had already been served, so she pecked Daddy quickly on the cheek and took her seat.

"Wait a minute, wait a minute," Daddy glared at them furiously. "For the Crane family we need no formal introduction, but for the queen, a formal blessing."

"Oh Daddy, goodness!" she said blushing, pleased in spite of herself.

They bowed their heads. "BARUCH, ATOAH,

ADONAI, ELOHANJO, MELACH, HOLUM, HA-
MOTZE, LECHUM, MIN-A-OHORITZ."

They began to eat, Brenda picking gently at the food.
"So this boy on the TV, he's picking you up for the
prom?"

Brenda nodded, until she swallowed her food. "Wasn't
he great?" She didn't notice her parents exchange glances.

"Well," Daddy said, "I'd like to test his pulse right now.
His blood pressure must be . . ." he made several
thoughtful gestures in the air.

"Oh Daddy, why do you always have to be a—a doctor.
I mean, you're absolutely wild—"

"No, no, just curious. Athletes have very low blood
pressure. So he was elected by the student body to escort
the queen to the Christmas prom? Isn't that odd? Don't
most queens choose their own escorts? At Columbia, at—"

Brenda shrugged, "It's the tradition. I don't care, really,
Able's a great guy. Imagine if they'd elected a dud. I
mean, *really.*"

"Well, he looks like a nice boy. Looks intelligent."

"And the papers will be full of the whole prom, what
with the mayor and the governor, and Able's race and all.
It'll be on TV, maybe the late news."

Brenda had one last sip of wine, made her excuses, and
rushed up the stairs to begin dressing, sure that she heard
her telephone in the bedroom.

"Hello," she blurted into the phone, bouncing into the
bed like a renegade rabbit, "Oh, hi. All set?"—"Swell. Ya
get your gown, I mean the flame one?"—"Really? Swell,
yeah, he's picking me up here."—"Huh? What do you
mean, do they know? Sure they know."—"No, they didn't
say anything. What's to say, it was an open election."—
"Well, I don't know about marriage either, but we're talking about a date, a prom, remember?"—"Now, really
dear, do you actually believe all that stuff?" A long pause.
"But I thought you went to college to *learn,* I mean to stop
hereditary thinking and all that?" Another pause. "Well,
maybe learning, by firsthand experience as you put it, may
not be a bad idea at that." And she placed the phone
gently in the cradle. Brenda wondered briefly what it would
be like to have his black arms around her, and she flirted
with the idea of a *real* good-night kiss. She had chalked up
a certain coolness from the girls as jealousy, easily borne
and readily forgotten. Now, a more vindictive scheme
seemed to be taking form.

The phone rang again and she grabbed it before it stopped, barking "Hello" into the mouthpiece.

"Brenda, this is Professor Nadir."

"Oh, hi, Professor," she said relaxing.

"All set? You're due at ten fifteen sharp, you know."

"Uh-huh. Able's picking me up."

"Good. Oh, there may be a few minor changes, some things the press boys want."

"Like what?" suspiciously.

"Oh, I don't know, I didn't get the details."

"Like ringing in a different escort, maybe?"

"Goodness, no. At Empire College, in the middle of New York City? The sheer volume of investigations would ruin the school."

"I hope to tell you."

"No, these are minor technical adjustments, so I understand. They may want you to pose for ten pictures instead of five, something like that."

"Oh."

"Well, we'll see you in—an hour?"

"OK, Professor, 'bye now."

She met him at the door, noting the wan smile and the blank face of the indescribably tired.

"Hi."

"Hi. You look great."

"Thank you, sir." She did a small curtsy. "The race was fabulous. Come; Daddy wants to meet you."

He went through the amenities as rapidly as possible, thinking intently about the ceremonies close at hand. Brenda was pleased with his formal wear. The tux was not a custom fit, but would do very well for his needs. She was surprised. They passed a couple on the street, friends of the family, and Brenda noted how their eyes barely acknowledged her, sliced Able to pieces and bore dead ahead. Suddenly she felt unclean, like a cockroach crawling from the woodwork and fouling the scenery. A chill not completely from the lake in Central Park tore at her bosom, making her happy to get inside the still-warm car.

It was a short trip to the park, the first of its kind in the East. Able kept thinking of what he would do, what he would say to the mayor and to the governor. The primary attention would be toward the queen, but as her escort, and with his own rep, he would not be ignored.

He parked the car easily, jumped out and went around to open the door for the queen. A TV cameraman and announcer moved in to cover the action.

"And the queen has arrived. The Queen *has* arrived. Here is this year's queen of the Christmas prom who will assist in the opening of this new educational park, Miss Brenda Crane—"

"Able? Able!"

"Oh, hi, Professor Nadir."

"Come over here a minute, there's a good fella."

"Well I don't know, I have—"

"This will just take a minute. There've been some changes in the schedule. Somebody else will escort Brenda for the opening ceremonies. Of course, you'll be the escort for the rest of the prom; it's just for the ceremonies."

"Huh?"

"Well, the TV people felt your relationship was a little too strong for home consumption. It would have knocked out the coverage, and it would've been mighty unfair to Brenda; I'm sure you understand. Now I want you to be bigger than this thing . . ."

Able reeled away from the advisor, confused and unclear as to what happened. He looked over to the ceremonial table. Brenda was smiling that way and smiling another, and there was someone with her, some redhead he had never seen before, talking earnestly to the mayor. "God?" he whispered.

He saw the TV camera with its great zoom lens for the first time as an enemy, as a stellar goliath of the great God Technos. "God?" he murmured, terrified.

He turned toward the students, spotting Sandy in the crowd, hoping that there was some kind of mistake, but Sandy was dancing with her tall, dark stranger. Dancing, dancing, distant.

The scene wobbled and danced before his eyes, the atmosphere crystalizing into a malignant sfumato. He lurched through the dancers, spinning and whirling in cohesive patterns of regimented motion until he stopped, furious, heaving a shoe at the TV cameras, screaming, "God! Motherfucker, where you at?"

Rough Diamond
or
Whatever Became Of
Good Old Gunga Din?

by John Oliver Killens

I'M SO MILITANT I'M SCARED SHITLESS OF MY
OWN SELF. RIGHT?

I'm so angry I sleep with my fists balled up. Check that
out, Buster.

Did you ever smell a Harlem bedbug after you'd cruelly
crushed him between your thumbnails? After the bloated
bugger had sucked your body dry? I'm so bitter ice cream in
my mouth taste like the smell of bedbugs, dead and
bloody on the warpath.

But for all that, I'm an all-around all-American boy.
Dig?

I mean I got the same stars in my eyes that any other
all-around all-American boy would have. I mean, I dreamt
the same mother-loving workingclass bourgeois dreams
that any other clean-cut all-American boy would dream.
Got it? I'm tall, dark, handsome, college-football type—
You dig? The only difference is: I'm colored. Know what
I mean? I'm black, tan Yank, I'm Negro, sepia fella—
Afro. Which means my dreams are always filmed realisti-
cally in black and white.

169

Dig—I'm a low-key dreamer with high aspirations. And I told myself, when I was a little biddy old baby sitting on my Mama's knee: "Boy," I said, "I know you'll have to work harder, you'll have to be sharper, smarter, quicker, but you'll make it just the same." I mean, I knew I would make it, just as sure as Willie Mays and Bill Russell and Jackie Robinson made it? Understand? Would you believe Harry Belafonte? And like I made it, sugar-pie. You can just like bet your two sweet tits I did. I made it big, baby, *BIG!* With a capital G! You can just bet your sweet ripe titties! You think Poitier is big?

I'm a writer, I mean, a novelist. Right? I mean I put down the kind of stuff that rips your phallic string aloose. I mean tear your natural chit'lings out, old faggot. Make you put a puddle in your panties. I write against racial prejudice. Right? At the same time, I don't blame the white man for all our mama-flipping woes. I'm much too bitter for that kind of unsophisticated shit. I mean, like there's some good niggers and some worthless ones. Right? I mean I don't go for those racist writers who seem to think that just because a man's skin is white his heart necessarily has to be black. Or vice versa. Jim Crow or Crow-Jim, I don't go for that racist crap at all. And I'm the kind of bitter nigger white folks like to listen to. Just check that out. And behind all that I'm universal.

As you may have gathered by now, I don't go for that hi-falutin' kind of language when I write. I mean I know all the big words, sweetie, I helped Webbie put the book together, old fag, but I prefer to write in the language of the people. I mean you've heard of folk singers. Check, I'm a folk writer. I mean I write with one foot on the black folk's back. Heh-heh-heh. I mean, in their lives I always keep my feet. I'm from the people, for the people, of the people, by the people, with the people, to the people— And so on.

Well enough of these personal irrelevancies. As you have guessed by now I am a very modest, extremely sensitive, self-effacing fellow. Shy, retiring and all that jazz. But to hell with that. To make a long story short, I won the National Book Award for fiction in 1964, for a book I wrote about Harlem. I am the only Negro to ever win the National Book Award. Oh yes, of course, there was, of course, ahem, Ellison, back there somewhere in the fifties. But would you call him a Negro? An invisible man? I'm visible, booby. Ask them bunnies at the Playboy Club. Well, anyhow, I won the damn thing. Like I say, it was a

book about Harlem, and it showed that jungle in all of its
true savagery and degradation. I mean I didn't hold nothing back, baby boy. I mean, in my book, cats all over the
place were smoking pot, horsing around, pimping, whor-
ing, nodding, I mean mainlining, sweetie pie. And kicking
their grandmothers in the ass, banging their baby sisters by
the numbers and peeping through the keyhole at their
mamas and daddies in the nightly hump. I mean, all kind
of action. He-ing and she-ing, she-ing and she-ing, he-ing
and he-ing and me-ing and me-ing. I mean, the natural
jungle, sweetie. I mean, I went Ellison one better, baby,
ten times better. The father of the hero of my book had
knocked up his wife, his mother, his three daughters, all in
the same damn month. The last of the goddamn baby-
makers. I laid it on so thick and hard, I believed it my
own self. I put it down so hard I'm scared to go to Harlem. I ain't been up there since the book came out. And I
wasn't ever scared to go to Harlem before my book came
out. I mean, the reviews of my book were so damn good, I
was conned into reading it my own damn self. I mean I
read the whole book through. Which is a thing a writer
should never be trapped into doing. A word of advice to
the young aspiring: Never read your own books. Never
take what you write seriously, even though you are a serious writer. Know what I mean?

I mean, imagine me, the boy wonder, the kid himself,
the intellectual hood in person, afraid to go uptown to get
a lousy haircut! How do you like them big ripe titties?
And, baby boy, what a hangup! Cause colored barber
shops downtown are as scarce as fourteen-year-old downtown virgins. Man! How I miss my Harlem barber! My
hair is so long cats have started whistling at me.

But I wrote a book, sweetie pie, even if I don't never
write another one. I wrote one one time. I mean, I made
cats like Hughes, Brown, Baldwin, Mitchell, Miller, Jones,
Clarke, Fair, Bennett, Kelley, Ellison look like apologizers
for the system. In my novel I made the colored city coun-
cilman a stone faggot that preyed upon poor little innocent
white boys who came up to the jungle just for a little old
sport. My hero raped his grandma on his mother's side.
Try to cap that. I had preachers hustling numbers and
running whorehouses. I had a saintly lady evangelist selling poontang. I was a living ass, and I was swinging.
When my novel first came out, all the rich important pad-
dies from downtown came uptown looking for me. But
they couldn't find me, cause I was already downtown liv-

ing in the Village. My publisher told me if I was going to be a Negro leader who had roots in the people like all the reviewers said I had my roots, I'd better get my fat black ass back uptown in a hurry. Else my image would be distorted. I told him like it was; I was scared to go uptown. Some of them jealous lumpen-bourgeois niggers might catch me up there and cut my throat. He told me I'd better rent a pad uptown in my name then. And that's exactly what I did.

I mean, the paddy boys really dug me. And that's where it's at, baby. Who're you kidding? Check, I was on Open End, Back End, Front End, Open Mind, Night Life, Hot Seat and all that other shit. Me and them television people were as tight as baby sister's twattie. I got invitations to speak about Harlem to all the universities, I mean, especially those in the North and particularly them throughout the South. Are you ready? I gave the commencement address at the University of Ole Miss. I was the angriest black writer to ever put a sentence together. In my speech at Ole Miss, dig, I attacked Adam Powell, Kenneth Clark, Fred Douglass, Louis Lomax, James Baldwin, LeRoi Jones and all those other Harlem phony faggots who make their reputations on the black backs of the people. Martin Luther King, Belafonte, Richard Gregory, Davis, Dee and Poitier, Roy Wilkins, James Farmer and Foreman, Young Whitney, Floyd McKissick, and Stokely Carmichael. Every living even if he wasn't swinging. I'm a militant. Good Lord! I'm frightful to my ownself. I'm so damn mean, I'm scared to face my own self. That's how come I stopped shaving. Check that out, you mother-bugger.

I mean, I'm not like most of these so-called black writers who confine their gunfire to attacking Negro leadership only. Negative, baby. I mean I exposed the big white Negro leaders too. I mean, the Good Lord made them and Mother do not pick them. Dig it. The bigger they are the harder they fall, I mean, on their natural tookus. Check, I didn't wait till I got back above the Mason-Dixie. You ready? I told that University of Ole Miss audience that Kennedy and Johnson had no understanding of the Southern situation. I mean, I was boss. I told them Kennedy was a phony. Yeah? I told them Johnson was a bigger phony. I told them M. L. King was a phony. Malcolm X and McKissick and Carmichael phonies! They gave me a standing ovation. I mean, in Mississippi, sweetie pie. Sippi, baby! Missi-goddamn-sippi! Mississippi goddamn! Are you ready, mother-lovers? The biggest paper in Mississippi wrote me up, I mean, *BIG!* They said I was the second coming of Booker Taliaferro Washington! Check, I'm a militant, pretty pussy. You better b'lieve me when I say so. I kick asses and take names.

The *London Times* did a story on me before anybody over there had read anything I ever wrote or ever heard about me. I had an American book-club contract and a paperback and a moving picture contract before I turned my manuscript in. Everybody loved me, sweet pussy. A man from one of the big national American magazines, really big, I mean the truly biggest, baby, had orders to follow me everywhere I went for a solid month. I mean uptown, downtown, eastside, westside, all around the frigging metropolis. To my lectures, to my publishers, to my agents. He even wanted to get into the bed with me and listen to me talking in my sleep. This kook followed me everywhere. I mean, even to places where nobody goes with me but me. I mean I got my doubts about the cat. I mean, following me to the onjay could not possibly be in the *line* of duty, I don't care what that little limp-wristed motherfucker says.

I was the first person ever to be interviewed by Red Badkins on that new teevee program, Folks to Folks. I built that program like the Babe built Yankee Stadium. You know, it's a real highbrow interview bit. Right? They brought all that television shit and set it up right there in my crib. It looked like there were about a hundred of them teevee people running around like cockroaches and fumbling about all over the place. Measuring this and setting up that. It took them half a day to get ready. One of them cats even measured my backside—for size, baby.

I said to one of the paddy sound men, I said, sarcastically, "This isn't going to be a spectacular, is it, sweet pussy? I mean, all this running around and wringing and twisting just to interview little old me?"

He giggled and bounced around and lisped, "Baby, *you are* spectacular. You big, tall, dark and handsome beastie, everything you do is spectacular." And the Oedipus Complexer pinched my hiney. I started to put him out of his misery.

At long damn last the famous interview began. Right off Red Badkins asked me what I thought of the other Negro writers. I told him like it was, sugarpie. "All of them stink on ice. None of them live in Harlem."

"Mr. Bill Yardbird, why do you use the word 'nigger' so

freely? In your book and in interviews, I mean, even when the author is speaking and not the characters."

I said, "Because I'm a free nigger. That's how come I use nigger freely."

That tore him up, but after a moment, he came back with: "But, sir, the word has negative connotations. It's derogatory to your people."

I came back, shooting from the hip, as per usual. "Red, baby, I have an original saying of mine. Sticks and stones may break my bones, but words will never do me in. And you can quote me on it."

"Very original indeed," he said. "I remember a variation of that one from my own childhood some thirty years ago."

"It just shows to go you," I shot back at him, "everything's been said before, even though you never heard it."

That stumped the clever bastard.

Then he asked me, "What do you think of Langston Hughes?"

I said, "He stinks on ice. He's not from Harlem."

Dig, Badkins is the sneaky kind of interviewer. All queers are sneaky bitches. Not that I'm saying he's definitely a fag—but—he said, "My understanding, Mr. Bill Yardbird, is that Mr. Hughes has lived in Harlem ever since he came to live in New York many many years ago."

See what I mean? Red's the kind of interviewer you got to keep your eye on every minute. Can't be trusted. White liberal. Probably Jewish, but you wouldn't guess it in a million years. I mean, I got more of a New York Jewish accent than he's got. He's in the Harvard bag. Kennedy New England style.

He tried to maneuver me into a corner so he could whale away at me, but I always have had clever footwork. I sidestepped that mother and counterpunched him— Chume! Chume! I said, "Well, Langston Hughes sure wasn't *born* in Harlem. *I* was born here. That's what I'm talking about."

He said, "But Mr. Baldwin, Mr. Mitchell and Dr. Clark and Mr. Belafonte were born in Harlem." See how sly the mother-buggers are?

But don't you worry, I capped the tricky bastard. I said, "But they don't live in Harlem any more. They escaped. They don't talk the people's language. I'm—"

That's another thing. They all have bad manners. The bugger cut me off. "You don't live there any more either, Mr. Yardbird."

"Don't you think I lived there long enough?" I told him, staring him straight into his baby blue eyes. "What do you people want to do? Keep us black folks in the ghetto all our lives? I thought you had a reputation of being a liberal." I put him on the defensive. Backed him into a corner. One-two-Chume! Chume! I whaled away. "I'm trying to burn the ghetto down," I said. "And you trying to keep me in it." I said, "I'm a man of the people, working class, bad nigger type, new-type bad nigger. My roots are rooted in the poor disinherited people, the speechless black masses. That's where my soul is, with the poor black people, may their tribes increase. I am them and they are me. Chitt'lings and pig knuckles and James Brown and black-eyed peas and Little Richard and hominy grits. That's me, baby, all the motherloving way."

That shook old Goldberg up. He said, "Very well put, and very interesting indeed, coming from a man wearing a two-hundred-dollar silk suit."

"It's imported mohair," I capped the mother. "And it costs two hundred and fifty dollars. And another thing, that's *my* Harlem up there, and I can wear anything I want to up there. What you folks want me to wear—sackcloth? And I don't buy my stuff from your people uptown either. I do my shopping on Fifth Avenue."

"My people?" he asked. "I don't have any relatives uptown."

I had the mother-bugger on the ropes now and I moved in for the kill. "The people up there love me and don't care what kind of suit I have on. They know I'm on their side. That damn half-white bourgeois preacher up there'd better watch out too, because there is a mandate up there to me from the black masses, and I might just one day answer the call to serve them. I've been resisting, but one day I might just let myself be drafted."

"You mean into the Army of the United States? Very admirable sentiments indeed."

"Heh-heh-heh-heh. I meant, drafted to run for the Congress of these United States. The people are saying in one loud strong voice: 'WE WANT YARDBIRD! WE WANT YARDBIRD!' How can I continue to deny them?"

The mother-bugger came off the ropes with: "But sir, isn't it true that you were making a speech on the corner of a Hundred and Twenty-fifth Street and Seventh Avenue a couple of weeks ago, and people threw things at you and chased you off the platform? You barely escaped with your very life?"

The bugger almost made me lose my cool. "Them weren't the people, bitch! They were nothing but a bunch of nobodies, a gang of poor-assed hoodlums. Junkies, hustlers, whores and whatnot."

"But, sir, Mr. Bill Yardbird, I thought the nobodies are precisely the people for whom you are the spokesman. I thought you were the personification of the Harlem nobodies, as you call them, so prosaically."

"I am *somebody,* baby. You'd better believe me when I say so. Ask any-damn-body if I ain't somebody."

That bugger's mother changed the subject again. They are some sly ones, sweetie. "You were chased off the streets of Harlem though, were you not?"

"It was a frame-up, mother. A bunch of Harlem middle-class niggers—"

"But, sir, I thought you said it was the nobodies, the, ahem, poor-assed hoodlums—"

"That's what I mean. Some poor-assed middle-class hoodlums up there plotting against the one-and-only. I got just as much right to be in charge of that graft up there as any-goddamn-body else. I'm as honorable a thief as any of them politicians up there. Elect me to office and I would systematize the graft. Everybody'd get a fair shake. But they agitated the people, they turned the beautiful honest noble unsuspecting masses against me."

He changed the subject again. "How do you react, Mr. Yardbird, to the very friendly critics who say that what they like about your novel is the pure and unadulterated animal spirit they find on every page. Nobody trying to be anything but what they are. The pure sweet beautiful black primitive animistic savagery of the jungle. No rancor, no bitterness, just pure subjective objectivity."

"That's right. We young niggers were pure and unadulterated hoodlums. We were happy nodding junky funky niggers. We weren't like our disgruntled maladjusted parents. We weren't trying to be nothing but niggers. That was the secret of our success. Give us some junk and some poontang or a nice fat boy and we could make it. We didn't study about no demonstrating and all that stupid unhip jazz."

He finally gave up. "Thank you very much, Mr. Yardbird, for this most enlightening interview. You are indeed a diamond in the rough. No middle-class fuzziness in your background. You are the real thing, the noble savage, here and now, and no two ways about it."

That was one of the best interviews I ever had. And, man, I really got some exposure that first month when my book came out. Talk about exposure! I mean, they exposed me twice on CBS, thrice on NBC, four times on ABC and all the time on NET. I mean I really was exposed good and proper those first few weeks. And everybody gave me good reviews excepting them handkerchief-head bourgeois colored publications. One of the interviewers asked me about it.

It was on CBS. He asked me: "Isn't it odd, Mr. Yardbird, that you got such rave reviews in the white press and such bad reviews in the Negro press? How do you account for that, sir?"

"No mystery about it. The white press knows what Harlem is all about. I mean, they can be objective—I mean—"

"But how can you say the white press knows, and the Negro press doesn't know? I mean, the Negro press is made up of Negroes, and they have called you, universally, a fraud, a phony, a rat fink, an illiterate. They say you gave a distorted image of the black community. They say you magnified the image the white man already had of Harlem—that it's a jungle, etcetera and so on."

"Them Uncle Toms—"

"They say *you're* the Uncle Tom, sir. Right here in this one here. I quote. 'Mr. Yardbird is a Gunga Din, all dressed up as an authentic diamond in the rough. We do not know where the white folks got him. We do not know from behind what white rock he crawled, but we do wish he would crawl back in a hurry. He has maligned the entire black community. We predict that white folks will make of him a new black leader. We predict for him all manner of television exposure and celebrity, and press interviews, the entire works, best-seller, book clubs, etcetera, etcetera, ad infinitum, ad nauseam. But the people of our community are getting weary of being described as jungle inhabitants, savages, beasts and the like, and it doesn't digest more easily when it is spewed from the mouth of a new black Messiah chosen by the white man, which is probably why Mr. Yardbird is seldom seen in this part of America. Harlem, that is. Mr. Yardbird often speaks of "house niggers" and "field niggers," but it is a peculiar thing how rapidly he made the transition from one class to the other!' Do you want to make a comment on this, sir?"

"No comment. They're just jealous niggers, and they're angry with me, because I refuse to prettify the place.

They're jealous because I'm making more money than them. They're angry because important white people listen to me more than they do to them. Them bourgeois niggers want me to hide the truth about the dialectics of the situation. But the truth is, wherever you find a group of niggers living together by themselves, it's a damn jungle pure and simple."

The interviewer cleared his throat. "Now, this one—a very reputable Negro publication, I must say. 'Mr. Yardbird speaks and writes as if ninety-nine percent of the hundreds of thousands of good people of Harlem are whores, hopheads and junkies. If this is true, will he kindly inform us, who are the people who keep all the thousands of stores and shops in business and the funeral parlors, and who maintains and sustains the hundreds of churches and lodges? Surely not the whores and the hopheads. Somebody up here must be putting in a honest day's work!' Would you care to comment on this, Mr. Yardbird?"

"I'd be delighted to. My comment is simply that, I mean, you know, it's a very tricky question and difficult to characterize to any definitive degree without the broader implications being taken into question."

He stared at me unbelievingly.

"That is my comment, sir." I stared back at the pecker-wood.

After I won the National Book Award and made my little acception speech—four hours long (it was the talk of the town for months), I was invited to a country which shall be nameless, situated as it is behind the Iron Curtain. The State Department told me they thought it would be a good idea for an angry militant writer like me to attend the conference behind the curtain. Are you ready? One of those State Department men, as busy as he was, and you know those cats stay busy, commuting as they do between Washington and Vietnam and Berlin and all those other places where we are keeping the torch of freedom burning; one of them cats dropped everything and made it up to the city just to see little old insignificant me. He said the big people in the government were very pleased and proud of me and my book the way I exposed the savagery of the jungle that was Harlem. I told him I couldn't care less what the government thought. "I'm a militant, I'm a man of the people, and I tell it like it is. And I don't care what that Georgia Baptist preacher from Montgomery thinks about me either."

We were sitting in the cocktail lounge of the Tudor

Hotel on East Forty-second Street. He stared at me with open admiration out of those pretty blue eyes of his. I thought he was going to try to kiss me any minute. He told me there were friends in high places in the government who agreed with my view of Harlem in its entirety. They agreed it was a jungle. And they were going to see that the government appropriated millions to civilize it.

"Civilize it!" I said indignantly, after my fifth martini. I believe he was trying to get me plastered. "Civilize it?"

He was flustered. His eyes were crossing now, and he had trouble keeping me in focus. He said, "What I mean is—sir—we thought—that is—"

"Civilize it!" I raged on. "Burn the mother-bugger down!"

He said, "Our sentiments exactly. Burn the mother-bugger down." He wasn't a bad paddy, when you come to think about it. Maybe a little limp-wristed, but what the hell? He said, "My department is very proud that you were invited to the conference. We want you to go and when you get there, we want you to tell it like it is!" He was a little shaky by now. Actually he was a *big* shaky.

I think he was trying to get me drunk and he got drunk instead. I mean, that's one thing, I can hold my licker. "We want you to represent the Free World, sweetie," he said, and I believe the switch-hitter winked at me.

But anyhow, I went to the conference. And it was something else. It was too much! I mean, too much!

First, because of an important teevee commitment in the States, I was two days late getting to the conference. They had come out to the airport to meet me every time a plane came in—for days. Banners waving, flowers strewed along the way and all that shit. But by the time I got there, there was no one there to meet me. Right? And nobody at the airport knew where the conference was, nor had they even heard about it. Can you imagine? I mean, those foreign cats out at the airport were so square they didn't even recognize me. Me! Big—black—handsome—me! Very tall and very dark and very handsome. Are you ready, I believe one of those suckers out there at the airport called me Louis Armstrong! Or Sammy Davis Jr.! Or Ralph Bunche! Would you believe—Sonny Liston! And another thing, hardly any of them could speak English. Well anyhow, after a few phone calls into the Writers Union, they finally sent someone out to the airport, sent a chauffeur and an interpreter for me. The interpreter was not my type. Tall, blond, blue-eyed, svelte, a real Nordictype, sexpot, of the Marxian persuasion yet. All the other writers from the other countries were jealous of her. At all the parties they were drawn toward me like I was some kind of a magnet or something. And Elsa would always be there right by my side. She spoke perfect English and she could interpret her sweet ass off. Her bust was well stocked with two enormous knockers, which would make any burlesque queen drool with envy, and she was plumpish at the backside, slim and round and fully stacked. I heard one of the British writers say of her: "It is undoubtedly jelly, since jam does not vibrate tremulously in quite that manner." In a word, she was zaftig. But she was not my type. But she was a great translator, a magnificent interpreter, as the other cats gathered at my side, like June bugs around a watermelon rind. Check, they threw questions at me going and coming, and with her translating on the spot, I caught them like Willie Mays and Bobby Hayes put together with Bobby Mitchell. But she was not my style, because I do not go for blonds. Check, I dig my chicks black and kinky-haired and double-breasted.

After the conference ended I was invited to spend another couple of weeks in the country, as an official guest of the government. They took me everywhere, and everywhere they took me she went with me as my guide. They let me look at everything. Collective farms, defense plants, workers rest homes, automotive plants, universities, parliament, football games, the whole megillah. She talked with me about the "Negro question in that cruel capitalist country known as the USA." She wept bitter tears about the plight of the poor black folks way down in Mississippi. She was sensitive was what.

My last evening in the country we went to a concert, the whole thing done in their native language. Are you ready? Not a word of English in the lyrics or the music. But near the end of the concert, the conductor turned to the audience and told them that in their midst this evening was a distinguished artist, who came to them from the wilds of Harlem in the USA (obviously he had read my book), but who had survived his ordeal as a child in the jungle and had emerged from the dung heap of capitalist rubbish to become one of the great writers of his time and of any time. I stood up (brimming over with humility) and they all cheered me and gave me a standing ovation.

Then the conductor dedicated the next number to me. In English. You ready? "Way Down Upon the Swanee

Mammy-Hunching River." See if you can top that, mother's little bugger!

They're singing Swanee River, check, and the whole audience is weeping and sniffling like grandmama has just booted the bucket, dig? And I'm sitting there like a knot on Dick's dog, and I'm ready to tear my ass with laughter. Even Elsa-baby had her handkerchief out. She put her hand out toward me and took my hand in hers. "You poor poor dear! You poor poor darling dear!" That kind of got by me too. Poor poor dear! Me! And I'm one of the richest niggers in the whole United States. I felt like telling her to bugger off, but I restrained myself. I let her continue to hold my hand all through that swampy Swanee River.

I spent four weeks in all in that country behind the curtain which shall be nameless, the country, that is, and Elsa-baby went everywhere with me, and chattered like a hustler selling goodies at a girlie show. But all during that time, everything was always on the up-and-up with us. Are you ready? She never made a solitary pass at me. I'll say this for them chicks behind the curtain—they are the most bourgeois-puritanical women I have ever come across. I mean, I said to myself, to her, I mean, but silently: "You are a beautiful, frigid, sexless sexpot." Notwithstanding, it did not make my business bad, since, being a blue-eyed, blond, she didn't appeal to me at all anyhow. Not in a sexual way. Never! Ever. Dig it!

That last night, after the concert, she was real tore up. I mean, she never got over that swampy river bit. She went up to my hotel suite with me to see that everything was in order, my suitcases packed and papers in order and things like that. It was the first time she had been up to my rooms since she had seen me checked in that very first day of my arrival. Right? She had always left me in the lobby and wakened me with a phone call every morning. This time she went up with me, and she saw to it that I was packed and she called the desk and arranged for them to pick up my baggage the next morning. She did this and that and the other. And then she ordered cognac, and we drank to a safe journey for me, as I would make my way back to the States. I planned to stop a couple of days in Copenhagen and then to Paris for a week, then to Rome for a couple of days, then to London for another week, and then—home to Harlem. On University Place. In the Village.

She stared at me and she must have thought of that mo-

ment at the concert. Her eyes begin to fill, and she spoke
to me in a trembling voice. "It is very hard, comrade, to
see you go back to that cruel capitalist country and to that
Harlem jungle."

I told her, "I don't do so bad, comrade. I have raised
myself up by my bootstraps and when I get back home
I'm going to raise my people to my level. And actually, I
myself live in a pretty swanky hotel downtown in Green-
wich Village."

She wiped her eyes, and her tone became hardened and
businesslike, as I had been accustomed to it being during
the month that I had known her. "This is no time for
cheap bourgeois sentimentality, comrade. It is time to take
stock. How has your trip been in our happy country?
Have you enjoyed our socialist hospitality? A little different from the old Southern hospitality. Yes?"

I said, "Yes, quite a difference."

She took a note-pad from her pocketbook. She was all
business now. She said, "Tell me of your reaction to these
four weeks in our socialist fatherland."

I stared at the beautiful blond one now, her face glow-
ing with a Marxian anticipation. Dig, she was that cock-
sure of herself. And this was the clincher. This was when
baby boy was supposed to sing for his supper. This was
why she had come up to my room. I'm not going to tell a
lie—she was a gorgeous wench, built like a brick outhouse
during the days of the Great Depression when bricks were
cheap and in abundance. And that socialist perfume was a
natural gas. And she knew how to wear it, baby. Seduc-
tion. Make a preacher put his Bible down. Make a faggot
move out of the YMCA. But for me, she was as cold as
fish on Fulton Street in the dead of winter. She was beauty
gone to waste. Cause she was not my type. But, like it had
been a long long time. Right?

I took another drink. I looked up at the ceiling and
back into her face again. She was ready with her pencil. It
was a very serious moment. She had her legs crossed and
she was as leggy a chick as I had glimpsed in my entire
stay in her glorious socialist fatherland. Seated, her dress
had slid to about an inch or two above her knees. She
stared at me and self-consciously pulled her dress down to
her knees, as if I had been staring at those precious knees
of hers, which were not bad to look at. Right? But she
need not have worried, because, like I said before, she was
definitely not my type. Check, but it had been a long long
time.

She cleared her throat. "Back to the subject, comrade. What are your impressions of us? Did we discriminate against you? Were we free and open? Did we withhold anything at all from you? I mean, from your eyesight. Yes?" She was warm and friendly, but she was all business. I'll say that much for her.

I began. "Well I certainly have had one of the most interesting experiences of all my life. I grant you that. I went everywhere I wanted to go; saw most of what I wanted to see. Everybody was cordial toward me. Like I talked to anybody I wanted to talk with. It's been a wonderful month, and I shall take home countless memories which will be among my souvenirs for life." I paused, to let her catch her breath, and I breathed freely, easily.

She said, "Yes, comrade. Please to continue." She was ever prim and proper—was this Marxist hunk of pulchritude. And she damn sure did smell good.

I cleared my scratchy throat and reached for another shot of cognac and wet my whistle one more time. "The women," I said, "are certainly different from the ones we are accustomed to back in the capitalist world."

She wrote furiously. Pimples of sweat above her socialist ruby-red lips now. She looked up from her notebook. "Yes?" Did I detect excitement in her voice, which was usually so businesslike? No, I didn't. Dammit!

"The socialist women of your country appear to be of a stock that comes very close to being of a bourgeois, Calvinistic, puritanical persuasion."

She looked up. She said, "Yes." Still prim and proper.

A kind of tiredness crept into my voice. "But a man is a man for all that bee-ess," I said. "And like in the culture I come from, a man is not complete without a woman by his side. You dig? I mean, you do understand?"

"Oh yes, comrade. And I have been by your side every waking moment since I met you at the airport. No?" Her wide eyes went back to her notebook and she scribbled away like any minute writing was going out of style forever.

"Affirmative," I said. "You have been constantly by my side. No two ways about it." Then I cleared my throat again, and my voice dropped a couple of octaves and sounded even wearier than I had ever heard it. I almost couldn't recognize my own voice. "I'm a very virile man. I like women. I mean, I'm known as a fighter for the rights of women. I am not what you would call a doctrinaire Marxist, I mean, I'm not a student of dialectical materialism. I don't dig that jazz, but I do believe that a unity of opposites is always necessary to produce a dialectical progression of the human race. Right? I mean like men and women must get together in any healthy situation. Right? This is stated purely from a historical perspective. Check." I paused. She didn't look up this time. She just kept writing, like the law was chasing her down a Hundred and Twenty-Fifth Street.

I continued. "Well, like it's been four long weeks, and I'm a man dedicated to the proposition of dialectical progression—I mean—men and women belong together— There should be no discrimination—segregation—What I mean is—togetherness should always be the goal—"

Suddenly she looked up into my face, and she erupted with laughter. I mean, she cracked up, disassembled. It was the first time she had laughed like that in four whole weeks. Like I had begun to think of her as the laughless one. She laughed, she laughed, she laughed and laughed.

I stared at her getting my "nigger" up and getting very warm around the neckbone. I mean, what the hell was so suddenly, I mean so everlastingly hilarious?

She said, "Comrade—" She started to laugh again. And then—"Comrade, are you—" Then more laughter. She wiped the laughing tears from her eyes. I was ready to go upside her head.

Finally she controlled herself. She said, "Comrade, are you trying to tell me you want to sleep with me?"

Behind her coming on like that, I mumbled something that sounded like it could have possibly been—"Yes— maybe—I mean—Like what the hell do you think I mean? I ain't whistling Swanee River."

She said, "There is no problem, comrade." And in all my life I never saw a chick get loose from her clothes as quickly as did darling Elsatanya. Notwithstanding, she was very prim and proper, even while disrobing. Dignity personified.

The Harlem Teacher

by Lorraine Freeman

She was late again. But she didn't care. Miss Jane Bottles hated teaching school in Harlem. "Oh, how I detest these people," she muttered to herself as she marched the three blocks from the subway to the school. She walked with her head down, deliberately ignoring the dark faces that surged past her. A shudder passed through her body when she came to the last hideous block just before the school. This was the street she hated the most. She felt the ugliness and the sordidness of the entire ghetto rushing up to claim her.

Miss Bottles had to pass the same jumping beer tavern every day. With the mean-looking men hanging outside. They seem to slouch in the shadows of the buildings. The smell of stale urine and rotting garbage penetrated the early morning air. Suddenly the doors of the bar swung open and flooded the sidewalk with wailing music. One of the young ones who had just come out of the bar stopped to watch her. Faint amusement on his face. He turned to his buddy and said something to him. They both laughed. "Hey lady, you can take your mask off now. Halloween is over." They went down the street laughing together. Others began to notice her and joined in the laughter. Her clawlike hands tightened on her pocketbook and gloves to escape their jeering faces.

Pausing for a moment in the doorway of her class, Miss

Jane Bottles surveyed the gray filmed-over room in which she was sentenced to spend another day. The bland faces of the children turned indifferently toward her. They were oddly alike. They talked and laughed flatly; they moved woodenly. She felt herself being drawn by an invisible vortex into the sunless room. Her buttocks tensed and relaxed as she eased herself under the scarred desk.

"Now the first thing," said Miss Bottles, glancing toward the center of the room without really seeing the faces of the children, "is to make sure that everyone is present." She opened the roll-call book and quickly made little marks next to each name. Her mind began to leap forward to the hours after school. Soon she would be on the subway riding away from this nightmarish land to the safety of downtown. Tonight she would go shopping; mingling blissfully among the crowds of another world. Such thoughts only made returning to her present more unbearable.

"Good," she lied, without looking up, "everyone is here today. Now children, today let us continue reading about Spots and his little friends. You children just love Spots, don't you?" They watched her out of their dead, dull eyes. Miss Bottles picked up a worn book and began to read: SPOTS IS A DOG. HE IS A GOOD DOG. HE IS THE DOG OF DICK AND JANE.

Her singsongy voice caressed the air as she glanced fondly into the reflecting vacuum of the room. She smiled softly to herself and felt a warm cozy feeling easing upward from the pit of her stomach.

"Why do we always have to listen to you read Spots every day?" came a voice from across the room, "while other second-grade classes do arithmetic and work on projects?" Miss Bottles was irritated at the interruption. The voice belonged to the sharp-faced little Linda Jane, a dark-skinned, plump child with tiny parts in her hair. Miss Bottles continued reading: SPOTS LIKES TO RUN. SPOTS LIKES TO PLAY. SPOTS—

"My big sister says that you're only teaching in this school because you're not good enough to teach anywhere else." The class began to stir.

"Nice little children don't talk that way to their teachers." The woman struggled to keep her face controlled. Oh, how she loathed this hateful little creature. Every day this annoying child intruded into Miss Bottles's private plans, asking endless questions or making rude remarks to upset the class. Linda Jane always complained whenever she gave the class needless tasks to do during the day when she did not feel like teaching. Her little alert eyes never missed anything. She was the only one who sometimes caught Miss Bottles during recess sneaking a drink out of her camouflaged Coca-Cola bottle.

She had wanted to be an artist. Ever since she was a tiny child she was always with a pencil in her hands drawing something. Her parents frowned upon it. It was so unladylike, they said. And she ended up being a respectable teacher to please them. But now they were dead and gone and she was in a field that she hated. "How did that weird-looking Miss Bottles ever become a teacher?" she overheard the new assistant principal remark to someone one day. It was too late for her to try to enter the art world. At the age of forty-two time was already running out. So she had to be satisfied with the *N. Y. Times* advertisements she sketched every Sunday.

"If only I could get a transfer that would take me to a nicer district with nice pupils from nice homes," she anguished through her cracked brown teeth. Her bracelets jangled as she opened her purse and withdrew her beloved bottle of camouflaged Coca-Cola. The hot, soothing liquid trickled down her parched throat. The street noises coming in from the open bathroom window seemed to soften. She smiled wickedly all the way back to the classroom.

At three o'clock class was dismissed. She walked happily around the room, straightening up and putting everything back in order. This was the part of day that she loved best of all.

"Thank God, today is Friday," she said, slipping into her coat. "A whole weekend to feel like a human being again." When she turned to leave the room, a shadow crossed over the doorway. It was Linda Jane.

"Miz Bottles, I'm sorry I misbehaved in class today but please don't send another note home to my mother." The teacher felt a surge of power flow through her body.

"You're such a nice little girl when you want to be," she began to lecture. "Why do you always misbehave in the classroom?"

"I dunno, I guess I jes' like to show off in front of the other kids."

"You don't see the little white girls on TV behaving like that, do you?"

"No ma'am."

"Don't you want to be like the nice little white girls on TV?"

"Yes ma'am."

"Well, let's try extra hard to see if you can change and be a nice little girl from now on." Her voice took on a patronizing air, "OK, honeybun?"

"Yes ma'am."

The child stood staring at the splintered floor. Miss Bottles felt uneasy. She wished the child would go.

"Miz Bottles, couldn't we please have more 'rithmetic and projects like the other classes, pl-eez, Miz Bottles." For one second she felt weak but her wrinkled face grew tight.

"Now you run along, Linda Jane, and don't tell me what to teach you and the others." Spots of rouge danced up and down her sunken cheeks. "I am your teacher and I know what's best for the class."

The older woman could feel the girl's attitude changing. Linda Jane did not move; she seemed like a black statue. "You ugly old hag, you drunken lush," she said quietly. There was an eerie tone to her voice; she should have been yelling but instead she seemed to be almost whispering. The teacher closed her eyes. "Oh God," she sighed. When she opened her eyes the child was gone.

Miss Jane Bottles went to the doorway and looked wistfully at the small angry figure retreating from sight.

"Forgive me, Linda Jane," she whispered softly. "Forgive me for having nothing else of myself to offer to you and the others but SEE SPOTS RUN." Suddenly she withdrew to that private place where the Linda Janes of the world could not reach her. "I hate them. I hate the dirty little niggers." She remembered the bottle in her pocketbook. It was empty. She would refill it at home.

All Day Long

by Maya Angelou

The first thing Jimmy B knew was that it was Saturday. Smelled like Saturday. It was Saturday and there was nothing to do. To have to do. Nothing to do, and all day long to do it in. He started to plan. He'd get up, feel under the sofa for his shoes, go get a glass of milk first. No, brush his teeth first. No. He wasn't going to plan. He'd just get up. That was what was so great about Saturday. You didn't have to plan anything. He rolled over and up out of bed. Today he was going to be a soldier. Not all day, just long enough to make the bed. Marching around. Hip, hut, he tightened the sheets. Three, four, now pull this like this, then put the pillows underneath, then push and the sofa is back to itself. He saluted the dark green sofa. Smartly turning on the half pivot that he learned last week in school, he marched to the bathroom. Hup two, three four, Hup two. Up to the bathroom mirror. He saluted himself. Good morning, Captain Jimmy. Good morning, Left-Tenant. Jimmy B popped his eyes, held his lips tight, tried not to laugh. Then he broke up. Watched himself laugh. That broken front tooth made him look like he was twelve years old. Well, he was. Not really. In two months he would be thirteen. Naw, really he was a good-looking fifteen-year-old. Looked like it. He could pass any day in the week for fourteen, at least. And what about Saturday. He whooped. It's Saturday. Boy! Bet Aunt Gloria left me something good. He brushed his teeth, minding the broken one. Aunt Gloria said he had to get it capped. He pictured a cap like Mr. Willie wears sitting on his tooth. That broke him up again. Boy!

There were all his clothes in little piles. Folded up like they were waiting to be bought. Hey, you're already mine. I got you. He took clean underclothes and opened the sofa again. Pajamas go with the pillows. They are never parted. They're together all night long and all day long. Back into the kitchen. The cool breath of the frigidaire was a greeting. Aunt Gloria must have brought milk in with her last night. And there was cold chicken and he knew where she left his rolls. Every Saturday it was the same thing. He ate alone. Cold nice food all by himself any way he wanted to. On weekdays and Sundays she got up and made his breakfast so he wouldn't be late to school or to church. But Saturday. He rushed. Got to get out in the street. See what's happening. He ate quickly, chose a clean pair of cords and a sweater, exchanged the sweater for a light blue short-sleeved shirt. Going to be warm today. And he was ready to hit the street. He checked the apartment. Kitchen was clean. The living room was all right. Thank goodness he never had to sweep the living-room floor, cause it had a rug and Aunt Gloria would vacuum it herself. She kept that house like white folks. Flowers from the store and thick curtains, drapes they called them. Nice, like in the movies. He felt for his key. Had it. OK, house, he saluted. So long, Captain House. And out the door. He three-at-a-timed the stairs and there was Harlem. People on the street. A fat woman, her behind sitting up on both sides like she had two basketballs under her clothes. Two men were talking to her. "Yeah, baby. That's right, baby, I know what you mean, baby." Jimmy B wanted to laugh. How could they call that big woman baby? Baby Big Fat Mama. He didn't move his hands or anything, but he saluted her. As you were, Sergeant Baby Big Fat Mama. Then he ran. Ran to Lenox Avenue. There it was. Sometimes when he went to sleep he prayed that Harlem would still be there when he woke up. Still be laughing and fighting and smelling like barbecue and sounding loud like Ray Charles. Today everything was still in place. The Virginia Hickory Pit was belching out that smoke and had slabs of ribs laid on top of each other like cords of wood. Now what made him think of cords of wood? They don't use things like that in New York. That was another life. True, he hadn't been here all during the winter, but it was still

pretty cold when he first came and they used coal then.
They don't know anything about stacking wood till your
hands get raw and the splinters get under your fingernails
and then somebody has to take a needle and scrape under
them till the blood comes or else you'll get infection and
never be able to stack cordwood again. He passed the
barbecue pit. Wouldn't look in the window again. In front
of the record shop some kids were dancing. He didn't
know the name of the dance. Oh but he could dance anything anybody else could, he just hadn't learned the names
of these dances in New York City. He started to join the
kids, but no. He didn't know them. Suppose they said
something. Maybe they wouldn't like it if he joined them.
Anyway, they were small kids. Anyhow they didn't know
any of the games the kids played in Greenstown. Not that
Jimmy B ever had much chance to play them. He was too
busy stacking cordwood, or picking cotton or picking peas
or feeding the hogs or something. They don't have anything like that in New York City. Let's see what's at the
Apollo. Aunt Gloria took him there when he first came.
He saw Duke Ellington. In person. Nobody in Greenstown
would have believed him if he told them that he had sat
about this far from Duke Ellington. In Person. Not that
he'd ever tell anybody in Greenstown anything. He wasn't
going back and he sure wasn't going to write nobody.

A drunk was leaning against the wall next to the shoe
store holding a Nina Simone album. "You sure can sing,
mama." He was crying, "Nina baby, sing to me." Jimmy B
slowed down, watched the man put the album up to his
ear and hold it there. "That's right, baby, sing that song."
Wonder can he hear something? Jimmy B hummed, "I
loves you, Porgy, don't let him take me." The man said
"That's right, baby, sing." Holding his laugh, Jimmy ran,
ran like a rabbit, dodging people, bumped into one lady
who had done her Saturday grocery shopping, bumped
into all those bags. He stopped. Nothing had fallen. I'm
sorry lady . . . he wanted to say it. But he just hadn't gotten into the habit of talking. Boy, these New York people
like to talk! And fast. Even when you tried, which Jimmy
B didn't, even when you tried to understand them, they
didn't sound like they were talking English.

The Apollo had a larger than true picture of Ella Fitz-
gerald. Boy, every important Negro in the world came to
the Apollo. Duke, Count Basie, Sarah Vaughn, Jimmy B
thought. I bet you Ralph Bunche and even Dr. DuBois

will be here someday. And maybe George Washington
Carver. No. He's dead. But I bet that's the only reason.

It was too early to go over to the corner where the
Black Nationalists preached. His aunt called them no-good
rabble-rousers, but he liked to hear them so much. It was
better than the outdoor church. Or like when they held re-
vivals along the riverbank in Greenstown. "Buy Black."
"Get the white man's hands out of your pockets." "Ethio-
pia for the Ethiopians." All the sayings that were like eating fire, like holding burning coals in your hand. But it
was too early for that. No. Better to go to the park.
Maybe he'd play softball. Maybe Ping-Pong. Maybe nothing, maybe just stand around and look at things.

On his way to the One Hundred and Thirty-eighth
Street school he thought about getting a job next summer
and buying his own mitt. Maybe he'd buy some perfume
for Aunt Gloria. There is no dresser in the whole world
that smelled as sweet as that dresser of Aunt Gloria. She
must have a million bottles of perfume. A zillion. It's suppose to help a woman find a man if she puts on enough of
it. Aunt Gloria doesn't put much on though. Still she
smells sweet and there is no man around the house but
him. Sure, next summer he'll buy her some perfume that's
guaranteed to catch a husband.

The park was nearly empty. Anyway there were some
kids over on the lot playing ball. Jimmy B stood watching.
Then a white man in shorts and tennis shoes came up,
grabbed him by the shoulders. "Hey," he said, "you want
to play?" How could you answer? Especially when the
man was white and you weren't sure whether you wanted
to or not. And what would he say if you said no? Or yes?
The man walked away. Nobody likes a kid that sulks.
That's what his teacher says all the time. Nobody likes a
wise guy. If you don't talk in New York City they think
you're a wise guy. Someone yelled, "Hey!" Jimmy B
turned around, the white man threw the mitt to him and
he caught it. Didn't mean to, but he couldn't let a nice
mitt like that drop on the ground. The man started running out to the lot. He looked around for Jimmy B and
yelled, "Come on, kid." Jimmy B ran, following the man
and before he knew it he was in the game. Catching, missing the balls. Falling down and sliding. His pants got dirty.
But this wasn't Greenstown. His aunt wouldn't be mad.
Well, she'd just say, "Boy, you sure got dirty." And then
she'd give him some clean clothes. The other guys won.
That was OK too. He had a good time. The white man

was collecting the mitts and ball and bat. All the kids threw the things to him. Jimmy B couldn't do that, so he walked up to the man and handed him the mitt and turned to walk away. The man said, "Hey wait, kid, you live around here?" Jimmy B looked at him. "Can't you talk?" Jimmy B nodded and started to leave again. The man caught his arm. "Well, what's your name?" Jimmy B got all his strength together in his arm and in his mouth all around the jaws like wind. He yelled, "Jimmy B," and laughing, jerked his hand away and ran, ran down the lane and out of the park. He was so tired, but that was fun. Pure fun. His breath was coming in hurtful little pieces. But it was fun.

He was hungry. A sandwich. Pulled out his wallet. Never in his life had a new wallet before. Aunt Gloria said every man needed something to keep his money in. She gave him the brown wallet. It had a picture of John Wayne and Susan Hayward in it. Someday he was going to have a pretty picture of Aunt Gloria and himself in it. But it was nice just as it was. He took out some change and bought a roll, pointing it out in the candy store, and a carton of milk. Everybody liked milk in New York City. And everybody had money to buy it. It was after two o'clock and Jimmy B had three hours before he had to be back in the house. Aunt Gloria always wanted him home by five on Saturday, because she liked to make sure that he had eaten and taken his bath before she went to work.

A woman with two small children passed, carrying two Safeway shopping bags, and another boy, couldn't be her son, he was too raggedy, was pushing a Safeway cart. That's it. Jimmy B lit out for the supermarket. Maybe he could carry some packages for the folks doing their Saturday shopping.

In front of the market about ten boys were standing, waiting, offering to carry bags. Jimmy B didn't stop. He didn't know them, and then they were very particular who carried bags from what store. Something like a union. He had almost passed the store when a boy called him. Hey, Jimmy B. He turned. It was Charlie. He went back. Charlie was much older, about fifteen or seventeen or something. Almost a man. Charlie said, "Hey man, what's happening." Jimmy B smiled. It's something to be called a man, even when you knew you weren't. Charlie told his friends, "This is Jimmy B. He lives in my building. He just came up here from Hang-em High Alabam." All the guys said Hi man. Charlie told them he didn't talk much, but he's a nice little cat. "Hey," he said to Jimmy B, "why don't you stay here and try to get somebody to let you carry their bags. They'll tip you a quarter or fifty cents or something." He asked the other guys, "Is it all right?" They shifted their shoulders, some said it was OK or it's all right or something like that. So Jimmy B stood with them. They told funny stories about how little some people tipped, and how their houses looked, and how much some people tipped them, and girl stories and girl-and-boy stories. Some of them were dirty, and Jimmy B thought what would Aunt Gloria think if she heard some of these? Boy, she'd get mad. She didn't like smut. That's what she called it, smut.

Then some old gray-haired woman asked Jimmy B if he'd like to take her bag. Charlie had gone on a job, but one of the other guys said, "On't day ake tay er hay ag bay, ee shay ill way ive gay ou yay a ickel nay." Jimmy didn't understand what he said, any more than he understood what anybody else said. He took the bag and was walking behind the woman, but she began to talk to him. "What's your name? Where do you live? Do you work here every Saturday? I never saw you before." Things like that. Jimmy B kept walking. She said, "Well, I guess you're not much of a talker. That's all right. What's the matter with this whole world is that people are talking too much. Nowadays words don't mean a thing. People ought to stop up their mouths so all the mean nasty things wouldn't get said, or they ought to plug up their ears so they couldn't hear all the stuff about wars and rumors of wars . . . don't mind if you're not a talker. And don't let anybody change you neither. Folks'll say Cat's got your tongue, but don't you let that bother you none. The Good Book says the tongue is a little member and boasteth of great things. And the tongue is a fire, a world of iniquity." Then they had reached her house and up the stairs. So slow. Jimmy B noticed that the woman couldn't go very fast. That's because she's so old her legs have gone to sleep and her feet are afraid. They went into her room, small, smaller than Aunt Gloria's room and not nice. Lots of papers around and no kitchen. Just a hot plate and table. Jimmy B put the package down on the oil-clothed table, and waited. The old lady took out a smaller purse from her large one and fished with wrinkled fingers and offered Jimmy B a nickel. A nickel. He was sure he'd get at least a quarter. They had walked about ten or twenty blocks. What could he do with a nickel. Then the old lady

said, "I'm sorry I can't give you any more. . . . See I'm
on relief. I mean they don't give me much money. Listen
to me, little boy. I just get stamps to buy food and a few
cash dollars. You understand?" He heard her. He heard
her sorryness about the money. Oh that didn't matter.
Anyway Aunt Gloria gave him spending money. She
opened a box of graham crackers and gave him a whole
package. He thought: Thank you, ma'am. I don't mind
about the money. It's all right. He just looked at her and
turned and left. "Least you could say is thank you. You
mean, nasty boy. Surely you could have said thank you."
He was down the stairs and back in the street before she
finished saying that. Now back to the store and maybe
he'd listen to some more of the stories. Or maybe not.
When he got back Charlie was back. He teased him about
taking that old lady's bag. "What'd she give you? A
nickel?" The other guys laughed. Jimmy B laughed with
them. He found one more person during the afternoon to
help, but that time the woman was younger and gave him
fifty cents and she lived in a building with an elevator. He
went up with her but walked back down. He still wasn't
sure about being in an elevator by himself. Charlie said
when he returned that it was time for him to go home and
if he was ready they could walk home together. Jimmy B
nodded. That's fine. He had never had a brother, but it
must be nice. All his cousins in Greenstown were brothers
and sisters and they protected each other and loved each
other and even fought each other. His uncle gave them all
work to do, but they ganged up on him and made him do
it and then lied for each other. Walking home with Charlie would be the perfect end to an outdoor Saturday. They
started up Amsterdam. Charlie was talking. Jimmy B
heard Gloria something. He really had to start listening or
trying to listen to what people said. Here he had missed
something. What was it about Gloria? His aunt was named
Gloria. He couldn't ask, just couldn't get the words out,
but what was it about Gloria? Charlie started talking
again. This time Jimmy turned his ears on. Yeah, all the
women in the building signed a petition. Now what's a petition? They wanted to get her out. Said she was having
too much male company. Really they said that she was a
whore and they didn't want that kind of carrying on
around their children. What Gloria was he talking about.
That's when she sent for you. "Who? Me? Only my Aunt
Gloria sent for me." Charlie said, "So after you came she
started going out in the streets. They have these places

where prostitutes rent rooms. Transient room they call them. Well, when I saw your aunt go into one last Friday night, I knew Momma and them other ladies were right." Jimmy B stopped. Dead still. My Aunt Gloria. Can't be. How could anybody say a ' thing like that! Charlie, they lied to you. Not my Aunt Gloria, she's good and sweet. Nothing they say like my mother was. Uncle always said that running around was what killed my mother, but Aunt Gloria is not like that. She works at night. That's so. But she's not a wild woman. A harlot. Charlie wouldn't let Jimmy B disbelieve. She's sharp. I mean your aunt is the best-looking woman in that block and when I get a little older and have some money I'm going to buy some . . . Jimmy B hit him. Hit him without even taking the time to ball up his fist. Hit him and flung his arm up and hit him again with his elbow, hit him and ran . . . ran up Amsterdam, ran while the subway underneath the ground was shaking the world a-loose. He wasn't going to live with nobody like that. A double-minded adulteress . . . No sir! There wasn't no place to go, but he was going someplace. Couldn't go back to Greenstown. Wouldn't let his uncle and cousins know that Aunt Gloria was that way. Bringing men in the house. A Jezebel. Probably laid down with them right on his sofa. Jimmy B wiped his tears with his handkerchief, looked at the handkerchief and threw it away. She gave him that nasty handkerchief. Told him every little man had his own handkerchief. She ought to know. She knew every little man everywhere. Even Charlie was going . . . going to . . . He was crying out loud before he knew it. And was at home before he knew it. Could he go in . . . Yes. He had to go in and get his sweater and he was going to put on his winter coat. Just in case he had to sleep outside. Up the stairs. He went up slowly like the old woman with the graham crackers. He opened the door with his key . . . first time in his life he had ever had a key to a door . . . softly. The house smelled of roast pork and sweet potatoes and something else—yes . . . men! His aunt called out, "Is that you, Jimmy B?" Who else she think it is? "Is that you, Jimmy B?" She was in the kitchen making his dinner. Probably sweet-potato pie. Every Saturday she made some dessert, something he said he liked, and he could eat it all week long. She wouldn't eat any. She said she had to watch her weight . . . why? "Jimmy B?" He said yes'm . . . quietly. Yes'm . . . She came out into the living room . . . in a robe . . . He didn't want to look at her . . . But she was pretty . . . He never noticed her before . . . She just looked like Aunt Gloria before . . . Now she looked like . . .

"Jimmy B, I heard from your uncle and he wants you to come back home . . . He said it's time to clear the ground and get ready for summer crops . . . Said he wants you home . . . You hear me?" Jimmy B heard . . . heard and thought about his cousins and then about Charlie . . . and cotton and squash and your own potato pies . . . and men. He said, "Yes'm" . . . His aunt came close to him. "You've been crying. Did somebody do something to you?" He shook his head . . . "And Jimmy B, I told you you don't say yes'm to me . . . just say yes, Aunt Gloria . . . Now listen to me again. I sat right down after I heard from your uncle and wrote to him. I told him you weren't coming back down there to be no pack horse for him and them big strong kids he's got. I told him you were going to stay right here and get your education and have everything money can buy that a boy your size needs. And I told him that I need you, I need you more than he ever thought of needing anybody . . . And I signed it Gloria and Jimmy B."

Jimmy B started to cry, not wanting to, the tears streaked down his little brown cheeks and made dark stains on the blue shirt . . . She loved him . . . she loved him more than anybody in the world . . . more than the men, more than his uncle loved his children . . . loved him and gave him handkerchiefs and keys and sweet-potato pies and blue shirts and everything. "What's the matter, Jimmy B . . . Why are you crying? Don't you want to stay with me? Don't you love your Aunt Gloria? Aren't you happy?" She took him in her arms. He came up just to her breast. He smelled the perfume through her robe . . . Next summer he was going to get her some perfume that would let her get a man all her own . . . so he could tell Charlie that his aunt had her own husband and Charlie's mother wouldn't have to be afraid for her son . . . "Aren't you happy, Jimmy B . . . Don't I treat you good?" He nodded into her bosom and the tears darkened the yellow robe . . . Yes'm . . . Yes'm . . . Yes'm . . .

Daddy Was A Number Runner

by Louise M. Meriwether

"I dreamed about fish last night, Francie," Mrs. Mackey said when she opened the door to admit me. "What number does Madame Zora's dream book give for fish?"

Lord, I thought, don't let Mrs. Mackey stand here with her big, black self telling me about her dreams. If I was late getting back to school from lunch again, Miss Oliver would keep me in.

"I dreamed about fish last night too," I said. "I dreamed a big catfish jumped off the plate and bit me. Madame Zora gives five-fourteen for fish."

Mrs. Mackey chuckled, her eyes disappearing into slits, her broad cheeks puffed out as if she were chewing bubble gum.

"That's a good hunch, child, us both dreaming about fish. Wait a minute and let me add that number to my slip."

"Mrs. Mackey, I gotta eat my lunch and be back to school by one o'clock. My father asks would you please have your numbers ready by the time I get here."

"Okay, lil' darlin', they's ready."

She handed me a number slip and a dollar bill which I

198

slipped into my middy blouse pocket. I ran down the stairs holding my breath. Lord, but this hallway was funky, unwashed and funky. Garbage rotting in the dumb-waiter mingled with the smell of vomited wine, and a foul-ness oozing up from the basement meant a dead rat was down there somewhere.

Outside it wasn't much better. It was a hot, humid day, the first of June, 1934, and the sudden heat had tumbled the tenement dwellers out of their stifling rooms and into the streets. Knots of men sat on the stoops or stood wide-legged in front of the store fronts, their black ribs shining through shirts limp with sweat. "Get yore black ass out of that street 'fore a car knocks it off," one of them yelled at three kids playing ball in the gutter.

I turned the corner at Lenox Avenue and ran down for-bidden Hundred Eighteenth Street. Daddy had warned me to stay out of that street, upon pain of a whipping, be-cause of the prostitutes, but I knew all about them any-way. Sukie had told me and she ought to know. Her sister, Little Fannie, whored right in that block.

Five or six boys, acting the fool, were pretending they were razor-fighting in front of the drugstore, their knickers hanging loose beneath their knees to look like long pants. I tried to squeak past them but they saw me.

"Hey, skinny mama," one of them yelled. "When you put a little pork chops on those spare ribs I'm gonna make love to you."

The other boys folded up laughing and I scooted past, ignoring them. I always hated to pass a crowd of boys be-cause they felt called upon to make some remark, usually nasty, especially now that I was almost twelve. I was skinny and black and bad-looking with my short hair and long neck and all that naked space in between. I looked just like a plucked chicken.

I ran around the corner of Fifth Avenue, but ducked back when I saw Sukie playing hopscotch by herself in front of my house. That Sukie. She was going on thirteen, a year older than me, but much bigger. I waited until her back was towards me, then I ran towards my stoop. When she saw me her mooney face turned pinker and she took out after me like a red witch. I was galloping around the first landing when I heard her below me in the vestibule.

"Ya gotta come downstairs sometime, ya bastard, and the first time I catch ya I'm gonna beat the shit out of ya."

That Sukie. We were best friends but she picked a fight with me whenever she felt evil, which was often, and if she said she was going to beat the shit out of me that's just what she would do.

I kept on running to the top floor and collapsed on our door. The lock sprang open. Daddy was always promising to fix that lock but he never did.

Our apartment was a railroad flat, each small room set flush in front of the other. The door opened into the dining room, so junky with heavy furniture that the room seemed tinier than it was. The big buffet and matching round table, carved with ugly dragons and scratched with scars, was a gift from the Jewish plumber downstairs and was one year older than God.

"Mother," I yelled. "I'm home."

"Stop screaming, Frances," Mother said from the kitchen, "and put the numbers up."

I took the drawer out of the buffet, and, reaching to the ledge on the side, pulled out an envelope filled with number slips. I put in Mrs. Mackey's numbers and the dollar and replaced the envelope on the ledge and slid the drawer back on its runners. It stuck. I took it out again and shoved the envelope farther to the side. Now the drawer closed smoothly.

"Did you push that envelope way back so the drawer closes good?" Mother asked as I went into the kitchen.

"Yes, Mother."

I sat down at the porcelain table in the kitchen which tilted crazily on its uneven legs, and absentmindedly knocked a scurrying roach off the table top to the floor and crunched it under my sneaker.

"If you don't stop racing up those stairs like that, one of these days you gonna drop dead."

"Yes, Mother."

I wanted to tell her that Sukie had promised to beat me up again but Mother would only repeat that Sukie would stop bullying me when I stopped running away from her.

Mother was short and wide, her long breasts and broad hips all sort of running together. She was light brown with short, thin hair, and yellow, rotting teeth. She had more empty spaces in her mouth than she had teeth and she seldom smiled. Daddy shouted and cursed when he was mad and hugged you when he was feeling good, but you just couldn't tell how Mother was feeling. She didn't curse you, but she didn't kiss you either.

She placed a sandwich before me, potted meat stretched from here to yonder with mayonnaise, which I eyed with suspicion.

"I don't like potted meat."

"You don't like nothing. That's why you're so skinny. If you don't want it, don't eat it. There ain't nothing else."

She gave me a weak cup of tea.

"We got any cream?"

"No. Put some sugar in it and be thankful you got that."

I sighed and dropped a spoonful of sugar in my tea. Seemed like we were getting poorer every day. I sipped the tea, looking at the greasy kitchen walls lumpy with layers of paint over cracked plaster. Daddy called its color vomit green.

The outside door slammed and I could tell from the heavy tread that it was Daddy. I bounced up and ran into the dining room, hurling myself against him. He laughed and caught me up in his arms, swinging me off the floor. Mother was always telling me that men were handsome, not beautiful, but she just didn't understand. Handsome meant one thing and beautiful something else, and I knew for sure what Daddy was. Beautiful. In the first place he was so big, not just tall, but thick and hard all over. He was dark, black really, with thick crinkly hair and a wide, laughing mouth. I loved Daddy's mouth. It looked as if it had been chiseled from black marble.

He sat down at the dining room table and began pulling number slips and money from his pocket.

"Get the envelope for me, Sugar."

I removed the drawer and handed him the envelope, smiling. "I dreamed a big catfish jumped off the plate and bit me, Daddy. Madame Zora gives five-fourteen for fish."

Daddy laughed. "That's a good dream, Sugar. I'll put a dollar on it."

Daddy said that of all the family my dreams hit the most.

"Jessie," Daddy called. "Where are the boys?"

Mother came to the kitchen door. "They ain't come home yet."

Daddy's fist hit the table with a bang. "If those boys have stayed out of school again it's gonna be me and their behinds. They're hanging around with those damned Ebony Dukes, that's what's got into them lately." He turned to Mother, shaking his fist. "I'm warning you. Nobody in this family has ever been to jail and if those boys get into any trouble I'm gonna let their butts rot in jail. You hear me?"

Mother nodded. She knew as I did that Daddy would be

the first one downtown if anything happened to his sons. James Junior, fifteen, and Claude, fourteen, were suddenly making a career out of playing hookey and staying out late at night, and it was true, they were messing around with the Ebony Dukes.

The Dukes were the toughest gang this side of Mt. Morris Park. When they weren't fighting their rivals the Black Raiders with knives, they were jumping the Jew boys who attended the synagogue on Hundred Sixteenth Street, or mugging any white man caught alone in Harlem after the sun went down. I had been nervous enough before about my brothers—always afraid they might fall off the roof (all the boys had to jump from one rooftop to another to prove they weren't chicken) or get run over by a car—and now I also had to contend with them getting knifed or killed in a gang fight.

Daddy started adding up the amounts on his number slips and counting the money. Mother sat down beside him and said nervously she heard that Slim Jim had been arrested.

"Slim Jim is a fool," Daddy said. "The banker he works for thinks he can buck the syndicate and Big Dutch. But Big Dutch pays off the police each and every week and all he had to do was give the cops the nod and they busted Slim Jim and his banker."

"Maybe you'd better find another job," Mother began timidly.

"There ain't no jobs for the ofays so what in the hell you expect me to do?" Daddy asked. "And how many times I gotta tell you I'm in no danger as long as the syndicate is paying off the cops?"

Mother played the numbers like everyone else in Harlem but she was uneasy about Daddy collecting them. Daddy went to work for Frenchy on commission three months ago when he lost his house painting job which hadn't been none too steady. Frenchy was a brown-skinned Creole from Haiti with curly black hair and sleek looks. Now Frenchy was handsome, but he wasn't beautiful. He operated a candy store on Fifth Avenue as a front for his number business and was Big Dutch's right-hand man.

Daddy said the racketeers ran Harlem. They controlled the pimps who brought the white men to the prostitutes and they banked the numbers while the police looked the other way. If the police really wanted to clean up this shit, Daddy said once, they would stop picking on the poor niggers trying to hit the number for a dime, but would snatch the bankers downtown who were banking the action and making the real money.

Now he repeated to Mother that as long as Big Dutch paid off the police he was safe. Mother nodded slowly as if trying to convince herself. Then she noticed I was still there and yelled at me to get on back to school.

I went to P.S. 81 near St. Nicholas Avenue, which was second only to P.S. 136 as being the baddest girls' school in the world. Sister gangs to the Ebony Dukes also fought with knives and scared us younger students and the teachers plenty. It's a wonder any of us learned anything.

After school I sneaked home again, avoiding Sukie, and sat on the fire escape watching her jump rope downstairs with the other kids she also beat on when she wasn't picking on me.

That Sukie. I wondered what made her so mean? She was too pretty to be so evil—all red and yellow like a plump peach with long red-brown hair that I envied. When we were best friends Sukie shared everything with me. She stole money from her mother's purse every morning and we stuffed ourselves with candy on the way to school. Once, in order to keep up, I took a dime from Mother's pocketbook, but Mother had spent a half hour on her knees looking under the couch for that lousy dime and I never stole from her again. I saved the change from milk bottles and when I got a nickel I would tell Sukie I had picked Daddy's pocket and that seemed to make her happy.

Sukie didn't like anybody, not even her mother and father. It was true that Papa Maceo was a drunk, but he was good-natured and happy and being a drunk was no reason for Sukie to call him a sonofabitch. Her own father. Sukie cursed all the time as if there was a pot boiling inside her. Daddy didn't even want me to say darn. It's darn today and damn tomorrow and goddamn the next day, he was always telling me, and I was going to grow up to be a lady and ladies didn't curse. But I had to curse some to keep up with Sukie. I wouldn't play the dozens, though—that mother stuff—or take the Lord's name in vain.

Sukie cursed out everybody except her mother who would have knocked her into the middle of tomorrow if she did. Mrs. Maceo was a little yellow woman, always grumbling that her drunken husband and her no-good children didn't appreciate how hard she had to work in that laundry on the late shift. Sukie sure didn't seem to care, glad to be able to stay out late at nights, and her sister, Little Fannie, was too busy prostituting around the corner to even speak to her mother.

It was on account of Little Fannie that Sukie beat me up the last time. I had simply asked her why her sister hustled so close to home, and Sukie hauled off and punched me right in the nose. After she got through bloodying me up, she took me around the corner and we watched Little Fannie hustling the men in off the street. That Sukie. You never could tell what would set that inner pot of hers to boiling. This time she got mad at me on sight one day last week and asked if I was ready to fight. Naturally I wasn't ready and I had been dodging her ever since. I wondered what made her so mean? What I should do is go on downstairs and get my whipping over with so we could be best friends again.

I was fighting the bedbugs on the couch in the living room where I slept, and I was losing. Mother and I had pulled the couch away from the wall into the middle of the floor. Mother thought that if the couch was in the center of the room the bugs wouldn't get me. Her theory was they were in the walls. Every Saturday she scalded all of the bedsprings with boiling water and Flit but she couldn't do anything with the walls. But those bugs didn't buy Mother's theory. Every night they marched right down that wall and across the floor and got me just the same.

My brothers were in their room behind the kitchen. When they came home hours after dinner Daddy had yelled at them but he didn't beat their butts as he had promised, thank God. Now, Mother and Daddy were arguing in their bedroom right next to me and I could hear every word they were saying. Mother was asking Daddy again if she could go up in the Bronx and get some day's work.

"Why don't you stop nagging me, woman?" Daddy said. "You know I don't want you doing housework."

"It's not what we want any more," Mother said. "It's what we need. The children need shoes and winter coats. We're all practically in rags."

"They also need you to be home when they get out from school. Ain't I having enough troubles now, for Christ sakes? What you want to start that shit all over again for? We ain't starving yet."

"We ain't far from it."

Daddy didn't answer.

After a slight pause Mother said: "The relief people are giving out canned beef and butter. Mrs. Maceo is trying to get on. I don't know when is the last time we've had any butter."

"And we may never have any again if I've got to let those damned social workers inside my house to get it. Bastards act like it's their money they're handing out. For Christ sakes, baby, there's a depression on all over the country. We're not the only family that's up tight."

"So what we gonna do?" Mother asked.

After a slight pause, Daddy's voice was gentle. "It's going to be all right, baby. I'm gonna play the piano for three rent and whist parties this weekend. I oughta make ten bucks for each one. That will help. You stop worrying now and trust me. You hear?"

I trusted Daddy. I wondered how come Mother couldn't.

On Friday night we helped Daddy practice for his parties. The boys came home early and Junior, leaning against the battered piano in the living room—another gift from the Jewish plumber downstairs—sang all the new songs he had heard on the radio, while Daddy picked out the melody and then added his swinging bass. Daddy could play any piece after hearing it only once. He played by ear. Claude was writing down the names of the songs as Daddy memorized them, his dark, thin face tight and secretive as usual.

I was surprised that Claude was hanging out with the Ebony Dukes because he used to say boys who ran around with gangs were morons. Claude was smart. He had already passed Junior in school, and before he started that hookey playing he used to spend his spare time studying and shining shoes on Forty-Second Street. I don't think Junior knew the way downtown. He used to taunt Claude that he was a sucker to work so hard with that shoeshine box for so little.

Claude had a disposition like Sukie's. He didn't like anybody and he seldom smiled. Junior was just the opposite, with a sunny personality and handsome like Daddy. He had never been bright in school and had dropped so far behind that now he just didn't care. I didn't believe, though, that Junior was mean enough to be an Ebony Duke. How could he ever mug anybody? He was too gentle.

Mother sat on the couch, sewing, and patting her feet.

After Daddy learned all the new songs that Junior and I knew (Claude couldn't sing), Daddy bellowed out his favorite blues: "Trouble in mind, I'm blue, but I won't be blue always. The sun's gonna shine in my back door some day," and then he left to play for the parties. We used to have fun like that every evening after dinner, but now those good times came very seldom.

Daddy brought home only nine dollars from the three parties. For tips he had been offered whiskey instead of money, and since he was not a drinking man, he had switched the drinks to food, eating Hoppin' John and chitt'lins all weekend long.

Mother had a fit. She raved it was either relief or housework for her. Daddy wasn't earning enough off the numbers to feed us and God alone knew when he was going to hit that big one he was always talking about. She kept it up until finally Daddy hollered that a man couldn't have any peace in his own home and yes, goddammit, go on up in the Bronx and find some work if she wanted to.

On Monday morning, Mother took the subway to Grand Concourse and waited on the sidewalk with the other colored women. When a white lady drove up and asked how much she charged by the hour, Mother said twenty-five cents and was hired for three days a week by a Mrs. Schwartz.

I spent most of my free time reading fairy tales from the library on the fire escape, trying to avoid Sukie. Then, hallelu, five-fourteen played. Daddy's dollar had dwindled to a quarter, but Mother also caught it for ten cents straight and thirty cents combination. Together they collected two hundred and fifteen dollars. A fortune.

"Where else can a poor man get such odds?" Daddy asked. "Six hundred dollars for a buck. If only I hadn't cut that number down to a quarter." But he had dreamed about his mother and had switched the dollar to nine-oh-nine which played for the dead.

That night Mother and Daddy sat at the dining room table counting that money over and over. There was something different about them, some soft way they looked at each other with their eyes and smiled. I went to bed and didn't even bother to pull the couch away from the wall, I was that happy. Let the bedbugs bite. Everybody, even those blood-sucking bugs, had to have something sometime.

We ate high off the hog for about a week. It sure was

good to get away from that callie ham which you had to soak all night to kill the salt and then save the juice and skin to flavor beans and greens. I think the reason why I was so skinny was that I just didn't like poor mouth collards and salt pork. Daddy stuffed a turkey with his secret Geechie recipe and nobody had to beg me to eat that.

Daddy paid up the back rent and Mother bought us all winter coats and shoes. But before long we were back to fried cabbage and ham hocks and it was just as if the big hit had never been. It wasn't long before the explosion came.

That Saturday Mother was at work and Daddy had already left on his rounds. I was in the kitchen scorching the rice for dinner when the two plainclothes cops pushed past that rotten lock Daddy had never fixed and walked right in. By the time I got to the dining room they were poking around as if they had been invited in. I knew instantly they were cops. The oldest one was huge with loose purple jaws like a bulldog. The other one was younger and nervous.

"Where does your old man hide his numbers?" Bulldog asked me, pulling open the buffet drawers.

I was so scared I couldn't speak, so I just shook my head.

Bulldog pulled out the drawer and placed it on the table. The young one sorted through it, pushing aside Mother's sewing bag and the old rags she was saving to sell to the rag man. He replaced the drawer and it jammed. I almost cried out loud. Then he gave it a shove and it closed.

They went through the other drawers in the same manner, then Bulldog went into the kitchen and began banging the pots and pans around in the cupboard.

I heard Daddy coming up the stairs and I ran towards the door yelling: "Don't come in, Daddy! It's the cops!"

Bulldog hollered, "Grab her!"

The young cop swung me off my feet. I screamed and kicked, aiming for his private parts like Mother had told me to do if a man ever bothered me.

Daddy came through the door. With one long stride he was at the young cop's side. He grabbed me, at the same time pushing the cop backwards.

"You all right?" Daddy asked.

I nodded. He put me down and straightened up.

"Hold it right there," Bulldog said. He was pointing his gun at Daddy's chest.

"You all got a warrant to mess up my house like this?" Daddy asked. "And stop waving that gun around. I ain't going nowhere. You're scaring my little girl to death."

Bulldog put the gun back inside his shoulder holster. "Don't need no warrant," he said. "Now hand over your numbers and come along quietly."

"You ain't got no warrant," Daddy repeated.

"Search him," Bulldog ordered the young one, who approached Daddy with hesitation and went through his pocket. He pulled out an envelope. Lord, I thought, they're gonna put Daddy underneath the jail. The cop opened the envelope and pulled out an unpaid gas bill.

"The only house where we can't find a number slip," Bulldog said, "is a number runner's house. Nobody else is that careful." He reared back on his heels. "Tell you what I'm gonna do, though. I'm gonna run you in for assault and battery for pushing my partner like you did. Let's go."

I was crying loudly by this time. "Hush," Daddy said. "You're a big girl now and you know what to do."

I nodded. He meant that after he was gone I was to take the numbers downstairs to Frenchy and tell him Daddy had been arrested. And that's exactly what I did do after the police had driven Daddy away in an unmarked blue car, and I cried every step of the way.

Mother and I were drinking tea at the dining room table, very silent and glum, when Daddy returned home around midnight. My brothers hadn't been home since they left that morning, and that worried Daddy more than his arrest.

"Damn cops," he muttered, as he sat down heavily. They hadn't found any numbers on him because the people on the stoop had warned him that two strange men were lurking about. Everybody in Harlem was a lookout for the cops.

"I thought the syndicate paid off so good that this wasn't supposed to happen," Mother said.

"There was an argument about the payoff," Daddy explained. Frenchy told him the police wanted a bigger take and the syndicate balked, so the police made a few arrests to show who was boss. "They didn't touch the big boys though," Daddy said, "just a couple of small runners like me."

"You'd better stop taking numbers now before something worse happens," Mother said.

Daddy was gloomy. "The worse has happened. Frenchy

says they'll probably throw my case out of court. But I've got a record now. Fingerprints. The works." He looked at Mother and shook his head sadly. "How can I keep those boys from running wild now that I've done gone and got a record?"

Silence was his answer. Mother finally cleared her throat and said: "I'm sorry this happened now because . . . well, I gotta tell you sometime and it might as well be now."

"What."

Mother averted her eyes. "If it was just you and me I wouldn't mind. We could scuffle along. But I can't even scrape together enough food for the children no more. We've got no money coming in now except for those few pennies I get from Mrs. Schwartz. Lately you've been playing back all your commission on the numbers."

"So I play all the commission back. I guess you don't help, huh?"

"Yes, I do. And when I hit for two cents last week all of my money went to help repay what you owe Frenchy."

"All right. All right. I'll give you back your damn ten dollars."

"It's not that. It's having nothing coming in steady I can count on."

"All I'm trying to do is hit a big one again," Daddy said. "Nine-oh-nine almost played today and I had two dollars on it. Lord, how I prayed that last figure would be a nine and out pops a goddamned six. We almost had us twelve hundred dollars, baby. That's all I'm trying to do. Hit us a big one."

"We can't wait until you hit a big one," Mother said, her voice cracking. Then it steadied. "I went to the relief place yesterday and put in an application. The social workers will be here Monday to talk to you."

Daddy jumped to his feet, his face twitching with rage, his lips working soundlessly.

"There's no other way," Mother said. "Your pride won't feed these children."

They stared at each other in a silence that wasn't quiet at all, as if they were arguing loudly without words.

"Goddammit," Daddy screamed, banging his fist down hard on the table, "I'm a fucking *man*. Why can't you understand that?"

"Your pride won't feed these children," Mother repeated quietly.

Suddenly Daddy collapsed back into his seat. His head

fell forward on his folded arms. He was crying. I ran to him. "Daddy. Daddy." But he pushed me away roughly and I fell to my knees. I was up in a rush, blindly groping for the door. I heard Mother yelling at me to come back as I stumbled down the stairs.

I ran down the street looking for Sukie. I found her jumping rope with some kids on Hundred Seventeenth Street.

"You ready to fight now?" I demanded.

Sukie took a step backwards, confused.

"Fight, goddamn you!" I screamed.

She kept backing away, her mouth slack with surprise.

"Motherfucker!" I screamed, and that did it.

"Don't play the dozens with me," Sukie cried, and suddenly we were all tangled up together.

It was a one-sided battle. If Sukie landed a blow I didn't feel it. I pressed forward and she fell beneath my weight. I jumped on top of her, pinning her body to the ground, and, grabbing her by the hair, I banged her head against the sidewalk again and again. A crowd of adults joined the shrieking children.

A woman yelled: "My God! Somebody stop her! She's murdering that child!" It was Mrs. Mackey.

Strong, black arms lifted me up bodily. I screamed and kicked, aiming at the man's privates, but my kicks fell short.

Sukie was sobbing: "She tried to kill me." Mrs. Mackey led her away. Blood dripped from her swollen mouth down her chin, and the skin on her face was grated raw where it had scraped the pavement.

I stopped kicking and the man put me down. I felt lifeless, numb, and the crowd was hemming me in. I was suffocating. I pushed against the black, shoving mass until I was free of them. There was something evil in their sweating black faces, and that something was in me also.

"Goddamn," I whispered, waiting for the lightning to strike me dead. "Goddamn them all to hell." But I was not chastised for my blasphemy. Even the Lord didn't care.

I walked to the corner and, turning my face away from home, I made my way aimlessly down Fifth Avenue.

Harlem On The Rocks
"I'd Rather Have
Snakes in my Nightmares"

by Loyle Hairston

When Soul Brother failed to show up at my house for dinner, I became worried. I can imagine the sun not rising; Strom Thurmond joining the civil rights movement; even Eldridge Cleaver becoming an Uncle Tom—but Soul Brother missing a soul feast? Never. Immediately, I called his landlady.

The good woman promptly shocked me with a cheerful account of what had happened to her pet tenant. A spine-chilling scream had shattered the peace of her humble home during the night. And upon investigation she found it had originated from Soul's rooms. Had his throat been cut? No. But her heart nearly stopped at the thought of what *had* happened to the poor man. His being her lodger, however, had proved to be his salvation; which meant—he was now in the capable hands of her favorite *psychoanalyst!*

My mission to rescue my troubled friend turned up the following circumstantial evidence:

"It was one of the most horrible nightmares I've ever had, Doc," Soul Brother said to the analyst as he stretched himself on the comfortable, polished leather couch.

211

"Just try to relax, my dear man, and tell me all about it," purred the bespectacled headshrinker, professionally pleased with the gloomy cast of his patient's face.

"Aw, it's terrible, Doc. Terrible!" Soul Brother shuddered. "I dreamt I was the house guest of . . . Lurleen Wallace."

"Extraordinary," conceded the good doctor. "How often have you had this dream?"

"Only once, thank God—last night. That's how come I'm on your couch this mornin'. It is not a dream I want to have again."

The headshrinker licked his lips and, crossing his legs under his notebook, urged his patient to relate the most nightmarish aspects of the dream.

". . . We was *friends,* Doc," groaned Soul. "Cut-buddies. Imagine, me—a genuine, pure, one-hundred percent, fullblooded, gutbucket, black nationalist—even *dreamin'* of bein' on good terms with the gov'nor of Alabama. Like, you gotta help me, Doc . . . before I flip my *lid!*"

"Indeed, indeed," sighed the good doctor, frowning significantly and jotting hurried notations on his writing pad. "Why don't you simply start at the beginning and try to recall the whole dream."

"Damn, Doc, you sure that's necessary?" argued Soul Brother, eyeing the doctor with grave suspicion. But the air-conditioned offices, the luxuriously comfortable couch and the smooth analytical prodding of the headshrinker finally undermined his willpower. Within a few minutes the patient had purged himself of as much of his dreadful dream as prudence would allow, the good doctor gurgling in malicious delight as shameful admissions boiled up from the patient's subconscious.

Soul confessed to having even *liked* the lady governor in his dream, and he had actually enjoyed his tête-à-tête with her, despite her treating his blackness as an irrelevance. It was plain his psyche had blown a fuse. He trembled, broke into a sweat; his head throbbed; his very soul felt sick as though suddenly polluted with white power structure fall-out.

At one point in the dream he had had no choice but to rebuke the Southern lady's scandalous endorsement of Brotherhood:

" 'Why—if an *ex*-"coon" might be so bold to ask—are you treatin' me like this, Madam Gov'nor?'

" 'Like what, sir?'

"I just stared at the woman, at how *she* was flabbergasted. Plain the gov'norship done addled her brains, done reduced her to a stark ravin' compassionate human bein'. I mean it was too much, Doc."

"Extraordinary," punctuated the analyst. "Extraordinary indeed." As indeed an extraordinary excitement gleamed in his eyes. Never in his illustrious career as a head-shrinker had a patient confessed to such extraordinary aberrations. But—even nightmares have a certain logical irrationality. However distorted the content might be, the subject matter of dreams is generally confined to a patient's experiences. Thus a black nationalist dreaming of a friendly engagement with the governor of Alabama seemed a violation of the laws of psychic gravity.

Noticing the anxiety building in the good doctor's face, Soul gave him a consoling pat on the knee.

Returning to his nightmare, he told how determined the governor was of converting him into "a black nationalist turncoat." Somehow his virtue managed to withstand the onslaught of her Southern hospitality. But his natural weakness for soul food nearly proved disastrous.

"Imagine, Doc," said Soul Brother with feeling. "I'm settin' there in the state house dinin' room lickin' my chops on . . . *imported* chitt'lin's *à la newburg*—with *truffles, creamed* black-eyed peas, collard greens *au gratin*, and candied yams in mushroom sauce—like do you hear me, Doc?—when the gov'nor launched her mortar attack.

". . .'Now how can you set there and tell me, with a straight face, you're against integration, Mr. Soul Brother,' she fired point-blank. 'When already our integrated Alabama National Guard done just wiped out a whole passel of Ku Klux Klan guerrillas; when James Meredith has just been elected governor of Mississippi—by a landslide; when the President has just announced the engagement of his daughter to a Hottentot; when the Black Muslims have just merged with the Mormon Church. And on top of that—it has just been confirmed that Mr. Rap Brown is going to keynote the Daughters of the American Revolution's national convention.'

"I mean it was like bein' caught in the crossfire of the Tet offensive, Doc. 'Madam Gov'nor,' I said, tryin' to counterattack, 'do you believe in "mongrelization"?'

" 'I most certainly do, Mr. Soul,' she shot back. 'Lord knows, our menfolks been practicing it long enough. I say it's about time Southern white womanhood got into the "fray." ' "

"She would of given Strom Thurmond a heart attack. I

didn't know what to do, Doc; so I told her to call the *other* gov'nor.

" 'D'you mean my George? Why he's out of town—nigger-baiting up North. I declare, Mr. Soul Brother—but I do believe you all's being downright unfriendly. Now here I am ready to give my all to help the colored race and you're treating me like I was . . . well—like I was one of them lowdown, deceitful, two-faced, pseudo-nigra-loving Yankee liberals. Why, as hospitable as I am, sir, if George was home, I reckon I'd just have to let him flog you. Now you just set back down there and let me serve you another helping of these deelicious chitt'lin's—you heah!' "

Soul Brother fell silent, closed his eyes, and groaned, looking so wretched that tears of pity welled into the good doctor's eyes. At last the patient sat up and wiped his profusely sweating brow; and then he passed his handkerchief to the analyst who did the same. Putting on his best psychiatric expression, the headshrinker started to pace up and down the spacious office. Now Soul Brother too got up and commenced pacing in step with the doctor. Both men's faces now bore a funereal seriousness. Suddenly the analyst stopped pacing and stared at his patient with much sympathy and urgency. Soul also stopped and stood tottering like a once proud black warrior who was suddenly divested of his *negritude*. Even a massive dose of *black power* wouldn't restore his libido juices.

"This, my dear sir, is going to be a bit painful . . . I'm afraid," prefaced the good doctor before beginning his brilliant analysis.

"Like sock it to me, Doc," said Soul, returning to the couch and sensing the dreadful mental scalpel being whetted in the good doctor's mind. "I mean—get down to my subconscious nitty-gritty."

"Despite your strong black nationalist sentiments," said the analyst, "you seem to be suffering from an unconscious need to . . . to love white people."

Soul Brother grunted as though he had been pole-axed.

"All of the symptoms reveal very strong manifestations of what you would call in layman's terms—an Uncle Tom syndrome."

Soul Brother fell back on the couch with a gasp.

"Is it . . . *that* bad, Doc?" he said in an asphyxiated whisper, an expression of horror overspreading his face.

Having cut mentally to his patient's psychic bone, the analyst couldn't help admiring his handiwork. The diagnosis confirmed his prognosis. And now Soul Brother waited fearfully for the verdict, becoming unnerved by the evangelical zeal flushing the good doctor's face.

"In a few days, my lucky man," the headshrinker continued, "you will have made a most remarkable transformation—from a 'whitey'-hating black nationalist to a nonviolent, responsible Negro integrationist . . . darling of white liberals."

Soul Brother winced; his eyes started out of his head; never had his mind been ambushed with such devastation. Indeed, such a violent tremor shook his body, he fell off the couch. . . . But at last the shock began to subside and that old militance flared in his eyes.

"Either you're puttin' me on, Doc," scowled the black nationalist, "or you're a mother-Freudian fool!"

. . . I was delighted when my good friend called the next day and invited *me* to dinner. And he had slept so soundly the past night, even paid the tab—with the good doctor's fee . . .

BIOGRAPHICAL NOTES

JOHN P. DAVIS was educated at Bates College and later received his master's degree at Harvard Law School. He has been publicity director for Fisk University, head of the Washington bureau of the Pittsburgh *Courier*, and for a number of years he was editor and publisher of *Our World* magazine. Presently he is director-editor of Special Publications of the Phelps-Stokes Fund in New York. He also edited *The American Negro Reference Book* (1966).

CLAUDE McKAY was born in Jamaica, West Indies, in 1890. In 1912 he came to the United States and studied at the University of Kansas for two years. He was first known for his poems, particularly for the volume *Harlem Shadows* (1922). His novel, *Home to Harlem* (1928), is still the most famous book ever written about the world's best-known ethnic ghetto. He was the first Negro writer to receive the medal of the Institute of Arts and Sciences. Claude McKay died in 1948.

COUNTEE CULLEN (1903–1946) was educated in the public schools of New York City. His recognition as a poet began when he was still in high school. As a student at New York University he won the Witter Bynner Poetry Prize, open to all undergraduates in American colleges. He received a master's degree from Harvard in 1926. He later became a teacher in the public schools of New York City, the work in which he continued until his death. *Color*, Cullen's first volume of poetry, appeared in 1925, when the poet was only twenty-two years old. This book won him

217

the Harmon Gold Award for literature as well as notable critical approval.

RUDOLPH FISHER was born in 1897 in Washington, D.C. He prepared himself to be both a doctor and a writer —in fact, Fisher's first short story was published in the *Atlantic Monthly* as he completed his medical studies at Columbia University. Most of Rudolph Fisher's short stories were published in the years between 1925 and 1934. Several of his short stories were published in the annual anthology of *Best Short Stories*. Fisher died in 1934, just as his writing began to receive national attention.

DOROTHY WEST (1910–   ) born in Boston, attended Girls Latin School there, Boston University and later the Columbia University School of Journalism. Afterward, she lived for a time in New York and edited the Negro quarterlies *Challenge* and *New Challenge,* in which the early work of such well-known black writers as Richard Wright, Margaret Walker and Owen Dodson appeared. During the Depression, Miss West worked as a relief investigator in Harlem and began to write short stories which were syndicated in newspapers across the country. In 1948 her novel *The Living Is Easy* appeared.

ANN PETRY was born in Old Saybrook, Connecticut. She studied pharmacy at the University of Connecticut and later worked in her family's drugstore. After moving to Harlem she worked for several social agencies and was later a reporter for *The People's Voice*. Her first novel, *The Street* (1946), was written on a Houghton Mifflin Literary Fellowship. Her other books are *The Country Place* (1947), *The Drugstore Cat* (1949), *The Narrows* (1953), *Harriet Tubman: Conductor on the Underground Railroad* (1955), and *Tituba of Salem Village* (1965).

CHESTER HIMES was born in Jefferson City, Missouri, in 1909 and attended the public schools of that city. After a short stay at Ohio State University he held a variety of jobs while attempting to start his career as a writer. His first short story was published in *Esquire* in 1934. Among his most notable books are *If He Hollers Let Him Go* (1945), *Lonely Crusade* (1947), *Cast the First Stone* (1953), *The Third Generation* (1954), and *Cotton Comes to Harlem* (1965), which is one of a group of novels that

he calls "Harlem domestic stories." For over ten years
Himes has lived in Paris.

LANGSTON HUGHES was born in Joplin, Missouri, in
1902. He attended Central High School in Cleveland and
after graduation spent two years in Mexico with his father.
In 1925 he received his first poetry award in a contest
conducted by *Opportunity* magazine. He is the best-known
and the most versatile writer produced by the Harlem literary renaissance. His literary career extends over a period
of more than forty years. Among his books are *The
Weary Blues* (1926), *Not Without Laughter* (1930), *The
Big Sea* (1940), and the books about the urban folk-hero,
Jesse B. Simple. Langston Hughes died in May, 1967.

JAMES BALDWIN was born in New York in 1924. His
career as a writer began while he was a student of P.S. 24
in Harlem—he wrote the school song. His first novel, *Go
Tell It on the Mountain* (1952), was acclaimed by the
critics. His stories and essays have since appeared in *Harper's, Esquire, Atlantic Monthly, The Reporter,* and many
other publications here and abroad. Among his other
books are *Notes of a Native Son* (1955), *Giovanni's
Room* (1956), *Nobody Knows My Name* (1961), *Another Country* (1962), *Going to Meet the Man* (1965),
and *Tell Me How Long the Train's Been Gone* (1968).
Two of his plays, *Blues for Mr. Charlie* (1964) and *Amen
Corner* (1965), have been successfully produced.

JOHN HENRIK CLARKE has been a teacher of both
African and Afro-American history for over twenty years.
Born in Union Springs, Alabama, he grew up in Columbus, Georgia. During the early part of his career he was a
poet, short-story writer and a journalist. He has been a
staff member of five publications and was co-founder and
literary editor of the *Harlem Quarterly*. After being discharged from the U.S. Air Force, where he was a master
sergeant, he studied at New York University and was an
occasional lecturer on African history at the New School
for Social Research. Since 1962, he has been the associate
editor of *Freedomways* magazine. In 1964 he became the
first director of the Heritage Teaching Program of HAR-
YOU-ACT, the antipoverty program in Harlem. His articles and special papers on African and Afro-American history have been published in leading journals throughout

the world. His published books are *Rebellion in Rhyme* (poetry, 1948) and *The Lives of Great African Chiefs* (history, 1958). He has edited the following anthologies: *Harlem, A Community in Transition* (1964), *Harlem, U.S.A.* (1965), *American Negro Short Stories* (1966), *William Styron's Nat Turner: Ten Black Writers Respond* (1968), and *Malcom X: The Man and His Times* (1969).

WILLIAM MELVIN KELLEY was born in New York City in 1937. From the Fieldston School he went to Harvard University, where he studied under Archibald Mac-Leish and John Hawkes. For his first novel, *A Different Drummer* (1963), he received the Richard and Hilda Rosenthal Foundation Award of the National Institute of Arts and Letters. His other books are *Dancers on the Shore* (1964) and *A Drop of Patience* (1965).

PAULE MARSHALL was born of Barbadian parents in Brooklyn, New York, in 1929. Her parents immigrated to America after the First World War. After graduating from Brooklyn College she worked in libraries and was a feature writer for the magazine *Our World,* traveling on assignments to Brazil and the West Indies. Her first novel, *Brown Girl, Brownstones,* was published in 1959. She is also the author of a book of short stories *Soul Clap Hands and Sing* (1961).

CLAYTON RILEY is an actor, short-story writer and journalist. He is drama and film critic for the *Liberator* magazine, and drama critic for the *Manhattan Tribune.* He lives in New York City. He is married and has two daughters.

LEROI JONES was born in Newark, New Jersey, in 1934. He attended high school in Newark and graduated from Howard University at the age of nineteen. A John Hay Whitney Fellowship in 1961 helped him continue his writing. He has produced two volumes of poetry and a book on jazz, *The Blues People*. His first novel, *The System of Dante's Hell,* was published in 1965. *The Dutchman, The Slave,* and *The Toilet,* among his one-act plays, have enjoyed successful off-Broadway runs.

RAY J. MEADDOUGH (1935–   ) was born in New York City, and graduated from New York University in 1960. After serving in the Marine Corps from 1954 to

1957, attaining the rank of sergeant, he worked at various jobs, and is presently assistant director of arts and culture for HARYOU-ACT. He is a member of the Harlem Writers Guild, has completed a collection of short stories, *A White Negro with a Button-Down Mind,* and is presently working on a first novel, *We Who Are About to Die.*

JOHN OLIVER KILLENS was born in Macon, Georgia, in 1916 and educated in schools on both sides of the Mason-Dixon line. He served with the National Labor Relations Board before and after the Second World War. His career was launched in 1954 with his highly successful novel, *Youngblood.* His second novel, *And Then We Heard the Thunder* (1963), was drawn in part from his experiences as a soldier in the amphibious forces in the South Pacific. Besides his two novels he has contributed a number of articles to various publications and has written for television and motion pictures. His first nonfiction book, *Black Man's Burden,* was published in 1965. Killens has served as chairman of the Harlem Writers Guild.

LORRAINE FREEMAN was born in New York City in 1931 and attended school in Manhattan and New Jersey. She has worked in the public libraries of New York City and has been a contributor to the *Catholic Worker* newspaper. She is presently living in upstate New York where she is in charge of a day-care center. Her present writing consists of finishing a novel about the black explorer, Matthew Henson.

MAYA ANGELOU is a short-story writer, poet, actress and singer. She spent a number of years teaching in Africa, mainly Ghana, and participating in the African Liberation Movement. During 1968 she completed a series of programs on African and Afro-American history and culture for Educational Television. Her first novel was completed in 1969.

LOUISE M. MERIWETHER, who grew up in Harlem and writes mainly about this famous black community, is an instructor in the Watts Writers Workshop in Los Angeles, California. Her short story "Daddy Was a Number Runner" is part of a novel in progress. She also works in the story department of Universal Studio in Hollywood.

LOYLE HAIRSTON was born in Mississippi in 1926. He

served in the Navy during the Second World War and afterward moved to New York City. His articles and book reviews have been published in *Freedomways* and other magazines. He recently completed his first novel, *Honeysuckle Across the Tracks.*

SELECTED TITLES *from A&B Books*

Blackmen say Goodbye to Misery	10.00
Education of the Negro	9.95
Heal Thyself	9.95
Heal Thyself Cookbook	9.95
Vaccines are Dangerous	9.95
Columbus and the African Holocaust	10.00
Columbus Conspiracy	11.95
Dawn Voyage	11.95
Aids the End of Civilization	9.95
Gospel of Barnabas	8.95
African Discovery of America	10.00
Gerald Massey's Lectures	9.95
Historical Jesus and the Mythical Christ	9.95
First Council of Nice	9.95
Arab Invasion of Egypt	14.95
Anacalypsis (set)	40.00
Anacalypsis Vol. 1	25.00
Anacalypsis Vol. 11	20.00
Harlem Voices	11.95
Harlem U.S.A.	11.95

Mail to A&B BOOKS 149 LAWRENCE STREET NEW YORK 11201
TEL: (718) 596-3389 · FAX (718) 596 -0968
$ 2.00 first book $ 1.00 each additional book. NY & NJ residents add sales tax.
Please find enclosed check/money order for $_____
Name:_____
Address:_____
City:_____ ST_____ Zip_____
Card Type:_____
Card Number:_____ Exp_____/_____

We accept *VISA MASTERCARD AMERICAN EXPRESS & DISCOVER*